ON KIM PHILBY

"Many people in the secret world aged the night they heard Philby had confessed. . . . It is one thing to suspect the truth; it is another to hear it from a man's lips. Suddenly there was very little fun in the game anymore; a Rubicon had been crossed. . . . To find that a man like Philby, a man you might like, or drink with, or admire, had betrayed everything; to think of the agents and operations wasted: youth and innocence passed away, and the dark ages began."
  —PETER WRIGHT, former assistant director of MI5

"Kim Philby is a legend—a demon or an antihero, depending on one's philosophical bent. Philby himself, or a thinly disguised fictional counterpart, stalks through many modern spy novels."
  —ROBERT J. LAMPHERE, FBI special agent

"[Philby] never revealed his true self. Neither the British, nor the women he lived with, nor ourselves ever managed to pierce the armour of mystery that clad him. His great achievement in espionage was his life's work, and it fully occupied him until the day he died. But in the end I suspect that Philby made a mockery of everyone, particularly ourselves."
  —YURI MODIN, KGB controller of "the Cambridge Spies"

"Philby has no home, no women, no faith. Behind the inbred upper-class arrogance, the taste for adventure, lies the self-hate of a vain misfit for whom nothing will ever be worthy of his loyalty. In the last instance, Philby is driven by the incurable drug of deceit itself."
  —JOHN LE CARRÉ

MY SILENT WAR

KIM PHILBY

MY SILENT WAR

THE AUTOBIOGRAPHY OF A SPY

Introduction by Phillip Knightley

Foreword by Graham Greene

THE MODERN LIBRARY

NEW YORK

This work was originally published in Great Britain in 1968 by MacGibbon &
Kee Ltd. This edition published by arrangement with The Estate of Kim Philby.

Grateful acknowledgment is made to David Higham Associates for permission to
reprint the foreword by Graham Greene to *My Silent War,* by Kim Philby
(Granada Publishing Ltd., London). Reprinted by permission.

Library of Congress Cataloging-in-Publication Data
Philby, Kim.
My silent war: the autobiography of a spy / Kim Philby.
p.   cm.
Originally published: New York : Grove Press, 1968.
Includes index.
ISBN 0-375-75983-2 (tradepaper)
1. Philby, Kim.   2. Espionage, Soviet—Great Britain—History—20th century.
3. Spies—Great Britain—Biography.   I. Title.   II. Series.
UB271.R92 P45 2002
327.124041'092—dc21
[B]   2002021948

Modern Library website address: www.modernlibrary.com

Printed in the United States of America

2 4 6 8 9 7 5 3

CONTENTS

INTRODUCTION

Phillip Knightley

Harold Adrian Russell Philby—"Kim" to his friends and family—has been part of my life for the past thirty years. I have written hundreds of thousands of words about Philby, appeared in many television and radio documentaries discussing him, and once spent a whole week talking to him in Moscow for six or seven hours a day. I have read every word of the more than twenty books written about him. I know his children and grandchildren and I keep in touch with his widow. Yet when people ask me, "What was Philby really like?," I have to reply, "I'm not certain I know."

So before you embark on the journey of reading this, the only book Philby ever wrote about himself, before you decide whether it is a frank confession, a fascinating justification for his life, or an insidious piece of Communist propaganda—or possibly all three—let me tell you what I know about a man whose motives and exploits continue to intrigue a new generation fifteen years after his death.

We should begin by giving Philby his professional due. In the history of espionage there has never been a spy like him, and now, with the Cold War over, there never will be. His achievements seem incredible. He joined the British Secret Intelligence Service (MI6) in 1940 and in three years rose to be head of its anti-Soviet section. Yet right from his Cambridge University days this urbane, pipe-smoking paragon of the English middle class had been an agent of the KGB. So the man running British operations against the Russians was actually working for the Russians himself. No wonder so few British plans worked. No wonder so many Western agents who slipped behind the Iron Curtain were never heard of again.

Worse was to come. In 1949 Philby was promoted to be the British Secret Service's liaison officer in Washington with the CIA and the FBI. This gave him access not only to British operations against Moscow but to American ones as well. The result: at the height of the Cold War, every move the West made against the Communist bloc was betrayed by Philby before it even began. And there was every possibility that had it not been for one mistake, Philby would have gone on to become CSS, Chief of the British Secret Service. The KGB would, in effect, have been running MI6, a disaster that could have changed the course of the Cold War.

This did not happen because Philby had shared his house in Washington with a fellow KGB agent, the British Foreign Office official Guy Burgess, and when Burgess fled to Moscow in 1951, Philby came under suspicion in the United States. He lingered on as a spy until 1963, doing freelance work for MI6 in Beirut under cover as a journalist, until his KGB masters, fearing that the British now had sufficient evidence to prosecute him and that the CIA might try to kill him, "brought me home to Moscow."

Back in 1968, with two colleagues on the *Sunday Times* of London, I wrote the first book about Philby—*Philby: The Spy Who Betrayed a Generation*. I then corresponded with Philby for twenty years and, in 1988, just three months before he died, spent a week with him, taking him step by step through his life.

We used *My Silent War* to jog his memory. He told me that he had been working on the book intermittently ever since he had come to Moscow, but had been doubtful that the KGB would ever let him publish it. When my book came out in Britain, the KGB arranged for Philby's book to be rushed into print. "But a lot of it was cut out," Philby said. "And I didn't have enough time to add new material." It was clear that the book had enhanced his reputation within the KGB, although there were still some officers who wanted nothing to do with him. He was invited to give lectures to training classes, and occasionally he was shown files concerning difficult operational cases and asked for his view. He warned his masters against becoming too involved in Africa and did his best to deter them from invading Afghanistan. Then, in the stultifying years of the Brezhnev regime, he slumped into a long period of despair. He cheered up when the former head of the KGB, Yuri Andropov, became leader, and when Mikhail Gorbachev took over, Philby was ecstatic. "This is the man we've been waiting for," he said. He was annoyed that American commentators were suggesting that the West should wait to see whether Gorbachev meant what he said about peaceful coexistence, or whether his words concealed an aim to control Western Europe, China, and Japan. "Such a suggestion is ridiculous," Philby said. "We have enough problems of our own without taking on other people's. This is just another myth, like all that talk of the Soviet Union being a 'Threat to the West' since the end of the war. In 1945, the Soviet Union was exhausted. The United States had the atomic bomb. What would we hope to gain by deliberately attacking Western Europe? No one wants to be incinerated."

My main impression of Philby during these talks was that here was a man at ease with himself in the twilight of his life, happy to exist quietly in his comfortable Moscow apartment and, since he was not sorry that his career as a spy was over, prepared to speak frankly about what it had involved. I did my best to get to the core of the man, no easy task with a master spy for whom deception is a professional skill. He was a charming, witty, and amusing host with a mind as sharp as a cut-throat razor. Although we mostly discussed espionage and politics, I sought his views on marriage, friendship, patriotism, honor, loyalty, treachery, betrayal, and the human condition. He talked about his favorite spy-thriller writers, today's youth, modern music, and the difficulties of life in the Soviet

Union—but also its rewards. He touched on his health, Soviet medicine, his finances, a trip he had made to Cuba, his travels within the Eastern bloc, and his memories of his colleagues in the CIA, including a list of those he would like to see again. But since then I have learned things he never even hinted at, such as his role in the exposure and eventual execution of the American atom spies Julius and Ethel Rosenberg; the missing year in his life as a spy; what the KGB really thought about him; and, most astonishing of all, how MI6 tried to persuade him to re-defect to Britain.

Philby came from an adventurous family. His father was Harry St. John Bridger Philby, a former magistrate in the Indian Civil Service, an explorer and an Arabist who became an adviser to King Saud. He held perverse political views and was interned at the start of the Second World War for telling Saud that he thought Hitler would win and that Saud should get his money out of pounds sterling. He felt that life should be lived to the hilt, an example he passed on to Kim. Women found the mix of idealism and love of action in both men an almost irresistible combination. After a tempestuous marriage, St. John Philby ended up with a Saudi slave girl. Kim had numerous affairs and married four times—a Viennese, an Englishwoman, an American, and a Russian. (The American joined him for a while in Moscow but left him when he expressed amazement that she should even bother to ask "If you had to choose between Communism and me, which would you choose?")

Kim Philby was in the thick of events in the thirties as the lights began to go out over Europe. He helped smuggle Jews and Communists out of Vienna. He was wounded in the Spanish Civil War, which he covered for *The Times* from the Franco side—while reporting to the KGB on German and Italian weapons being used there. He was still with *The Times* in France in 1940 and got out just ahead of the Germans. His expense account for the belongings he lost as he fled via Boulogne is still in the archives of the newspaper—"Dunhill pipe (two years old but all the better for it) one pound ten shillings." No wonder he looked an ideal recruit for MI6.

Yet this ideal recruit had already been signed up by the KGB back in 1934. Spotted while still at Cambridge because—like his fellow students Guy Burgess, Donald Maclean, and Anthony Blunt, later known as the Cambridge spy ring—he believed that the Western democracies were unable to check the rise of Fascism and that only the Soviet Union could save the world. His critics—and, of course, there are many—while conceding that his initial commitment to the Soviet Union might have been understandable at the time, wonder how he could possibly have remained in the service of Moscow after the Nazi-Soviet nonaggression pact of 1939.

One new piece of information is that he did not. According to KGB files, he was worried that valuable secrets he was providing about the British Expeditionary Force and the French army might now be passed on to the Germans. He demanded of his controller, "What's going to happen to the single-front struggle against Fascism now?" On February 20, 1940, the London resident of the KGB reported to Moscow that Philby's controller in Paris no longer knew where Philby was and that efforts to find him had failed. Moscow replied that such efforts should cease—Philby was finished; he was to be left out in the cold.

But in 1941 the KGB learned to its surprise that without its orders and without its help, Philby had got into MI6. It hastened to get in touch with him again. This was a surreal period in the master spy's career. It was clear that Germany was about to invade the Soviet Union: he could resume the anti-Fascist fight with a clear conscience.

But having reestablished contact with Philby, the KGB was suddenly very wary. What if he was part of a devilish MI6 plot to penetrate the KGB? It ordered counterintelligence officer Elena Modrzhinskaya (she is said to be still alive and well and living in Moscow) to examine Philby's file and decide whether he was a genuine recruit to Communism or a British penetration agent.

The first point Modrzhinskaya raised with her bosses was the volume and value of the material Philby had sent to the KGB. Could MI6 really be run by such fools that no one had noticed that precious information was leaking to Moscow? Next, was it really possible that Philby—with his Communist views, his work for the Communists in Vienna, and his Austrian Communist wife—had sailed through MI6's vetting procedures? She concluded that Philby was really working for the British and that so too were all the other members of the Cambridge spy ring—except, perhaps, Donald Maclean.

Her report split the KGB. Many of its officers believed that she was wrong and that Philby was an outstanding and loyal agent. In the end they prevailed, and the KGB continued to use Philby and the Cambridge ring. But there was always a group within the KGB who refused to trust him, and their nagging influence made his early years of exile in Moscow a misery. Word of Philby's unhappiness leaked back to London, and MI6 mounted an operation to convince him to return, to redefect. This was a secret, long-term, and persistent plan. How do I know of it? Maurice Oldfield, who had been head of MI6 at the time, told me after he had retired that persuading Philby to return had been a ongoing operation. And in 1997 I met the former East German spymaster Markus Wolf, who had been host to Philby on his visits to East Germany. Wolf said, "I was responsible for his security arrangements and I entertained him—we did a bit of cooking together at my place in the country. He had a KGB escort, and one evening this officer told me that the KGB lived in fear that Philby would go back to Britain, a move that would deal a propaganda blow to Moscow. He said that the British Secret Service in Moscow had found ways of making several offers to persuade Philby to return." This was puzzling, because in his twenty-five years in the Soviet Union, Philby had kept his Moscow address a secret. He avoided all other Westerners. If he wanted to go to a restaurant, his KGB minder arranged it, usually reserving a private room. So the "several offers" could only have been made in person by someone who had access to him on more than one occasion, someone he knew well. What follows now is speculation, because it is often impossible to prove matters in the secret world, but only one man fits the bill—the British novelist Graham Greene.

Greene, who had been a colleague of Philby's in MI6, had been corresponding with him since 1968, when, to the amazement of the literary world, he accepted an invitation from Philby's British publishers and wrote the introduction to the first edition of this book. Then, in 1986, Greene went to Moscow and the two old spies got together for a reunion in Philby's flat. Five months later, Greene went back to Moscow; he went again in September 1987, and then again in February 1988. He saw Philby each time.

From recent biographies of Greene, we now know that he reported on all these visits to MI6. Further, Greene has said that Philby would have expected him to do just that: "I knew that Kim would know that I would pass it on to Maurice Oldfield [then head of MI6]."

Greene would never have made the offer to Philby without authorization, and it would appear most likely that it was Oldfield who gave him the go-ahead. Greene even gave a tantalizing hint of the operation in interviews with his official biographer, Professor Norman Sherry. Sherry told me, "Greene said he had this dream of seeing Philby come walking down the street towards him in Britain. I suspect that this was not a dream but Greene's roundabout way of saying what he had been up to with Philby."

Philby had no moral qualms about the agents he had betrayed during his spying career. He saw the struggle between Western intelligence and the KGB as a war. "There are always casualties in war," he told me, adding, "Anyway, most of them were pretty nasty pieces of work and quite prepared themselves to kill if necessary."

He told me at our Moscow meetings that he had regrets about the way he had handled some things but no regrets whatsoever about the life he had chosen. He was uneasy, however, when our talk turned to the American spies Julius and Ethel Rosenberg, who had been sent to the electric chair in 1953 for betraying American atomic secrets to Moscow. But there was doubt at the time about their guilt, and allegations that they had been made scapegoats to appease American public concern that the Soviets had exploded their own bomb in 1949—years before the CIA had predicted that they would. A worldwide campaign appealing to President Eisenhower for clemency was whipped up by national Communist parties, and there was international outrage when the president ignored it. Over the years, debate over the Rosenbergs' guilt had not died out, so I asked Philby's view. But apart from saying that all the Rosenbergs were guilty of was being "lowly couriers with no link to the main KGB atomic spy rings" and that he could not understand why Eisenhower denied them a reprieve, he refused to talk about them.

I did not learn why until 1996, when stories began to appear about the "Venona decrypts," the successful American deciphering of radio traffic between Moscow and the Soviet consulate in New York in 1944–45. This material, which began to be decoded in the early 1950s, gave clues as to the identity of KGB spies in the West and was ultimately behind the uncovering of nearly every major Soviet spy in the postwar period. As MI6's liaison officer in Washington, Kim Philby had had access to the Venona material and knew the way the FBI was using it. This was a great break for the KGB, but it put Philby in a difficult and dangerous position. What should he do as he followed the FBI's homing in on his Soviet intelligence service comrades? If he were to use his knowledge of Venona to warn those most at risk so that they could flee, the FBI would suspect a leak. It would investigate everyone who had had access to Venona, including Philby, and he would never again enjoy the same degree of confidence. He made a brutal decision—he would tip off those agents who were of most importance to Moscow and sacrifice the others.

So he tipped off Donald Maclean, then a rising star in the Foreign Office, who fled to Moscow in May 1951. He tipped off Morris and Lona Cohen, responsible for couriering atom secrets stolen from Los Alamos to the Soviet consulate in New York, who fled the United States on an hour's notice in June 1950.

But no one tipped off the Rosenbergs, because the KGB considered them expendable. And no one imagined that the Americans would execute them. In the KGB's eyes, according to Philby, "They were minor couriers, not significant sources, [and] provided no valuable secrets." Philby felt guilty about the Rosenbergs for the rest of his life.

Why are we so intrigued by Philby? That someone was capable of such treachery puzzles and frightens us. If Philby did not do it for money—as has been the case with most American traitors—what did he do it for? Philby made a total ideological commitment when he was only twenty-one and had the strength of purpose to stick to it for the rest of his life. Like a character in a Graham Greene novel, he mixed duplicity and charm. In his treachery he risked all for his convictions, and he got away with it.

He recognized at one stage that things were going wrong in the Soviet Union but he told me that his choices were limited. "I couldn't give up politics altogether. I'm too much the political animal. I could whine, as some have, that the cause had betrayed me. Or I could stick it out in the confident faith that the principles of the Revolution would outlive the aberrations of individuals, however enormous." He had no doubt whatsoever about the verdict of history on this point, and four months later, before his beloved Communism collapsed, he died happy and fulfilled—perhaps his greatest coup of all.

———

PHILLIP KNIGHTLEY is an author and journalist who lives in London. He is best known for *The First Casualty,* a history of war correspondents and propaganda; *The Second Oldest Profession,* an examination of the role of intelligence services through the ages; and *Master Spy: The Story of Kim Philby.*

FOREWORD

Graham Greene

This is not at all the book that Philby's enemies anticipated. It is an honest one, well-written, often amusing, and the story he has to tell, after the flight of Burgess and Maclean, is far more gripping than any novel of espionage I can remember. We were told to expect a lot of propaganda, but it contains none, unless a dignified statement of his beliefs and motives can be called propaganda. The end, of course, in his eyes is held to justify the means, but this is a view taken, perhaps less openly, by most men involved in politics, if we are to judge them by their actions, whether the politician be a Disraeli or a Wilson. "He betrayed his country"—yes, perhaps he did, but who among us has not committed treason to something or someone more important than a country? In Philby's own eyes he was working for a shape of things to come from which his country would benefit.

Like many Catholics who, in the reign of Elizabeth, worked for the victory of Spain, Philby has a chilling certainty in the correctness of his judgement, the logical fanaticism of a man who, having once found a faith, is not going to lose it because of the injustices or cruelties inflicted by erring human instruments. How many a kindly Catholic must have endured the long bad days of the Inquisition with this hope of the future as a riding anchor? Mistakes of policy would have had no effect on his faith, nor the evil done by some of his leaders. If there was a Torquemada now, he would have known in his heart that one day there would be a John XXIII. "It cannot be so very surprising that I adopted a Communist viewpoint in the thirties; so many of my contemporaries made the same choice. But many of those who made the choice in those days changed sides when some of the worst features of Stalinism became apparent. I stayed the course," Philby writes, and he demands fairly enough what alternative there could possibly be to the bad Baldwin-Chamberlain era. "I saw the road leading me into the political position of the querulous outcast, of the Koestler-Crankshaw-Muggeridge variety, railing at the movement that had let *me* down, at the God that had failed *me*. This seemed a ghastly fate, however lucrative it might have been."

His account of the British Secret Service is devastatingly true. "The ease of my entry surprised me. It appeared later that the only enquiry made into my past was a routine reference to MI5, who passed my name through their records and came back with the laconic statement: Nothing Recorded Against." (He was luckier than I was. I had a police record, for after a libel action brought against me by Miss Shirley Temple, the papers had been referred to the Director of Public Prosecutions, and the trace had therefore to be submitted to C himself.) There was even a moment when Philby wondered whether it really was the Secret Service which he had entered. His first factual reports inclined his Soviet contact to the view that he had got into the wrong organization.

His character studies are admirable if unkind. Don't talk to me of ghost writers: only Philby could have been responsible for these. Anyone who was in Section V will agree with his estimate of its head, Felix Cowgill, whom he was to displace. "Cowgill revelled in his isolation. He was one of those pure souls who denounce all opponents as 'politicians.'" The Deputy Chief of the Secret Service is immediately recognizable. "Vivian was long past his best—if, indeed, he had ever had one. He had a reedy figure, carefully dressed crinkles in his hair, and wet eyes." To C himself, Brigadier Menzies, Philby is unexpectedly kind, though perhaps the strict limitations of his praise and a certain note of high patronage will not endear the portrait to the subject. For Skardon, the MI5 interrogator who broke Fuchs down, he has a true craftsman's respect.

If this book required a sub-title I would suggest: The Spy As Craftsman. No one could have been a better chief than Kim Philby when he was in charge of the Iberian section of V. He worked harder than anyone and never gave the impression of labour. He was always relaxed, completely unflappable. He was in those days, of course, fighting the same war as his colleagues: the extreme strain must have come later, when he was organizing a new section to counter Russian espionage, but though then he was fighting quite a different war, he maintained his craftsman's pride. He was determined that his new section should be organized better than any other part of the ramshackle SIS. "By the time our final bulky report was ready for presentation to the Chief, we felt we had produced the design of something like a service, with enough serious inducements to tempt able young men to regard it as a career for life." He set about recruiting with care and enthusiasm. "The important thing was to get hold of the good people while they were still available. With peacetime economies already in sight, it would be much easier to discard surplus staff than to find people later to fill in any gaps that might appear." No Soviet contact this time would be able to wonder whether he had penetrated the right outfit. A craftsman's pride, yes, and of course something else. Only an efficient section could thoroughly test the security of the Russian service. It was a fascinating manoeuvre, though only one side knew that it was a mock war.

The story of how, to attain his position, he eliminated Cowgill makes, as he admits, for "sour reading, just as it makes sour writing"—one feels for a moment the sharp touch of the icicle in the heart. I saw the beginning of this affair—indeed I resigned rather than accept the promotion which was one tiny cog in the machinery of his intrigue. I attributed it then to a personal drive for power, the only characteristic in Philby which I thought disagreeable. I am glad now that I was wrong. He was serving a cause and not himself, and so my old liking for him comes back, as I remember with pleasure those long Sunday lunches at St. Albans when the whole sub-section relaxed under his leadership for a few hours of heavy drinking, and later the meetings over a pint on fire-watching nights at the pub behind St. James's Street. If one made an error of judge-ment he was sure to minimize it and cover it up, without criticism, with a halting stammered witticism. He had all the small loyalties to his colleagues, and of course his big loyalty was unknown to us.

Some years later, after his clearance by Macmillan in the House of Commons, I and another old friend of Kim were together in Crowborough and we thought to look him up. There was no sign of any tending in the overgrown garden and no answer to the bell when we rang. We looked through the windows of the ugly sprawl-ing Edwardian house, on the borders of Ashdown forest, in this poor man's Surrey. The post hadn't been collected for a long time—the floor under the door was littered with advertising brochures. In the kitchen there were some empty milk bottles, and a single dirty cup and saucer in the sink. It was more like an abandoned gypsy en-campment than the dwelling of a man with wife and children. We didn't know it, but he had already left for Beirut—the last stage of his journey to Moscow, the home which he had never seen. After thirty years in the underground surely he has earned his right to a rest.

———

GRAHAM GREENE (1904–91), one of the greatest and most widely read English writers of the twentieth century, was the author of, among many novels, *The Man Within, England Made Me, The Power and the Glory, The Quiet American, Our Man in Havana,* and *Travels with My Aunt.* He was, as well, a noted short-story writer, essayist, film reviewer, and occasional playwright.

AUTHOR'S NOTE

This short book is an introductory sketch of my experiences in the field of intelligence. More will follow in due course. But already at this stage I must draw attention to a problem by which I am confronted.

The public naming of serving officers whose work is supposed to be secret cannot fail to cause personal embarrassment. I have no desire to cause such embarrassment to former colleagues in the British, American and sundry other services, for some of whom I feel both affection and respect.

I have tried therefore to confine the naming of names to officers whom I know to be dead or retired. On occasion, however, it has proved impossible to write a lucid story without naming officers who are still in service.

To these latter I apologize for any embarrassment caused. I, too, have suffered personal inconvenience through my connection with secret service.

Moscow, 1968

INTRODUCTION

This book has been written at intervals since my arrival in Moscow nearly five years ago. From time to time in the course of writing it, I took counsel with friends whose advice I valued. I accepted some of the suggestions made and rejected others. One suggestion which I rejected was that I should make the book more exciting by heavier emphasis on the hazards of the long journey from Cambridge to Moscow. I prefer to rest on a round, unvarnished tale.

When the book was brought to a provisional conclusion last summer (1967), I gave long consideration to the desirability of publishing it, again consulting a few friends whose views might be helpful. The general consensus of opinion, with which I agreed at the time, was that the question of publication should be shelved indefinitely. The main reason for this was that publication seemed likely to cause a rumpus, with international complications the nature of which was difficult to foresee. It seemed unwise to take action that might have consequences beyond the range of reasonable prediction. So I decided to sit on my typescript.

The situation has been completely changed by articles which appeared in the *Sunday Times* and the *Observer* in October 1967.

Those articles, in spite of a number of factual inaccuracies and errors of interpretation (and, I fear, gratifying exaggeration of my own talents), present a substantially true picture of my career. It was immediately suggested, of course, by rival newspapers that the *Sunday Times* and the *Observer* had fallen victim to a gigantic plant. The absurdity of this suggestion has already been exposed in the *Sunday Times*. For my part, I can only add that I was offered an opportunity to vet the typescript of the *Sunday Times* articles before publication and, after reflection, deliberately declined. I felt that the Editor should be prepared to stand by the conclusions reached by his own staff, and that the objectivity of the articles would be open to attack if I, so interested a party, intervened.

As I say, these articles completely charged the situation. The consequences of the truth being disclosed are on us irrevocably, for better or worse. I can therefore offer my book to the public without incurring the charge of wanting to muddy waters. My purpose is simply to correct certain inaccuracies and errors of interpretation, and to present a more fully rounded picture.

The first serious crisis of my career was long drawn out, lasting roughly from the middle of 1951 to the end of 1955. Throughout it, I was sustained by the thought that nobody could pin on me any link with Communist organizations, for the simple reason that I had never been a member of any. The first thirty years of my work for the cause in which I believed were, from the beginning, spent underground. This long phase started in Central Europe* in June 1933; it ended in Lebanon in January 1963. Only then was I able to emerge in my true colours, the colours of a Soviet intelligence officer.

Until quite recently, when the *Sunday Times* and the *Observer* let some large and fairly authentic cats out of the bag, writers who

---

*After leaving Cambridge a convinced Communist, Philby went to Vienna, where he joined in the struggle of the Austrian Socialists against the government. In Vienna in 1934 he married a Communist— Litzi Friedman.

[The author's footnotes are distinguished from those created by the 1968 publisher of *My Silent War* (some of which have been updated for this Modern Library edition) by being printed in roman type.]

touched my case in newspaper articles and books thrashed around wildly in the dark. They cannot be blamed for their ignorance since, throughout my career, I was careful not to advertise the truth. But some blame perhaps attaches to them for rushing into print in that blissful state, and for their insistence on looking for complex explanations where simple ones would have served better. The simple truth, of course, crumbling Establishment and its Trans-atlantic friends. But the attempt to wash it away in words, whether ingenious or just nonsensical, was futile and foredoomed to failure.

After nearly a year of illegal activity in Central Europe, I returned to England. It was time for me to start earning my own living. Then something evidently happened. Within a few weeks I had dropped all my political friends and had begun to frequent functions at the German Embassy. I joined the Anglo-German Fellowship, and did much of the legwork involved in an abortive attempt to start, with Nazi funds, a trade journal designed to foster good relations between Britain and Germany.* In spite of my best efforts, this strange venture failed, because another group got in ahead of us. But while the negotiations were in progress, I paid several visits to Berlin for talks with the Propaganda Ministry and the *Dienststelle Ribbentrop*. No one has so far suggested that I had switched from Communism to Nazism. The simpler, and true, explanation is that overt and covert links between Britain and Germany at that time were of serious concern to the Soviet Government.

The Spanish war broke out during one of my visits to Berlin. The Nazis were cock-a-hoop, and it was not until I returned to England that I learnt that General Franco had not taken over the whole country, but that a long civil war was in prospect. My next assignment was to Fascist-occupied territory in Spain with the aim of bedding down there, as close to the centre of things as possible, on a long-term basis. That mission was successful, for within a few weeks I became the accredited correspondent of *The Times* with

---

Philby was covering up traces of his early enthusiasm for Communism; Burgess, who was also a member of this Fellowship, appears to have been doing exactly the same thing.

Franco's forces, and served as such throughout the whole heart-breaking war. Again, no one has suggested that this made me a Falangista. The simpler explanation still holds the field; I was there on Soviet service.

In August 1939, when the war clouds were piling up fast over Danzig, *The Times* told me to forget Spain and hold myself in readiness for attachment to any British force that might be sent to the Western Front. It was as good as I could have expected in the circumstances. Any war correspondent with an enquiring mind could amass a huge amount of information which censorship would not allow him to publish; and my experience in Spain had taught me the right sort of question to ask. As it turned out, British headquarters were established in Arras, within easy reach of Paris. I spent most of my weekends in the heaving anonymity of the capital, not only for the obvious purpose of philandering. But, good as it was, the Arras post was not good enough. I had been told in pressing terms by my Soviet friends that my first priority must be the British secret service. Before the press corps left for France in early October, I dropped a few hints here and there. All that I could then do was sit back and wait. This book describes in some, though not complete, detail how this new venture was crowned with success.

In case doubt should still lurk in devious minds, a plain statement of the facts is perhaps called for. In early manhood, I became an accredited member of the Soviet intelligence service. I can therefore claim to have been a Soviet intelligence officer for some thirty-odd years, and will no doubt remain one until death or senile decay forces my retirement. But most of my work has lain in fields normally covered, in British and American practice, by agents. I will therefore describe myself henceforth as an agent.

"Agent," of course, is a term susceptible of widely different interpretations. It can mean a simple courier carrying messages between two points; it can mean the writer of such messages; it can imply advisory or even executive functions. I passed through the first stage rapidly, and was soon writing, or otherwise providing, information on an increasingly voluminous scale. As I gained in knowledge and experience, consultative and executive functions were gradually added to the mere acquisition and transmission of intelligence. This process ran parallel to my rising seniority in the British service, in which, from about 1944 onwards, I was consulted on a wide range of policy problems.

Some writers have recently spoken of me as a double agent, or even as a triple agent. If this is taken to mean that I was working with equal zeal for two or more sides at once, it is seriously misleading. All through my career, I have been a straight penetration agent working in the Soviet interest. The fact that I joined the British Secret Intelligence Service is neither here nor there; I regarded my SIS* appointments purely in the light of cover-jobs, to be carried out sufficiently well to ensure my attaining positions in which my service to the Soviet Union would be most effective. My connection with SIS must be seen against my prior total commitment to the Soviet Union which I regarded then, as I do now, the inner fortress of the world movement.

In the first year or two, I penetrated very little, though I did beat Gordon Lonsdale to the London School of Oriental Studies by ten years. During that period, I was a sort of intelligence probationer. I still look back with wonder at the infinite patience shown by my seniors in the service, a patience matched only by their intelligent understanding. Week after week, we would meet in one or other of the remoter open spaces in London; week after week, I would reach the rendezvous empty-handed and leave with a load of painstaking advice, admonition and encouragement. I was often despondent at my failure to achieve anything worthwhile, but the lessons went on and sank deep. When the time came for serious work, I found myself endowed with much of the required mental equipment.

It was just as well, for my first challenges came in Germany and in Fascist Spain, both countries with a short way of despatching enemy intelligence agents. My reward came during the Spanish

---

* *Secret Intelligence Service, formerly MI6, the British secret service department in charge of all secret intelligence work, both espionage and counter-espionage, on non-British soil.*

war, when I learnt that my probationary period was considered at an end; I emerged from the conflict as a fully-fledged officer of the Soviet service.

How did it all begin? My decision to play an active part in the struggle against reaction was not the result of sudden conversion. My earliest thoughts on politics turned me towards the labour movement; and one of my first acts on going up to Cambridge in 1929 was to join the Cambridge University Socialist Society (CUSS). For the first two years, I attended its meetings with regularity, but otherwise took little part in its proceedings. Through general reading, I became gradually aware that the Labour Party in Britain stood well apart from the mainstream of the Left as a world-wide force. But the real turning-point in my thinking came with the demoralisation and rout of the Labour Party in 1931. It seemed incredible that the party should be so helpless against the reserve strength which reaction could mobilise in times of crisis. More important still, the fact that a supposedly sophisticated electorate had been stampeded by the cynical propaganda of the day threw serious doubt on the validity of the assumptions underlying parliamentary democracy as a whole.

This book is not a history or a treatise or a polemic. It is a personal record, and I intend to stray as little as possible from my main theme. It is therefore enough to say at this point that it was the Labour disaster of 1931 which first set me seriously to thinking about possible alternatives to the Labour Party. I began to take a more active part in the proceedings of the CUSS, and was its Treasurer in 1932–3. This brought me into contact with streams of Left-wing opinion critical of the Labour Party, notably with the Communists. Extensive reading and growing appreciation of the classics of European Socialism alternated with vigorous and sometimes heated discussions within the Society. It was a slow and brain-racking process; my transition from a Socialist viewpoint to a Communist one took two years. It was not until my last term at Cambridge, in the summer of 1933, that I threw off my last doubts.

I left the university with a degree and with the conviction that my life must be devoted to Communism.

I have long since lost my degree (indeed, I think it is the possession of MI5).* But I have retained the conviction. It is here, perhaps, that a doubt may assail the reader. It cannot be so very surprising that I adopted a Communist viewpoint in the thirties; so many of my contemporaries made the same choice. But many of those who made the choice in those days changed sides when some of the worst features of Stalinism became apparent. I stayed the course. It is reasonable to ask why.

It is extremely difficult for the ordinary human being, lacking the gift of total recall, to describe exactly how he reached such-and-such a decision more than thirty years ago. In my own case, an attempt to do so would make appallingly tedious reading. But, as the question will be asked, it must be answered, even if the answer takes the form of gross over-simplification.

It seemed to me, when it became clear that much was going badly wrong in the Soviet Union, that I had three possible courses of action. First, I could give up politics altogether. This I knew to be quite impossible. It is true that I have tastes and enthusiasms outside politics; but it is politics alone that give them meaning and coherence. Second, I could continue political activity on a totally different basis. But where was I to go? The politics of the Baldwin-Chamberlain era struck me then, as they strike me now, as much more than the politics of folly. The folly was evil. I saw the road leading me into the political position of the querulous outcast, of the Koestler-Crankshaw-Muggeridge variety, railing at the movement that had let *me* down, at the God that had failed *me*. This seemed a ghastly fate, however lucrative it might have been.

The third course of action open to me was to stick it out, in the confident faith that the principles of the Revolution would out-

Secret service department responsible for counter-espionage and security in Britain and in all British territory overseas.

live the aberration of individuals, however enormous. It was the course I chose, guided partly by reason, partly by instinct. Graham Greene, in a book appropriately called *The Confidential Agent*, imagines a scene in which the heroine asks the hero if his leaders are any better than the others. "No. Of course not," he replied. "But I still prefer the people they lead—even if they lead them all wrong." "The poor, right or wrong," she scoffed. "It's no worse—is it?—than my country, right or wrong. You choose your side once and for all—of course, it may be the wrong side. Only history can tell that."

The passage throws some light on my attitude in the depths of the Stalin cult. But I now have no doubt about the verdict of history. My persisting faith in Communism does not mean that my views and attitudes have remained fossilized for thirty-odd years. They have been influenced and modified, sometimes rudely, by the appalling events of my lifetime. I have quarrelled with my political friends on major issues, and still do so. There is still an awful lot of work ahead; there will be ups and downs. Advances which, thirty years ago, I hoped to see in my lifetime, may have to wait a generation or two. But, as I look over Moscow from my study window, I can see the solid foundations of the future I glimpsed at Cambridge.

Finally, it is a sobering thought that, but for the power of the Soviet Union and the Communist idea, the Old World, if not the whole world, would now be ruled by Hitler and Hirohito. It is a matter of great pride to me that I was invited, at so early an age, to play my infinitesimal part in building up that power. How, where and when I became a member of the Soviet intelligence service is a matter for myself and my comrades. I will only say that, when the proposition was made to me, I did not hesitate. One does not look twice at an offer of enrolment in an elite force.

LIST OF ABBREVIATIONS

Abwehr	German Military Intelligence
ACSS	Assistant Chief of the Secret Service
BSC	British Security Co-ordination
CUSS	Cambridge University Socialist Society
GB	State Security Service of the USSR
GC & CS	Government Code & Cypher School
GUR	Soviet Military Intelligence
MI5	Originally the counter-espionage section of British Military Intelligence—the usual name for the Directorate-General of Security Service
NKVD	Narodnyi Komissariat Vniutrennikh Del (People's Commissariat of Internal Affairs)
OPC	Office of Policy Co-ordination
OSO	Office of Strategic Operations
OSS	Office of Strategic Services (USA), the American counterpart of SIS
PWE	Political Warfare Executive
SCI	Special Counter-Intelligence
SIS	Secret Intelligence Service (MI6)
SOE	Special Operations Executive

MY SILENT WAR

CURTAIN RAISER: A WHIFF
OF THE FIRING SQUAD

It was quite early in my career as a Soviet intelligence official that I first ran into serious trouble, escaping, almost literally, by the skin of my teeth. It was in April 1937, when my headquarters were at Seville in the south of Spain. My immediate assignment was to get first-hand information on all aspects of the Fascist war effort. The arrangement was that I should transmit the bulk of my information by hand to Soviet contacts in France or, more occasionally, in England. But for urgent communications, I had been provided with a code and a number of cover-addresses outside Spain.

Before I left England, instructions in the use of the code were committed to a tiny piece of substance resembling rice-paper, which I habitually kept in the ticket-pocket of my trousers. It was this tiny object that nearly brought me face to face with the firing squad.

After a few busy weeks in Seville and the surrounding country-side, my eye fell on a poster advertising a bull-fight to be held on the following Sunday in Córdoba. The front line then ran just twenty-five miles east of Córdoba, between Montoro and Andújar, and the chance of seeing a bull-fight so close to a front which I had not yet visited seemed too good to be missed. I decided to spend a long weekend at Córdoba, including attendance at the Sunday *corrida*. I went to the *Capitania,* the military headquarters in Seville, to get the necessary pass, but a friendly major waved me away. A pass was not required for Córdoba, he said. All I had to do was get on the train and go.

On the Friday before the bull-fight, I boarded the morning train at Seville, sharing a compartment with a group of Italian infantry officers. Always on the job, as the saying goes, I asked them to have dinner with me in Córdoba, but they explained courteously that they would not have time. They would be too busy in the brothels before moving up to the front next day. I took a room in the Hotel del Gran Capitan, enjoyed a solitary meal, and walked the scented streets in a happy daze until about midnight when I returned to the hotel and went to bed.

I was aroused from a deep sleep by thunderous hammering on the door. When I opened, two Civil Guards stamped into the room. They told me to pack my bag and accompany them to headquarters. To my question why, the senior of the two, a corporal, answered simply, *"Ordenes."*

I slept heavily in those days. Besides, I was at the disadvantage of confronting, in my pyjamas, two heavily booted men with rifles and revolvers. Half asleep and half scared, my brain reacted with less than the speed of light. I was conscious that something might have to be done about the tell-tale paper tucked away in my trousers; but how to get rid of it? My mind moved vaguely in the direction of bathrooms, but I had taken a room without a bath. By the time I had dressed and packed, and the Civil Guards had turned over my bed-clothes, I had got no further than a sluggish resolve to get rid of my scrap of paper somehow on the way from the hotel to Civil Guard headquarters.

When we got into the street, I found that it was not going to be easy. I had only one free hand; the other gripped my suitcase. My escort, evidently well trained, kept a steady pace behind me all the way, watching me, for all I knew, like hawks. So the incriminating material was still on me when I was shown into an office lit by a single bright naked bulb shining on a large, well-polished table. Opposite me stood an undersized major of the Civil Guard, elderly, bald and sour. With eyes fixed to the table, he listened perfunctorily to the report of the corporal who had brought me in.

The major examined my passport at length. "Where," he asked me, "is your permission to visit Córdoba?" I repeated what I had been told at the *Capitania* in Seville, but he brushed my words aside. Impossible, he said flatly; everyone knew that a permit was necessary for Córdoba. Why had I come to Córdoba? To see the bull-fight? Where was my ticket? I hadn't got one? I had only just arrived and was going to buy one in the morning? A likely story! And so on. With every fresh outburst of scepticism, I became aware, with growing unease, that my interrogator was a confirmed Anglophobe. There were plenty of Anglophobes in those days in Spain, on both sides of the line. But by this time my brain was beginning to work normally, and I began to see possibilities in that wide expanse of gleaming table.

With an air of utter disbelief, the major and the two men who had arrested me turned to my suitcase. With unexpected delicacy, they drew on gloves and unpacked it item by item, probing each article with their fingers and holding it up to the light. Finding nothing suspicious in my change of underwear, they next examined the suitcase, tapping its surface carefully and measuring its inner and outer dimensions. There was a sigh when its innocence was established beyond doubt. For a second, I hoped that that would be the end of it, and that I would simply be told to get out of town by the first available train—but only for a second.

"And now," said the major nastily, "what about you?"

He asked me to turn out my pockets. I could no longer postpone action. Taking first my wallet, I threw it down on that fine table, giving it at the last moment a flick of the wrist which sent it spinning towards the far end. As I had hoped, all three men made a dive at it, spreadeagling themselves across the table. Confronted by three pairs of buttocks, I scooped the scrap of paper out of my trousers, a crunch and a swallow, and it was gone. I emptied my remaining pockets with a light heart, and the major fortunately spared me the intimacies of a rigorous body-search. He gave me instead a dry little lecture on the Communists dominating the British Government, and ordered me to get out of Córdoba next day. I was paying my hotel bill in the morning when my two friends of the Civil Guard emerged from a recess in the lounge and asked if they might share my taxi to the station. As I boarded the Seville-bound coach, I gave them a packet of English cigarettes, and they waved to me happily as the train pulled out.

It was not a heroic episode. Even if my coding instructions had been found, my British passport would probably have saved me from the death sentence. But in subsequent years I have often had occasion to reflect that the really risky operation is not usually the one which brings most danger, since real risks can be assessed in advance and precautions taken to obviate them. It is the almost meaningless incident, like the one described above, that often puts one to mortal hazard.

I. Taken On by the Secret Service

It was in the summer of 1940, to the best of my knowledge, that I first made contact with the British secret service. It was a subject that had interested me for some years. In Nazi Germany and later in Spain, where I served as correspondent for *The Times* with General Franco's forces, I had half expected an approach. I was confident that I would recognize my man the moment he made his first cautious soundings. He would be lean, and bronzed, of course, with a clipped moustache, clipped accents and, most probably, a clipped mind. He would ask me to stick my neck out for my country and frown austerely if I mentioned pay. But no, nothing happened. If anybody did size me up during that time, he found me wanting. The only intelligence officer who took the slightest interest in me during my Spanish days was German, a certain Major von der Osten, alias Don Julio, who died early in the World War in a motor accident in New York. He used to take me to Abwehr headquarters in the Convento de las Esclavas in Burgos, and explain his large wall maps dotted with the usual coloured pins. He dined and wined me in desultory fashion for a year or so, and it proved a useful contact as far as it went. It emerged in due course that his real interest in me was to get an introduction to a lady of my acquaintance. When I obliged him, he propositioned her forthwith, both espionage-wise and otherwise. She turned him down indignantly on both counts, and his manner to me became distant.

When the World War broke out, *The Times* sent me to Arras as their correspondent accredited to the Headquarters of the British Army. By June 1940 I was back in England, having been evacuated twice, from Boulogne and from Brest. In London, I had written two or three pieces for *The Times*, winding up the campaign and pointing its various morals. I have no idea what I wrote and, having just read the pungent comments on the campaign in Liddell-Hart's memoirs, I am grateful for the lapse of memory.* I must have produced dreadful rubbish. The main point was that, by the end of June, I was at a loose end. *The Times* showed no disposition to get rid of me or to overload me with work. Thus I had ample leisure to plot my future, if only I could make a good guess at the nature of the background I had to plot it against.

I decided early to leave *The Times*, considerate though they had always been to me. Army field censorship had killed my interest in war correspondence. Try writing a war report without mentioning a single place-name or designating a single unit and you will see what I mean.† Besides, the idea of writing endlessly about the morale of the British Army at home appalled me. But, in deciding to leave *The Times*, I had to remember that my call-up was fast approaching. I had no intention of losing all control of my fate through conscription into the army. It was therefore with increasing concern that I watched various irons I had put in the fire, nudging one or other of them as they appeared to hot up. I had one promising interview, arranged by a mutual friend, with Frank Birch,‡

---

*Basil Liddell-Hart, The Liddell-Hart Memoirs, *2 vols. (New York: G. P. Putnam's Sons, 1965).*

†British army censorship relaxed as the war went on. During the phony war period, its mutton-headed restrictiveness compared unfavourably with the much-criticized practice of General Franco's censors.

‡*Before and after the war, a don at King's College, Cambridge.*

a leading light in the Government Code & Cypher School, a crypt-analytical establishment which cracked enemy (and friendly) codes. He finally turned me down, on the infuriating ground that he could not offer me enough money to make it worth my while. Disconsolately, I went to Holloway for my medical.

A few days later, Ralph Deakin, then Foreign News Editor of *The Times,* summoned me to his office. He bulged his eyes at me, puffed out his cheeks and creased his forehead, habits of his when upset. A certain Captain Leslie Sheridan, of the War Office, had telephoned to ask whether I was "available for war work." Sheridan had not impressed Deakin. He had claimed to be a journalist on the grounds of a previous association with the *Daily Mirror.* In short, Deakin wanted no part of the affair, and pressed me to let the matter drop. I was sorry to disappoint him. Although I had never heard of Sheridan, I strongly suspected that one of my irons was glowing bright. I decided to strike before it cooled, and immediately followed up the enquiry.

Soon afterwards I found myself in the forecourt of St. Ermin's Hotel, near St. James's Park station, talking to Miss Marjorie Maxse. She was an intensely likeable elderly lady (then almost as old as I am now). I had no idea then, as I have no idea now, what her precise position in government was. But she spoke with authority, and was evidently in a position at least to recommend me for "interesting" employment. At an early stage of our talk, she turned the subject to the possibilities of political work against the Germans in Europe. For ten years, I had taken a serious interest in international politics; I had wandered about Europe in a wide arc from Portugal to Greece; I had already formed some less than half-baked ideas on the subversion of the Nazi regime. So I was reasonably well equipped to talk to Miss Maxse. I was helped by the fact that very few people in England at that early date had given serious thought to the subject. Miss Maxse's own ideas had been in the oven very little longer than mine.

I passed this first examination. As we parted, Miss Maxse asked me to meet her again at the same place a few days later. At our second meeting, she turned up accompanied by Guy Burgess,* whom I knew well. I was put through my paces again. Encouraged by Guy's presence, I began to show off, name-dropping shamelessly, as one does at interviews. From time to time, my interlocutors exchanged glances; Guy would nod gravely and approvingly. It turned out that I was wasting my time, since a decision had already been taken. Before we parted, Miss Maxse informed me that, if I agreed, I should sever my connection with *The Times* and report for duty to Guy Burgess at an address in Caxton Street, in the same block as the St. Ermin's Hotel.

The Times gave me little difficulty. Deakin huffed and sighed a little, but he had nothing spectacular to offer me. So I left Printing House Square without fanfare, in a manner wholly appropriate to the new, secret and important career for which I imagined myself heading. I decided that it was my duty to profit from the experiences of the only secret service man of my acquaintance. So I spent the weekend drinking with Guy Burgess. On the following Monday, I reported to him formally. We both had slight headaches.

The organization to which I became attached called itself the Secret Intelligence Service (SIS). It was also widely known as MI5, while to the innocent public at large it was simply the secret service. The ease of my entry surprised me. It appeared later that the only enquiry made into my past was a routine reference to MI5, who passed my name through their records and came back with the laconic statement: Nothing Recorded Against. Today, every new spy scandal in Britain produces a flurry of judicial statements on the subject of "positive vetting." But in that happier Eden positive vetting had never been heard of. Sometimes, in the early weeks, I felt that perhaps I had not made the grade after all. It seemed that somewhere, lurking in deep shadow, there must be another service, really secret and really powerful, capable of backstairs machination on such a scale as to justify the perennial suspicions of, say, the

---

Burgess and Philby were both at Trinity College, Cambridge. Burgess had been in Section D of SIS since January 1939.

French.* But it soon became clear that such was not the case. It was the death of an illusion. Its passing caused me no pain.

Guy first took me to the office that had been assigned to me. It was a small room with a table, a chair and a telephone, and nothing else. With a snort of annoyance, Guy disappeared down the corridor and came back with a sheaf of foolscap which he laid on the table. Satisfied that I was now fully equipped for my duties, he told me that my salary would be the same as his: £600 per annum, paid monthly in cash and no nonsense from the Inland Revenue. No snooping after a single secret shilling! In fact, the secrecy of pay-scales concealed gross inequalities. Each contract was theoretically a private, secret one between the Chief and his subordinate. And if the Chief could get A cheaper than B, whatever their respective merits, he would be silly not to do so. However, I was quite happy with the arrangement, and I was then taken off to be introduced to some of my future colleagues. As they play no substantial part in my story, I shall not embarrass them by mentioning their names.

The section of SIS in which I found myself was known as Section D (for Destruction). I never saw its charter—if it had one. From talks with my colleagues, I gathered that the object of the section was to help defeat the enemy by stirring up active resistance to his domination and destroying, by non-military means, the sources of his power. The head of the section was Colonel Lawrence Grand,† to whom I was introduced a few days after joining his staff. Tall and lean, he looked startlingly like the dream-figure who should have approached me in Germany or Spain. The difference was that his mind was certainly not clipped. It ranged free and handsome over the whole field of his awesome responsibilities, never shrinking from an idea, however big or wild.

Much attention was focused at that time on attacking the Iron Gates of the Danube, to interrupt the supply of Rumanian oil to

---

*This thought was put into my head by my Soviet contact. My first factual reports on the secret service inclined him seriously to the view that I had got into the wrong organization.

†*Section D, under Grand, was set up in March 1938.*

the Germans. I had seen the Iron Gates, and was duly impressed by the nerve of colleagues who spoke of "blowing them up," as if it were a question of destroying the pintle of a lock-gate in the Regent's Canal. Such an attempt was hopelessly out of keeping with the slender resources of Section D in 1940. When it was finally made, it was discovered and nipped in the bud by the Yugoslav police, causing the British Government some embarrassment. The same disparity between ends and means appeared in suggestions that Hitler's oil supply could be seriously interrupted by "putting the Baku oilfields out of action." I have since seen the Baku oilfields, and amused myself mildly by wondering how I would launch such an enterprise, assuming that I started from a base in Cairo. Even in 1940, I would have dismissed such talk as fantasy, if I had not attended a press conference in Arras given by General Pownall, then Chief of Staff to Lord Gort,* in which he said that, given the strength of the Siegfried Line, better prospects might be offered by an attack through the Caucasus. If successful, such an attack would open "Germany's weak eastern defences" to Anglo-French assault.

Grand never had the resources to carry out his ideas, though they were given freely to his successors. His London staff could fit easily into a large drawing-room. We regularly did so on Sundays at his headquarters in the country, where plans, plans, plans were the inexhaustible topics of discussion. In the field, he had little more than bits and scraps. His efforts to get a larger slice of the secret cake were frowned on by the older and more firmly based intelligence-gathering side of the service. Starting from the valid premise that sabotage and subversion are inherently insecure (the authors of bangs are liable to detection), the intelligence people rushed happily to the invalid conclusion that bangs were a waste of time and money, diverting resources from the silent spy. Thus

---

To sever his connection with The Times *in July 1940, just before he joined SIS, Philby put out the story that he was being taken on by Lord Gort, Commander of the British Expeditionary Force (BEF), to write up the official records of the campaign. This story is confirmed in a letter written by Ralph Deakin in 1944: "Lord Gort became so well-disposed to Philby that he took him away from* The Times *to do work on the record of the Expeditionary force before Dunkirk."*

Grand's demands on the Treasury and on the armed services were often blocked within the service. At best, they were given lukewarm support.

On the side of political subversion, the difficulties were even more serious, because they involved fundamental aspects of British policy. By and large, the British Government had accustomed itself to supporting the monarchs and oligarchs of Europe. Such men were strongly averse to any form of subversion. The only people likely to support any sort of resistance to Hitler were the Left-wing movements: the peasant parties, the Social-Democrats and the Communists. Only they were likely to risk their lives by continuing resistance after the Germans had engulfed their countries. Yet they were extremely unlikely to stir for the sake of a British Government which insisted on playing footsie with the King Carols and the Prince Pauls who had systematically persecuted them between the wars. Thus the ideologues of subversion in Britain started out under a heavy handicap imposed by the Foreign Office which failed to see until much too late that, whatever the outcome of the war, the sun of its favourite puppets had set for ever. Small wonder that, when the crunch came, the resistance movements leant so heavily towards the Soviet Union, and that the balance was only restored in France, Italy and Greece by a massive Anglo-American military presence.

For reasons of security and convenience, all SIS officers are given symbols which are used in correspondence and conversation. Grand was naturally D. His sub-section heads were known as DA, DB and so on; and their assistants were distinguished by the addition of numerals, e.g. DA-1. Guy was DU. According to normal practice, therefore, I should have been DU-1. But Guy explained, with heavy delicacy, that the symbol DU-1 might have implied some subordination of myself to him; he wanted us to be regarded as equals. He solved the dilemma by giving me a third letter instead of a final numeral, and he chose the letter D. Thus he launched me on my secret service career branded with the symbol DUD.

DU was not the ideal starting-point for what I had in mind. I wanted to find out how it was organized and what it was doing. But Guy, following his own predilections, had turned DU into a sort of ideas factory. He regarded himself as a wheel, throwing off ideas like sparks as it revolved. Where the sparks fell he did not seem to care. He spent a long time in other people's offices, propounding his ideas. As he warmed to his themes, shouts of raucous laughter would drift down the corridor to my office where I sat thinking or reading the newspapers. After a hard morning's talking, Guy would return to my office, chortling and dimpling, and suggest going out for a drink.

One day in July, Guy came into my office bringing some papers for a change. They were pages of a memorandum written by himself. Grand had given general approval to its contents, and had asked for further study and elaboration of the subject. For that Guy needed my help. I was excessively pleased. From long experience, I knew that "helping" Guy meant taking all the donkey work off his hands. But as I had done literally nothing for two weeks, I would have been glad of any work. I took the papers and Guy sat down on my table to watch my face for signs of appreciation.

It was a characteristic production: lots of good sense embedded to the point of concealment in florid epigram and shaky quotation. (Guy had quotations to meet almost any emergency, but he never bothered to verify them.) What he proposed was the establishment of a school for training agents in the techniques of underground work. It was an astonishing proposal, not because it was made, but because it had not been made before. No such school existed. Guy argued the case for its necessity, obvious now but new then. He outlined the subjects of a syllabus. At the end, he suggested that such a college should be named the "Guy Fawkes College" to commemorate an unsuccessful conspirator "who had been foiled by the vigilance of the Elizabethan SIS." It was a neat touch. He could hardly have proposed "Guy Burgess College."

At last, I had got my teeth into something. I broke the subject up into its component parts: syllabus, selection of trainees, security, accommodation and so on, and produced a memorandum on each.

I have forgotten most of what I wrote and, in view of the huge training establishment that gradually developed, I hope that my first modest paper on the subject no longer exists. Having deposited his shower of sparks into my lap, Guy seemed to lose interest in a fresh riot of ideas. But it was not so. He saw that Grand read my papers, and arranged committees to discuss them. I did not take to committee work then, and have never taken to it since. Every committee has a bugbear. My bugbear on the training committee was a certain Colonel Chidson.* He had played an astute part in rescuing a lot of industrial diamonds from Hitler in Poland, but to me he was a pain in the neck. He had visions of anarchy stalking Europe, and resisted bitterly the whole idea of letting a lot of thugs loose on the continent. One day, I spotted him coming towards me in Lower Regent Street. A moment later, he saw me and froze in his tracks. In a swift recovery, he turned up his coat collar and dived into a side-street. Our training school had evidently become very necessary.

Guy's refrain at the time was "the idea must be made to *catch on*"; and somehow it did. In due course, I learnt to my surprise that Brickendonbury Hall, a former school building standing in spacious grounds near Hertford, had been acquired for training purposes.† I was introduced to a Commander Peters, RN, who had been seconded to us to act as commandant of the school. He often took Guy and me to dinner at the Hungaria, to listen to our views on the new project. He had faraway naval eyes and a gentle smile of great charm. Against all the odds, he took a great and immediate fancy to Guy, who ruthlessly swiped the cigarettes off his desk. As will be seen, his connection with us was brief. He was later awarded a posthumous VC for what was probably unnecessarily gallant behaviour in Oran harbour. When I heard of the award, I felt a pang that he should never have known about it. He was the type of

---

*In D Department of SIS. Later Chief Security Officer in Ankara Embassy when Philby went to Istanbul in 1947.

†In his excellent *Baker Street Irregular*, Colonel Sweet-Escott erroneously locates the first training school at Aston House. Aston was an explosives depot run by a Commander Langley, RN.

strong sentimentalist who would have wept at such honour. Our trainees came to adore him.

There were other additions to the training staff. There was jolly George Hill* who had written books about his secret exploits in Soviet Russia. He was one of the few living Englishmen who had actually put sand in axle-boxes. Immensely paunchy, he looked rather like Soglow's king with a bald pate instead of a crown. He was later appointed head of the SOE Mission† in Moscow, where the Russians hailed him with delight. They knew all about him. A very belated security check of his conference room in Moscow revealed a fearsome number of sources of leakage. Then there was an explosives expert named Clark, with a rumbustious sense of humour. Asked to arrange a demonstration for the Czech DMI‡ and his staff, he planted booby-traps in a copse through which they had to walk to his training-ground. He had assumed that they would go through the wood in Indian file like ducks. Instead, they walked abreast, and the officers at each end of the line suffered nasty shocks. It was a fluke that no one was hurt.

Then there was a melancholy Czech printer, who was recommended as having run an underground press in Prague. He was pale and podgy; after one look at him, the Commander decided that he must mess with the students. Another sad figure was an Austrian Social-Democrat who called himself Werner. He was being groomed to bear-lead any Austrian trainees we might get. No such recruits ever appeared and, as he spoke only German, I had to spend a lot of time holding his hand. He finally resigned, and was earmarked for other employment. He was killed when a submarine taking him to Egypt was sunk by dive-bombers in the Mediterranean.

---

*He had been with Bruce Lockhart, one of the British secret agents in Russia after the Revolution of 1917; also a friend of Sidney Reilly who had plotted to assassinate Lenin and Trotsky. During the Second World War he occupied a high post in SOE, and was sent to Moscow by Churchill as SOE/SIS representative.

†Special Operations Executive, formed under Churchill's orders in 1940 to assume all responsibility for undercover action against the Axis, especially sabotage and subversion. See Chapter II.

‡Director of Military Intelligence.

Our outstanding personality, however, was undoubtedly Tommy Harris, an art-dealer of great distinction.* He was taken on, at Guy's suggestion, as a sort of glorified housekeeper, largely because he and his wife were inspired cooks. He was the only one of us who acquired, in those first few weeks, any sort of personal contact with the trainees. The work was altogether unworthy of his untaught but brilliantly intuitive mind. He was soon snapped up by MI5 where he was to conceive and guide one of the most creative intelligence operations of all time. It will be seen that those days at Brickendonbury were days of almost unrelieved gloom, as far as I was concerned. They were illumined only by the beginning of a close and most highly prized friendship with Tommy Harris.

A few trainees were tossed our way: two small groups of Belgians and Norwegians, and a somewhat larger group of Spaniards. In all, there were about twenty-five of them. Perhaps they picked up some useful tips at Brickendonbury, but I doubt it. We had no idea what tasks they were supposed to perform, and neither Guy nor I had any success in digging the necessary information out of London headquarters. Otherwise, we had little to do, except talk to the Commander and help him draft memoranda for headquarters which seldom vouchsafed a reply. One thing only was clear. We had little to teach the Spaniards, most of whom were ex-*dinamiteros* from Asturias. "All instructors are the same," remarked one—a boy of about eighteen. "They tell you to cut off so much fuse. We double it to be quite safe. That is why we are still alive."

We might have learnt a useful lesson in security procedure if we had but known it. The truth did not emerge for some years. As we proposed to deal with agents to be sent to enemy territory where they were likely to be captured, it was decided that the identities of officers on the training staff should be protected by aliases. Peters became Thornley, Hill became Dale and so on. Guy, indulging his

---

He paid for the education of at least one of Philby's children; he also suggested to André Deutsch, the publisher, that Philby might write an account of his career, but Philby waited until after he arrived in Moscow.

schoolboyish sense of fun, persuaded the Commander to impose on me behind my back a name so inappropriate that I refuse to divulge it. The only exception was Tommy Harris who, for reasons which escape me, was allowed to retain his own name. Sometime after the war, Tommy ran into the head of our Belgian group, a nasty man of carefully obtruded aristocratic origin, and repaired to a teashop with him. While reminiscing about Brickendonbury, the Belgian remarked that the trainees had penetrated all our aliases save one. Tommy tested him and found that he did indeed know all our names, and asked him who the exception was. "Actually it was you," replied the Belgian.

Guy Burgess will soon disappear temporarily from these pages, so I may perhaps be forgiven a story which brings out his love of innocent mischief. Night had just fallen after a fine summer day. The Commander was in bed, nursing a sharp attack of eczema, to hide which he was growing a beard. A visiting instructor, masquerading under the name of Hazlitt, was at his bedside sipping a glass of port. There was a sudden shout from the garden, which was taken up by a babel in five languages. Trainees poured into the house, claiming to have seen one, three, ten, any number of parachutes falling in the vicinity. On hearing the news, the Commander ordered the Belgians to get into uniform and mount a machine-gun in the French windows. It commanded a nice field of fire, right across the school playing grounds. I do not know what would have happened if the enemy had come in by the front door. "If the Germans have invaded," the Commander told Hazlitt, "I shall get up."

He then made a disastrous mistake. He instructed Guy to ascertain the exact facts of the case, and telephone the result to the Duty Officer in London. Guy went about the business with wicked conscientiousness. I heard snatches of his subsequent telephone report. "No, I cannot add to what I have said. . . . You wouldn't want me to falsify evidence, would you? Shall I repeat? . . . Parachutes have been seen dropping in the neighbourhood of Hertford in numbers varying from eighty to none. . . . No, I cannot differentiate between the credibility of the various witnesses. Eighty to none. Have you got that? I will call you again if necessary. Goodbye." He went to report in triumph. "I don't know what I shall do if I do get up," said the Commander, "but I shall certainly take command."

An hour or two passed, and nothing more happened. The Belgians sadly took apart their Lewis gun, and we all went to bed. Next morning, Guy spent a lot of time on the telephone, and periodically spread gleeful tidings. The Duty Officer had alerted his Chief, who had communicated with the War Office. Eastern Command had been pulled out of bed, its armour grinding to action stations in the small hours. Guy made several happy guesses at the cost of the operation, upping it by leaps and bounds throughout the day. I should add that the nil estimate given him the night before was my own; the eighty, I should think, came from Guy himself. Both of us were wrong. One parachute had fallen. Attached to a landmine, it had draped itself harmlessly round a tree.

As the summer weeks went by without any clear directives from London, the Commander's aspect changed for the worse. He became more than usually taciturn and withdrawn. At first, I thought that his eczema was bothering him more than he cared to admit. But then I began to hear from the grapevine things which had never been told us officially. Section D had been detached from SIS and reformed under the aegis of Dr. Dalton, the Minister of Economic Warfare; Grand had gone, his place taken by Frank Nelson,* a humourless businessman whose capacity I never had an opportunity to gauge. After a visit to Brickendonbury from Colin Gubbins† and a posse of fresh-faced officers, who barked at each other and at us, the Commander fell into a deep depression. He minded not being told. It was no surprise when he summoned Guy and myself one morning and told us that he had spent the previous evening composing his letter of resignation. He spoke sadly, as if conscious of failure and neglect. Then he cheered up and the charming smile

---

*He made a fortune early in life as a partner in the merchant firm of Symons, Barlow & Co. in Bombay. While working for SIS he became Conservative MP for Stroud.

†In 1939 he was Assistant to the Head of Military Intelligence Department of the War Office— MI/R (Military Intelligence/Research).

came back, for the first time in many days. He was clearly happy to be going back to his little ships after his brief baptism of political fire.

The Commander's resignation was accepted without difficulty. Listlessly, we set about disbanding our establishment. The steps taken to this end are no more than a blur in my memory. We must have stashed the trainees away somewhere for future use, as I heard later that, in addition to Werner, at least two of them were dead. One, a nice Norwegian wireless operator, had been caught by the Germans and shot soon after his return to Norway. The other, the best of the Belgian group, had been flown to a dropping place in Belgium. But his parachute had somehow caught on the under-carriage of the aircraft, and he had been hurtled at mercifully high speed to unconsciousness and death. The Spaniards I was to see again.

Tommy Harris left us in pretty high dudgeon and soon found his true level as a valued officer of MI5. Guy and I reported to the new headquarters of Special Operations at 64 Baker Street which afterwards became famous (or notorious, according to the point of view) as plain "Baker Street." An awful lot of office furniture was being moved in and around; every time we visited the place, partitions seemed to be going up or coming down. Below us, the staff of Marks & Spencer watched and wondered. There were many new faces confronted with new jobs. Banking, big business and the law had been combed for recruits. There was also a distressing dearth of old colleagues. Nelson's purge had been thoroughgoing. He had been gleefully assisted by some senior officers on the intelligence side of SIS, notably Claude Dansey and David Boyle, of whom more will be heard. They were determined not only to "get Grand," but to get all his closest henchmen as well.

The purge was to come yet nearer before it was called off. One evening, Guy dropped in for a drink in an unusually tongue-tied condition. Finally it came out; he had fallen "victim to a bureaucratic intrigue," by which I understood that he had been sacked. I assumed that my own days, if not hours, were numbered, and Guy obviously looked forward to having me as a companion in distress.

But next month, and the month after that, my pay envelope still contained ten £5 notes. Special Operations, it seemed, had need of me; or perhaps I was too insignificant to merit dismissal. Guy was nothing if not resilient. He soon found a desirable niche in the Ministry of Information, which gave him a wide range of cultivable contacts. He began to refer contemptuously to my continued association with "Slop and Offal."

II. In and Out of SOE

Although the failure of our first training venture was depressing, it had the advantage of getting me back to London, where I could at least feel nearer to the corridors of power and decision. In practical terms, it did me little immediate good. I had no specific duties, and therefore could not lay claim to office space. I drifted around Baker Street, trying to memorize the new faces and fit them into a coherent organizational pattern, a most difficult task for anyone at that time. Everybody seemed very busy, if only moving furniture. In the presence of such activity, my idleness embarrassed me. It was like a cocktail party at which everybody knows everybody but nobody knows you.

Improbable though it seemed at the time, I was witnessing the birth-pangs of what was to become a formidable organization. If I have described its origins, such as I saw them, in flippant terms, it is because flippancy is unavoidable. Between the wars, the intelligence service had enjoyed a mythical prestige; but the myth had little substance. This statement may strain the credulity of many, especially in the absence of published records. But is it any more incredible than the known fact that the prestigious fleet sent to

Alexandria to frighten Mussolini away from Abyssinia was incapable of action because it had no shells? The truth is that, under a succession of complacent and indifferent governments, the secret service had been allowed to wither, just as the armed forces had withered. Apart from financial starvation, there was little serious approach to staffing and system. Just as horse-minded officers were allowed to dominate the army twenty years and more after the battle of Cambrai, so the secret service, because its Chief happened to be an admiral, was overloaded with naval rejects. No particular blame can attach to Admiral Sinclair* for this; thrown entirely on his own slender resources, he naturally picked his subordinates from the circles he knew best.

As for system, there was virtually none. When, as a result of the Fifth Column scares in Spain, the potential importance of undercover action against an enemy seeped into what passed for British military thinking, the result was reluctant improvisation. Section D was grafted onto a sceptical SIS, to plan noisy acts of derring-do, while the theme of "black propaganda"† became the toy of a number of government fringe organizations which stumbled about in the dark, bumping into one another. Small wonder that the results in the first year of war were minimal. In case I should be thought to exaggerate, let me quote Colonel Bickham Sweet-Escott,‡ one of the ablest and most perceptive officers to serve SOE throughout the war: "Our record of positive achievement (Summer, 1940) was unimpressive. There were a few successful operations to our credit, but certainly not many; and we had something which could be called an organization on the ground in the Balkans. But even there we had failed to do anything spectacular . . . our essays in Balkan subversion had succeeded only in making the Foreign Office jumpy. As for Western Europe, though there was much to excuse it, the

---

*Known as "Quex." Director of Naval Intelligence until 1921. Head of SIS from 1936 until his death in November 1939.

† "Underground" or subversive propaganda.

‡ Came to SIS from the City. Served in Section D. Author of Baker Street Irregular, Methuen, 1965.

record was lamentable, for we did not possess one single agent between the Balkans and the English Channel."* Strange, but true.

This was the background of the changes described in the last chapter. But they were only small parts of a much bigger programme of reform. In July 1940 Churchill invited Dr. Dalton, the Minister of Economic Warfare, to assume the sole responsibility for all undercover action against the enemy. To discharge this responsibility, Dalton called into being an organization which he called the Special Operations Executive.† Originally, it was divided into three parts: SO1, for black propaganda; SO2, for sabotage and subversion; and SO3, for planning. SO1 was later rechristened Political Warfare Executive, and SO2 took over the name originally given to the organization as a whole, Special Operations Executive. For the sake of brevity, I will refer to them in future as PWE and SOE, even if the events described took place before the change of name. SO3 need bother us no longer, as it soon drowned in paper of its own making and died an unlamented death.

I was beginning to wonder how long I could go on drawing pay without working for it when I received a summons from Colin Gubbins. He had been put in charge, among other things, of our training programme, and must have heard my name in connection with the abortive Brickendonbury experiment. Gubbins, of course, was to achieve great distinction by the end of the war,‡ and I am pleased to think that at that first interview I sat up and took notice. The air of his office crackled with energy, and his speech was both friendly and mercifully brief. A friend of mine nicknamed him "Whirling Willie" after a character in a contemporary comic strip. It was rumoured that he could only find time for his girl-friends at breakfast. But he was man enough to keep them.

Gubbins began by asking if I knew anything about political

<hr>

*B. Sweet-Escott, Baker Street Irregular.

† Started on 22 July 1940. See E. H. Cookridge, Inside SOE *(Arthur Barker, 1966)*.

‡ Maj.-Gen. in 1943. DSO, CMG, KCMG, Polish Croix de Vaillance. Served in Poland during the war. Worked for SOE from 1940 to 1946, when he retired. Afterward Sir Colin MacVean Gubbins. Died in 1976.

propaganda. Guessing that he would like a monosyllabic answer, I replied: Yes. He went on to explain that the new training establishment was being planned on an ambitious scale. There would be a considerable number of technical schools for demolition, wireless communication and the rest. In addition, he was setting up a central school for general training in the techniques of sabotage and subversion. Underground propaganda was one of the techniques required, and he was looking for a suitable instructor. He wanted me to go away and produce a draft syllabus on the subject. He showed me to the door with the words: "Make it short."

When I got down to it, I realized that my knowledge of propaganda left much to be desired. I had no inside experience of modern advertising methods. My few years in journalism had taught me to report what was happening, often a fatal mistake in a propagandist whose task is to persuade people to do things. I consoled myself with the unconvincing reflection that the world had seen many successful propagandists who had been equally ignorant of the techniques of selling soap. But, to be on the safe side, I took the trouble to consult a few friends of mine in the advertising world from whom I picked up some basic principles that could be padded out to fill quite a few lectures. I have found that advertising people can be relied on for two things. First, they will warn you on no account to go into advertising; second, they will expatiate at length on the dirtier tricks of their profession.

Within a few days I felt that I had enough to sustain the draft syllabus which Gubbins wanted, provided I lent it reality by drawing on examples from European politics and from Fascism in particular. I compressed it all into a page and a half of foolscap and telephoned Gubbins to say that it was ready. In five minutes he was back again, saying that he had arranged a meeting in Charles Hambro's* office to discuss the paper that afternoon. It was the first time since the fall of France that I had seen any action to speak of.

During the war Churchill put his friends from the City into high posts in SOE and SIS, including his banker, Charles Hambro, head of SOE from 1942 to 1943.

Gubbins brought several of his staff officers along to the meeting. Hambro greeted us in his friendly, comfortable way, making us all feel at home. He took my paper and read it aloud, slowly and deliberately. At the end of it, he remarked that it all sounded very sensible. Gubbins's officers nodded in brisk, no-nonsense manner; they looked intensely military. To my surprise Gubbins himself was smiling happily. "Exactly what I wanted," he said emphatically. "*Exactly* . . . what do you say, Charles?" Hambro said nothing in particular. Perhaps the Great Western Railway was on his mind. "Go ahead and do just that," Gubbins told me. The meeting was over.

I had now got specific duties which entitled me to a desk in Gubbins's offices. These were not at No. 64, but farther up Baker Street towards Regent's Park. I set about expanding my draft syllabus into a series of full lectures. But I was still far from happy. The new school was to be located in Beaulieu, Hampshire, far from London. Such a distance would interfere horribly with my other pursuits. Sometimes it seemed that I would do better to throw my hand in, but I was deterred by two considerations. In the first place, it was essential to keep my foot in the door of the secret world to which I had gained access. It would be stupid to resign until I had a clear prospect of other employment in that same world. In the second place, knowledge is seldom wasted, and I could not lose by finding out what was going on in the Special Operations' far-flung establishments. I decided to stay on until something more rewarding turned up.

I had little doubt that the training people would let me go when the moment came. I knew that I would make a lousy lecturer. Since the age of four, I have had a stammer, sometimes under control, sometimes not. I also had qualms about the subject matter of my course. The prospect of talking about political subversion did not worry me. There were very few people in England at that time who knew anything about it, and I had at least had a little practical experience in that field. But I was disturbed by my rudimentary acquaintance with propaganda techniques. I had drafted leaflets before but had never printed one.

It was some time before we foregathered at Beaulieu, and I used it to fill some of the gaps in my knowledge. As often as possible, I visited Woburn Abbey, where Leeper* presided languidly over the black propaganda people in PWE. (More than four years later, I found him little changed. It was the summer of 1945; he was languidly swatting flies in the British Embassy in Athens while Greece came to the boil.) But I was surprised to learn that he could be pettish on occasion. It was said that he clashed with Dalton more often than not, and gave the good Doctor much food for exasperated thought.† There is some confirmation of this story in Dalton's memoirs.

If the new Baker Street was the preserve of banking, big business and the law, Woburn had been stormed by the advertisers. Outside Leeper's own sanctum, the place sounded like a branch of J. Walter Thompson. There were exceptions, of course: Dick Crossman, Con O'Neill, Sefton Delmer‡ and Valentine Williams, to mention a few. But the majority, so it seemed, had just the sort of expertise I stood most in need of.

At first, I was treated with some reserve. Like all departments, especially new ones, Woburn was on the lookout for trespassers. But they soon realized that my interest in getting to know them was sincere, and that I was more than ready to accept advice. It was clear that secret agents in Europe would indulge in propaganda, whether we wanted it or not. That being the case, it was good policy for Woburn, as the authority responsible for black propaganda, to get a foot in the door in the shape of a co-operative instructor. After a few visits, I qualified for a lunch with Leeper. Valentine Williams, who was present, offered to drive me back to London in his official Rolls-Royce. I would have liked to talk to him about Clubfoot. But we had lunched well and he slept all the way.

There was another, perhaps more important, field for my re-

Electra House, a secret department, established by the Foreign Office. Leeper worked as an assistant to Sir Stuart Campbell. Later it was merged with SOI of D-Department into the PWE.

†*SOE was directly responsible to the Minister of Economic Warfare, Dr. Hugh Dalton.*

‡*Like Philby he had been a journalist covering the Spanish Civil War—for the* Daily Express.

searches at this time. It was all very well to teach agents the forms of propaganda. But the content of propaganda was just as important. Doubtless, the agents would get their orders on the day; but it was necessary to prepare them in advance for the sort of orders they would receive. This required a certain amount of political indoctrination, so that they would reach their fields of operation with at least some general idea of what the British Government had in mind for the future. Woburn was not a good place to seek answers to such questions. Leeper and his men were themselves complaining of the lack of political direction from London.

For this purpose, I turned to Hugh Gaitskell.* I had known him slightly before the war, when we had discussed Austrian problems. I cannot remember the nature of his interest, and I am quite sure that he did not know mine. At the time of which I am speaking, he was Principal Private Secretary to Dalton, sitting right under the horse's mouth. He was closely associated with Gladwyn Jebb,† whom Dalton had made responsible for Baker Street operations. Gaitskell was a very busy man and usually suggested our meeting for dinner at a pub off Berkeley Square. We would discuss my problems over sausages and mash. Sometimes we would go back to his office and consult Jebb or perhaps the Doctor himself. The latter was always ready with a hospitable whisky-and-soda. (I have already boasted of having recognized Gubbins as a man of distinction. To restore the balance, I must confess that I never suspected in Gaitskell the first-class Front Bench material which emerged later.)

On the whole, the result of these meetings was disappointing. Dalton was having his troubles with the Foreign Office. It was facile then, as it is now, to speak of a Foreign Office view. There are a lot of people in the Foreign Office and quite a few views. But when all

---

*Gaitskell had also been in Austria in 1934. He was supposed to have been alarmed at the news of Philby's marriage to "that young communist girl, Alice [Litzi] Friedman." Apparently Gaitskell saw Philby as "a rather altruistic left-winger, mixed-up and Byronic in outlook, eager to assist the left-wing cause without leaning quite as far as communism." Gaitskell, it appears, also underrated Philby!

†He later interrogated Krivitsky, who reported that there was a Soviet agent in the Foreign Office— probably Donald Maclean.

the objections to a given course of action were taken into account, the common denominator which was left was usually unexciting. It often appeared that the British wanted a simple return to the status quo before Hitler, to a Europe comfortably dominated by Britain and France through the medium of reactionary governments just strong enough to keep their own people in order and uphold the *cordon sanitaire* against the Soviet Union.

This view of Europe was incompatible with the very existence of SOE. Its aim, in Churchill's words, was to set Europe ablaze. This could not be done by appealing to people to co-operate in restoring an unpopular and discredited old order. It could not even be done by working on the feelings of the moment; they were conditioned largely by Hitler's uninterrupted sequence of victories. We could operate effectively only by anticipating the mood of Europe after a few more years of war and Nazi domination had steeled them to take the future into their own hands. This would, without doubt, be a revolutionary mood. It would sweep away the Europe of the twenties and thirties.

Dalton and Gaitskell, of course, saw the contradiction between their SOE mission and the Foreign Office view. But they had to walk warily because they themselves had no clear alternative. Both were sure, like good Socialists, that the European trade unions held one of the most important keys to the situation. But it was doubtful whether the unions would take the risks involved at the behest of a British Government, even if it contained Attlee, Bevin, Dalton and other Socialists. To many, it seemed that wartime Britain was very different from the Britain of Baldwin and Chamberlain. But how could a foreigner be sure that it was not just a different cloak for the betrayer of Abyssinia, Spain and Czechoslovakia? Suspicion was kept alive by the failure of the British to unfold a truly revolutionary propaganda. The lack of suitable political direction dogged us through the war. All resistance groups took our money and supplies; very few paid heed to the voice of London. They emerged only when they saw their own way to the future, not the way envisaged for them by the British Government. Thus the comparative success of SOE on the side of physical demolition and harassment was matched by its comparative failure in the political field.

This is not the place for a discussion of the limitations of SOE, whether imposed from outside or inherent in its own weaknesses. I mention these problems only to illustrate the doubts which beset me as I joined the teaching staff at Beaulieu. They explain why, in spite of the good companions I found at the school, my stay there was almost wholly unsatisfactory. My own shortcomings, and the enforced neglect of my other interests, contributed substantially to the unhappy state of affairs. I escaped to London whenever I could, usually on the pretext of visiting Woburn for talks on technical matters. But it was not enough. No wonder that my mess bill was consistently the highest.

My discontent was in no way due to my colleagues at Beaulieu, in whom I was lucky. Our commandant, John Munn, was a young colonel of the sensible military type, as opposed to the no-nonsense military, the mystical military and the plain-silly military. He neither barked nor advocated Yoga. He held together a shoal of pretty odd fish in a net of personal authority. His treatment of us was adult, and his attitude to his own superiors was loyally critical. His Chief of Staff was an older man who had seen service in the First World War. He was fond of saying that he had security in his bones, and looked as if he had little marrow in them. But he was only occasionally a nuisance and had a pretty talent for the piano.

The Chief Instructor was a colourful character called Bill Brooker, who afterwards made a great success of the subsidiary training school established in Canada. He was the dynamic-salesman type, with an inexhaustible armoury of wisecracks and anecdotes, including a series in brilliant Marseilles argot. As far as I am aware, he had never lived an underground life. But, after a little research, he could talk to trainees as if he had never lived otherwise. He was assisted by a paler imitation of himself, who described himself as a drysalter. Drysalting, I learnt, was one of the more respectable of City occupations.

We had one of the pottery Wedgwoods, pale and wild-eyed, who would break long silences by unexpected and devastating sallies. There was Trevor-Wilson, who later displayed a gift for captivating both the French and the Chinese, which proved invaluable when he was posted to Hanoi. He used to visit Southampton regularly on private business about which he would smile savourously and say nothing. One day he was refused official transport for the purpose and resolutely walked the whole way, there and back—some fifteen to twenty miles. It was the most determined act of gallantry in my experience. In abrupt contrast to Trevor-Wilson, there was a Buch-manite* who unhappily marked me down for conversion. The end came when he gave me his views on sexual intercourse and I re-marked that I felt sorry for his wife. After that, our contacts were limited to table-tennis, which he played with a dexterity suggesting human origin.

The star of our team was Paul Dehn,† who had now fulfilled his early promise as an entertainer. He proved that deep waters do not have to be still. At bottom, he was a serious man with a warm and generous strain of romanticism. On the surface, he bubbled and frothed like a trout stream. His tomfoolery at the piano shortened the long summer evenings, and some of his images are still with me. He claimed to have heard at a Manchester bus stop the following snatch of conversation. First prosperous grocer to second prosper-ous grocer: "Adabitacunt last night. Aaaah, it was luvly . . . just like a velvet marse-trap."

The one of us who achieved most public recognition after the war (if we except Paul Dehn) was Hardy Amies, the dress-designer. He was my first and only contact with that profession, and he looked the part in a large and elegant fore-and-aft, green for the Intelli-

<hr />

Frank Nathan Daniel Buchman, an American evangelist and missionary, founder of the Oxford Group Movement, who carried on an extensive campaign for Moral Rearmament in Great Britain, 1939.

†*In SOE during the war. Scriptwriter. Won the British Film Academy Award (Best British Screen-play) for screenplay of Anthony Asquith's* Orders to Kill, *1958. Wrote screenplays for* The Spy Who Came in from the Cold, *1965, Zeffirelli's film version of* The Taming of the Shrew, *1966, and* Murder on the Orient Express, *1974. Died 1976.*

gence Corps. He was not a regular member of our mess, as he was liaison officer between the school and headquarters in Baker Street, one of his main duties being to dig out of headquarters material of potential value to our instructing staff. As our requirements were, at that stage, almost limitless, he could have made for himself a pretty wide field of enquiry. I felt unreasonably resentful of his presence as his job would have suited me better than my own.

The first fact to distinguish me from my colleagues was that I was alone in having had personal experience of life underground. Not one of the others had ever dreamt of lowering his voice when passing a policeman in the street. Yet subsequent experience convinced me that, in the circumstances, the choice of raw instructors was wise. Seasoned secret service officers were in desperately short supply. In practice, they could only have been drawn from SIS. It was clear that if SIS had been approached for suitable instructors, it would have followed time-honoured practice by off-loading duds (if even they could have been spared). It is awesome to think what would have happened to the trainees if they had fallen into the hands of such men. As it was, our staff instructors had more than their fair share of intelligence and imagination; beside them, some of the old hands would have looked imbecile. This view, I think, is borne out by experience. There has been much criticism of SOE; of its planning, its operations, its security. But attacks on its training establishment have been relatively and deservedly few.

The second fact that set me apart from my colleagues was that they were all in uniform. On occasion, Peters and Gubbins had both dropped remarks about the desirability of getting me into the army. As I have already said, I thought that such a step might seriously limit my freedom of movement without offering any countervailing benefit. I found that the best way to maintain my eccentric status was neither to agree or disagree; in face of my apparent total indifference, the subject was quietly forgotten. Long before the end of the war, I came to realize my good fortune. I was never inhibited by dreams of promotion nor by the envy of colleagues, and never had rank pulled on me by senior officers outside my service.

The great difference between Beaulieu and Brickendonbury was that we actually trained people at Beaulieu. We were no longer an overstaffed holding camp, but a real school. There was a group of Norwegians, who were remarkable at fieldcraft. In one night exercise, after only a few weeks of training, the whole group succeeded in reaching a particular upstairs room in a house after penetrating thick woods strewn with alarms and booby-traps, laid by the head gamekeeper at Sandringham,* and crossing an open garden heavily patrolled by members of the instructing staff. I was on patrol myself and could have sworn that no one had got through. There were my old Spanish friends from Brickendonbury, required to do a little work at last. After my first talk with them, they nicknamed me *el comisario politico.* These were presumably the same Spaniards whom my old friend, Peter Kemp,† met on the shores of Loch Morar, near Arisaig. In his instructive book, *No Colours or Crest,* Kemp writes of them: "A villainous crowd of assassins; we made no attempt to mix with them"—a remarkable case of telepathic judgement.‡ My own feeling is that after being mucked around for a year or so by the British Government, they would cheerfully have killed anyone in the uniform of a British officer. But they exercised restraint.

It is only with sadness that one can recall the party of Dutchmen who attended our first course. Too many of them, owing to an operational disaster, were soon to be sent to certain death. Herr Giskes,§ a former Abwehr officer, has written of the capture in Holland of an SOE wireless operator, who thereafter communicated with England under German control and was responsible for party after party being dropped straight into the arms of waiting Germans. Subsequent enquiry seems to have established that the cap-

---

*One of the few thousand Nobby Clarkes in Britain. He was seconded to us as fieldcraft instructor.

†*SOE officer. Fought alongside the Albanian partisans after the German occupation in 1943.*

‡My views on Spain and Spaniards naturally differ from those of Peter Kemp who fought for General Franco during the Civil War. But I fully appreciate his description of the shock he suffered on first exposure to Hugh Quennell, the head of the SOE Spanish section.

§*Herman J. Giskes, author of* Abwehr III F, *Amsterdam, 1948.*

tured operator did in fact send the emergency signal telling HQ that he was in German hands, but that somehow his message was wrongly interpreted, or just ignored.

Shortly after the school opened, we were sent a party of anti-Fascist Italians, recruited from among Italian prisoners-of-war in India by Alberto Tarchiani and his friends. They were unfortunate in the choice of the British officer put in charge of them. He spoke perfect Italian, but was of the barking type. I used to wonder, not very sympathetically, when he would get a stiletto in his ribs. There were also two Frenchmen, booked for some special mission which was not divulged to us. One was Right, the other Left; but both had an admirable hatred of Vichy. They turned out to be my star pupils, and within a fortnight they were producing leaflets of a high standard. I mention this because they were almost the only trainees who took the slightest interest in politics or political propaganda. The others were probably better SOE material; brave but pliable, content to do what they were told without worrying about the future shape of Europe.

I was clearly bad SOE material, since worry about the future shape of Europe was my chief preoccupation. The war situation was going from bad to worse. The Greek army, facing the Italians in Albania, had shot its bolt by spring. The Yugoslav revolution of April, for which SOE claimed some credit (our people had been there and *post hoc, propter hoc*), was followed by the prompt invasion of Yugoslavia and occupation of Greece. Worst of all was the loss of Crete, for the defence of which sufficient British resources should have been available. The retention of Suda Bay would have been substantial compensation for the loss of the Balkan mainland. It was difficult to discuss such matters in our mess, where a tendency to the stiff upper lip masked realities. But still greater events were looming.

One fine morning, my batman woke me with a cup of tea and the words: "He's gone for Russia, sir." After giving two rather perfunctory lectures on propaganda technique, I joined the other instructors in the mess for drinks before lunch. My colleagues were clearly plagued by doubt in this perplexing situation. Which way should the stiff upper lip twitch when Satan warred on Lucifer? "Russky's for the high jump, I'm afraid," said Munn reflectively, and his words were generally agreed, or rather approved. The spirit of the Finland volunteers was still very much alive. For the moment, the subject was closed by the announcement that Mr. Churchill would address the nation that evening. It was clearly wisest to wait until the Prime Minister had spoken.

As usual, Churchill settled the question. By the time he had finished his speech, the Russians were our allies, my colleagues approved, and the upper lip clicked back into place. The only casualty was the spirit of Finland. But in the next few days, we were increasingly alarmed by the informed estimates that seeped through from London of the Red Army's capacity to resist the German onslaught. The Russian section of the War Office Intelligence Directorate wavered between three and six weeks for the duration of Hitler's Russian campaign. SOE and SIS experts said much the same. The most optimistic forecast I heard in those days was attributed to a Brigadier Scaife, then employed, I think, in the Political Warfare Executive. He said that the Russians would hold out "at least three months, possibly much longer." As Evelyn Waugh once wrote: ". . . he was bang right."

It was now more than ever necessary for me to get away from the rhododendrons of Beaulieu. I had to find a better hole with all speed. A promising chance soon presented itself. During my occasional visits to London, I had made a point of calling at Tommy Harris's house in Chesterfield Gardens, where he lived surrounded by his art treasures in an atmosphere of *haute cuisine* and *grand vin*. He maintained that no really good table could be spoiled by winestains. I have already explained that Harris had joined MI5 after the break-up of the training-school at Brickendonbury. It must have been sometime in July that he asked me if I would be interested in a job that called for my special knowledge of Franco's Spain. He explained that it would not be with MI5, but with SIS.

In order to make sense of Harris's suggestion, it is necessary to anticipate, very briefly, matters that will be discussed in detail in subsequent chapters. SIS was responsible for all secret intelligence work, both espionage and counter-espionage, on foreign soil. MI5 was responsible for counter-espionage and security in Britain and in all British territory overseas. The counter-espionage section of SIS, known as Section V, and MI5 were in fact two sides of the same medal. The primary function of Section V was to obtain advance information of espionage operations mounted against British territory from foreign soil. It was clear that effective advance warning from Section V would go far to help MI5 in its task of safeguarding British security.

Section V, according to Harris, was not providing adequate service. MI5 had been pressing SIS hard to make the necessary improvements, even to the point of threatening to go into the foreign business itself. Such an extension of MI5's charter could not have taken place without a government decision, but some officials at least were prepared to take the issue up to the top. SIS, therefore, yielded to the pressure by substantially increasing Section V's budget to finance additional staff. As a high proportion of German intelligence operations against Britain were mounted from the Iberian Peninsula, the biggest expansion, from two officers to six, was planned for the sub-section dealing with Spain and Portugal. Harris told me that Felix Henry Cowgill, then head of Section V, was looking for someone with a knowledge of Spain to take charge of the expanded sub-section. If I was agreeable, Harris thought that he could put forward my name with good hope of success.

I decided at once to fall in with the suggestion, but I asked Harris for a few days to think it over. There might have been snags; in any case, I must rationalize my decision. Section V was located at St. Albans, not ideal, but immeasurably better than Beaulieu. My new job would require personal contacts with the rest of SIS and with MI5. There was also a suggestion of Foreign Office interest, not to mention the service departments. By accident, I discovered that the archives of SIS were also located at St. Albans, next door to

Section V. When I looked for drawbacks, I could only think that the job was not in all respects the one which I would have chosen, Spain and Portugal now lying far out on the flank of my real interest. But the same applied, a thousandfold, to Beaulieu.

A few days later, I told Harris that I would be most grateful if he took the matter further. He first interested his own boss, Dick Brooman-White,* who was then head of MI5's Iberian section, and was later to become a close friend, and I assume that the old-boy network began to operate. I rather think that the formal approach to Section V was made by Dick White,† then a senior officer of MI5, and about the only one whose personal relations with Cowgill remained tolerable. (Dick White, "Big Dick," is not to be confused with Dick Brooman-White, "Little Dick." The former was much later to become head of SIS while the latter was elected Conservative MP for the Rutherglen constituency.) It was not long before I received a telephone call from Cowgill, asking me to go and see him.

Meanwhile, I was busy disentangling myself from Beaulieu. By means of two spectacular failures in the lecturing line, I made it impossible for anyone to contend that I was indispensable, and Munn received my decision to resign in his sensible and sympathetic way. He only asked me to stay on until I could find a replacement. Here, again, I was lucky. I found at a loose end that same *soi-disant* Hazlitt, who, shoulder to shoulder with Commander Peters, had braved the German paratroops at Brickendonbury. The final arrangements took two or three weeks more, during which time I paid a visit to Cowgill at Markyate, on that detestably narrow stretch of the Great North Road. It is a measure of the informality of the times that I had not definitely applied for the job and

*Defended Philby in the House of Commons when Marcus Lipton accused Philby of being the Third Man in 1955.

†Mr. (afterward Sir Richard) Goldsmith White. Became head of MI5 in 1953, then head of SIS in 1965—the only man to have been in charge of both departments. When he became head of SIS in 1956 he was furious that Philby was still working for SIS and had him put under surveillance.

that Cowgill therefore could not have indicated his acceptance. Yet, in the course of a long evening, he told me exactly what my duties would be against a background of the structure of SIS as a whole. As his discourse was of a highly secret nature, I took it as a formal statement of intention. In other words, I considered myself hired.

III. "An Old-Established Racket"—SIS

My transfer, or rather my drift, from SOE to SIS was completed in September 1941. A dynamic lady who made the same move a year or so later was happy at the change, because, as she said: "If you have to work for a racket, let it be an old-established racket." I could have said the same earlier, if I had thought of it. It would have been stupid to underrate the ability of the new men flowing into Baker Street, and their objective was a thoroughly worthy one. Yet they brought with them a style of strained improvisation as they left their tidy offices in the City and the Temple to spread disorder and financial chaos throughout Europe, gamekeepers turned poachers one and all. It was great fun in theory with ideas whizzing up and down the corridors. But most of the hard work involved pleading with the Air Ministry and the Admiralty for an extra aeroplane or an extra small boat, and SOE had yet to establish itself with Britain's perennially conservative services.

SIS was also undergoing changes, and its staff was expanding, but all too slowly, to meet the growing hunger of the services for intelligence. But there was a hard core of established practice and a staff structure to correspond. The new accretions did little to

change its essential nature. SIS resembled the Chinese in their
ability to absorb and digest alien influences. Under pressure, it took
in representatives of the Foreign Office and of the service departments, of whom Patrick Reilly* alone left a significant mark. It even
survived more corrosive imports, such as Graham Greene and
Malcolm Muggeridge, both of whom merely added to the gaiety of
the service.† In short, I was happy to find solid ground beneath my
feet, and to get down to real work.

As is well known, the headquarters of SIS were then in Broadway Buildings, just across the road from St. James's Park station. But
the wartime organization had outgrown its original habitat. Both
Section V and Central Registry had been displaced to St. Albans,
while other odds and bits had been scattered around London and
the Home Counties. On arrival at St. Albans, I was billeted on some
horribly rich people, whose wealth was not the only horrible thing
about them. The husband was conveyed daily between his house
and the station in a chauffeur-driven Rolls-Royce, while the wife
locked up the sugar and counted jam-pots lest the maids should pil-
fer. In a mercifully short time, I found a convenient cottage on the
farthest outskirts of town, where I could be free of unwanted interruption. Within a few days, I bought a pheasant from a man at a bus
stop. He told me that he "sometimes got a chicken," so I fared well
thereafter.

Much will be heard of SIS in the following pages, and a general,
though far from comprehensive, picture of its activities should
emerge in due course. At this stage, it is necessary to give only a
summary account of its structure and proceedings, to assist the
reader in understanding my story from the outset. It should be understood that any summary account must be an over-simplification. If

*Principal Foreign Office adviser to SIS in 1944. See p. 97. Afterward British Ambassador in
Paris.

†Philby once defended Graham Greene when the latter was involved in a row because his agent sent
to the Azores, after the British take-over, failed to communicate; the result was that SIS was made to look
silly by MI5. For Greene's and Muggeridge's exploits, see p. 77.

the British genius leans towards improvisation, then SIS is a true reflection of it. The organization is like an old house, the original plan of which is still visible though dwarfed by subsequent additions.

SIS is the only British service authorized to collect secret information from foreign countries by illegal means. Its monopoly in this respect is sometimes infringed by enthusiastic amateurs. But whenever such infringements come to light, they lead at best to acrimonious inter-departmental correspondence, at worst to serious confrontations in Whitehall. The words "by illegal means" distinguish the secret service from other newsgathering agencies, such as the Foreign Service and the press, though some nations fail to appreciate this fine, and sometimes illusory, distinction. Thus, in the Middle East, as I know from personal experience, journalists are confused with spies—often rightly so. Yet, however blurred in practice, the distinction is real. SIS alone receives secret funds, for which it is not accountable in detail, so that it may get information from foreign countries which is not obtainable by ordinary, lawful means.*

The basis of SIS activity is the network of agents, almost always of foreign nationality. These agents work, directly or indirectly, under the control of an SIS office, known as a "station," housed in a British Embassy and thus protected from the action of local authorities by diplomatic convention. Their motives in working as agents are various, ranging from the heroic to the squalid. The great majority are paid for their work, though not too well. On the whole, SIS prefers to have agents on its payroll, since the acceptance of pay induces pliability. The unpaid agent is apt to behave independently, and to become an infernal nuisance. He has, almost certainly, his own political axes to grind, and his sincerity is often a measure of the inconvenience he can cause. As one SIS officer re-

---

*The latest figure available to me, for 1966–7, is £10 m.—a fourfold increase in twenty years of peace.

marked in disgust of the Vermehrens, the German couple who defected to the British in Istanbul during the war: "They're so God-awful conscientious you never know what they're going to do next."

Information collected by agents finds its way, directly or by devious means, to the local SIS station responsible for their recruitment in the first place. There it is given a preliminary assessment, for value and accuracy, by SIS officers disguised as diplomats. If considered of interest, the information is transmitted, with appropriate comment, to London headquarters. Transmission is normally by foreign service communications, radio or diplomatic bag, according to the degree of urgency. At the time of which I am now speaking, the pre-war disguise of Passport Control Officer* for the chief SIS representative was still in wide use, although it was already a little less than opaque. Its advantage was that the holder of that office was legitimately entitled to make enquiry into the records of visa applicants, and one type of enquiry could lead to another. Its disadvantage was simply that the device had become known. In a later chapter, I will deal with more recent disguises.

The structure of headquarters in London was based on a division of responsibility for the production and assessment of intelligence. Those who produced the stuff should submit their wares to independent scrutiny before the finished article was sent to government departments. In accordance with this principle, headquarters was divided into two groups of sections, known respectively as "G" Sections and Circulating Sections. The "G" Sections administered overseas stations, and supervised their operations. Each had a regional responsibility; one would manage Spain and Portugal, another the Middle East, a third the Far East and so on. Circulating Sections assessed the intelligence received, and passed it on to interested government departments; they would then pass back to the "G" Sections the judgement of those departments, together with their own. The Circulating Sections were divided, not regionally,

---

The first head of SIS, Captain Cummings, established a vast network of espionage in Europe based on Passport Control Officers.

but according to subject matter. One would handle political intelligence, others concerned themselves with military, naval, economic and other types of information.

Section V, to which I found myself attached, was in a peculiar position, in more than one respect. In name, it was a Circulating Section, and its subject matter counter-espionage. But, whereas the other Circulating Sections dealt with regular government departments, such as the Foreign Office, the Admiralty and the rest, whose knowledge of secret operations was marginal, Section V's main "customer" was itself a secret organization: MI5. This, it might have been thought, should have led to mutual understanding and smoother co-operation. In fact, the reverse was the case, and it was not until the war was nearly over that reasonable harmony between the two organizations was attained. This unhappy situation was partly due to personal factors, which were aggravated by the fog, not to mention the hysteria, of war. But it was also due to basic differences of opinion about the line of jurisdictional demarcation between the two organizations. MI5 argued that counter-espionage was indivisible, and that they were entitled to all information on the subject available to Section V. Cowgill, speaking for Section V, rejected that view, maintaining that MI5 were entitled only to information bearing directly on the security of British territory, with the implicit rider that he himself was sole judge of the relevance of information to British security. He claimed, apparently in all sincerity, that MI5 were planning to set up their own counter-espionage organization in foreign territory, while MI5, in their turn, suspected Cowgill of withholding from them essential information on the pretext of safeguarding the security of SIS sources. These clashes were to put me in a whole series of awkward situations, as my own sympathies in the debate were usually with MI5. To avoid needless trouble, many of my subsequent communications to MI5 had to be made verbally.

Partly out of this painful situation, there arose a second peculiarity of Section V. In the early days of the war, the demands of the service departments on SIS were urgent and overwhelming. As we shall see, there were also powerful people in SIS who regarded offensive intelligence as the only serious form of intelligence in wartime. As a result of these pressures, SIS stations abroad were concentrating more and more exclusively on getting information required by the armed forces, such as troop movements, naval concentrations, air potential, weaponry and so on. Counter-espionage was starved of resources, and MI5 was justified in complaining, not only that Section V was withholding information, but also that SIS was not getting enough anyway. This was a charge that Cowgill could not ignore; he felt much the same himself. But he was not strong enough to force through the necessary diversion of existing SIS resources to counter-espionage goals. He preferred to circumvent the existing establishment by having specialist officers of his own attached to overseas stations. Nominally, such officers came under the general administration and control of the "G" sections; but most of the latter were far too busy to pay them any attention, and their day-to-day instructions emanated direct from Section V. The "G" officer in charge of Spain and Portugal, for instance, was a certain Fenwick, who had come to SIS from the oil business. He acquiesced, with only a minimum of grumbling, in the posting of counter-espionage specialists to Madrid, Lisbon, Gibraltar and Tangier, and within weeks had practically forgotten all about them. So all went smoothly, provided I paid him a courtesy call every now and then and (in his own words) "munched a chop" with him. The general effect of this arrangement was that Section V, though still a Circulating Section in name, acquired some of the functions of a "G" Section. It became a hybrid, regarded with a degree of suspicious incomprehension by the rest of SIS. The position suited Cowgill well. It enabled him to claim that counter-espionage was an esoteric art, calling for wisdom not revealed to the common run of intelligence officers. He thus acquired a certain immunity from criticism within SIS. Unfortunately, he could not expect the same respectful hearing from MI5.

Although I have said that SIS is the only British organization authorized to collect information by illegal means, it does not follow that it is alone in collecting secret intelligence. By interception of wireless signals, it is possible to obtain huge quantities of secret intelligence without breaking any national or international law. Before wireless messages can be read, they must be decyphered. This was done in wartime Britain by the so-called Government Code & Cypher School at Bletchley. Much of their work was brilliantly successful. I must leave it to learned opinion to decide how much more could have been achieved if the wrangling inside GC & CS had been reduced to manageable proportions. (The same could be said of most government departments, not to mention the universities in peacetime.)

To sum up very briefly the place of Section V in the intelligence world: as part of SIS, it was responsible for the collection of counterespionage information from foreign countries by illegal means. The department chiefly interested in its intelligence was MI5, which was responsible for the security of British territory and therefore required as much advance news as possible of foreign attempts to penetrate British secrets. Some of the work of Section V was also of interest to other departments. For instance, the Foreign Office had a direct interest in the facilities offered by neutral governments to the German intelligence services. The efforts of Section V were at first supplemented by the Radio Security Service (RSS), which intercepted enemy intelligence signals, and by GC & CS, which read them. Before the war had gone on long, these roles were in fact reversed. Section V's investigations abroad were directed mostly to filling in the gaps in the extraordinarily comprehensive picture derived from signals intelligence.

It is now time to turn to some of the personalities involved, many of whom loom large in my subsequent story. The head of Section V, as I have mentioned, was Felix Cowgill.* He had come to SIS from the Indian police shortly before the war, and had already

---

Later Lt.-Col. Cowgill. Towards the end of the war Philby intrigued against Cowgill: see Chapter VI. Cowgill can hardly have been suspicious of Philby since he was one of his closest advisers. Cowgill later left the Service. In 1966 he retired from the task of liaising between the British Army and the local citizenry in Munich-Gladbach, West Germany.

made his mark. His intellectual endowment was slender. As an intelligence officer, he was inhibited by lack of imagination, inattention to detail and sheer ignorance of the world we were fighting in. His most conspicuous positive quality, apart from personal charm of an attractively simple variety, was a fiendish capacity for work. Every evening, he took home bulging briefcases and worked far into the small hours. Friday nights, as a regular habit, he worked right round the clock. Mornings would find him, tired but still driving, presiding over a conference of his sub-section heads and steadily knocking an array of pipes to wreckage on a stone ashtray. He stood by his own staff far beyond the call of loyalty, retaining many long after their idleness or incompetence had been proved. To the outer world, he presented a suspicious and bristling front, ever ready to see attempts to limit his field of action or diminish his authority. By the time I joined Section V, he was already on the worst of terms, not only with MI5, but also with RSS, GC & CS and several other SIS sections as well. Glenalmond, the St. Albans house in which Section V had established its headquarters, already felt like a hedgehog position; Cowgill revelled in his isolation. He was one of those pure souls who denounce all opponents as "politicians."

Unfortunately, Cowgill was up against a formidable array of brains. Most of our dealings with GC & CS on the subject of German intelligence wireless traffic were with Page and Palmer, both familiar figures in Oxford. RSS presented the even more formidable Oxonian combination of [Hugh] Trevor-Roper, Gilbert Ryle, Stuart Hampshire and Charles Stuart. Herbert Hart, another Oxonian, confronted him in MI5, though here Cambridge too got a look in with Victor Rothschild,* the MI5 anti-sabotage expert. All these men outclassed Cowgill in brainpower, and some of them could match his combativeness. Trevor-Roper, for instance, was never a meek academic; and it was characteristic of Cowgill's other-

---

*Also at Trinity College, Cambridge, in the 1930s. His mother employed Burgess soon after he left Cambridge—to report on her stock holdings, and later Burgess took over his flat in Bentinck Street. Later on in the war he trained Allied saboteurs for operations in Nazi-occupied Europe.

worldliness that he should have once threatened Trevor-Roper with court martial. It is a tribute to Cowgill that he fought this combination for nearly five years without realizing the hopelessness of his struggle. How often would he fling off a furious minute denouncing this or that colleague, and then softly murmur, with a gleam of triumph, "and *now* let's get on and fight the Germans!"

The main issue on which these personal battles were joined was control of the material derived from the interception of German intelligence-signals traffic. When the question first arose, the Chief of SIS had vested control in the head of Section V. There was plenty to be said for the ruling, and, to the best of my knowledge, it was never seriously challenged. What was challenged was the way in which Cowgill exercised his control. He realized at once that he had been dealt a trump card, and from the beginning he guarded it jealously, even to the point of withholding information that might have been put to effective use. His foes held him guilty of seriously restrictive practices, while he held them at least potentially guilty of disregarding totally the security of the source. After a hassle with Cowgill, Dick White, then Assistant Director of the MI5 Intelligence Division, claimed to have had a nightmare in which the material concerned was on sale at the newsstands.

Cowgill's relations with the rest of SIS posed problems of a different order. Here he was faced, not with what he regarded as excessive interest in his doings, but with the danger of total neglect. During the war, offensive intelligence absorbed most of the energies of SIS. Counter-espionage, with its emphasis on defence, was reduced to Cinderella status. This was largely due to the influence of Claude Dansey,* who was then Assistant Chief of the Secret Service, or briefly ACSS. He was an elderly gentleman of austerely limited outlook who regarded counter-espionage as a waste of effort in wartime, and lost no opportunity in saying so. His specialty

---

*Assistant to Stewart Menzies. Valentine Vivian and he were, to some extent, rivals; and Philby took Vivian's side against Dansey. In the First World War he worked in Intelligence in France, then tried to run an English-style country-club in America. After that he worked for SIS in Italy and Switzerland, then was brought back to London to organize "Z" Section. Dansey died shortly after D-Day, in 1944.

was the barbed little minute, which creates a maximum of resentment to no obvious purpose.

The cause of counter-espionage should have been defended, at that high level, by Valentine Vivian,* whose title was Deputy Chief of the Secret Service, or DCSS. He was a former Indian policeman, and had been head of Section V before the war. But Vivian was long past his best—if, indeed, he had ever had one. He had a reedy figure, carefully dressed crinkles in his hair, and wet eyes. He cringed before Dansey's little minutes, and shook his head sadly at his defeats, which were frequent. Shortly before I joined Section V, Cowgill had brushed Vivian aside, making little effort to hide his contempt. It was no thanks to Vivian that Cowgill finally won his battle for increased appropriations for Section V, and with Vivian that was to rankle. It may seem that the feelings of so ineffectual a man scarcely require mention in a book of this kind. But, at a later stage, they were to play a critical part in my career.

It was more than a year before I was directly affected by these high-level rivalries. My first duty was to do my job and learn it at the same time. I was given precious little guidance from above, and soon became indebted to my head secretary, an experienced girl who had been in the service before the war and was able, despite chronic ill health, to keep me from the worst pitfalls. The volume of work was monstrous. As a result of staff increases, we were now six in the Iberian sub-section, doing the work which two were supposed to have done before. Small wonder that one of them committed suicide. We were still regularly swamped with incoming mail. Some allowance must be made, of course, for Parkinson's Law; even so, like many of my colleagues, I could only keep pace with my towering "in-trays" by taking a fat briefcase home in the evenings. Every day brought a few telegrams from Madrid, Tangier or

*Known as "Vee-Vee." Son of a renowned Victorian portrait painter. Came to SIS in 1925 from Indian police. He was a friend of Philby's father—from the days when St. John Philby was in the Indian Civil Service. He was responsible for Philby's transfer from SOE to SIS, and later was used by Philby when he intrigued against Cowgill. See Chapter VI.

Lisbon. We received showers of minutes from other sections of SIS and of letters from MI5. Once a week, we received depressingly heavy bags from the Peninsula, where our representatives were still thrashing around in the dark. For every lead that produced results of any kind, a dozen lured us tortuously into dead ends.

A typical muddle confronted me at an early stage. An SIS agent in Madrid stole the diary of a certain Alcazar de Velasco, a particularly nasty Falangist from the Spanish Press Office, who had visited England a month or two previously. The diary stated explicitly that he had recruited a network of agents on behalf of the German Abwehr; names, addresses, and assignments were given in detail. It was not until many weeks' work had been wasted that we reached what was surely the correct conclusion, namely, that the diary, though undoubtedly the work of Alcazar de Velasco himself, was fraudulent from beginning to end, and had been concocted solely for the purpose of extracting money from the Germans.

Yet the theft was not entirely fruitless. We had long suspected Luis Calvo, a Spanish journalist working in London, of passing to Spain information that might comfort, and possibly aid, the enemy. The fact that his name appeared in the diary as a recruit for the Alcazar de Velasco network suggested a promising means of extracting a confession, spurious though we thought the entry to be. Calvo was accordingly arrested and taken to the "tough" interrogation centre on Ham Common. No physical violence was used to break him down. He was merely stripped naked and propelled into the presence of the camp commandant, a monocled Prussian type called Stephens who punctuated his questions by slapping his riding-boots with a swagger-stick. We had made a correct assessment of Calvo's nerve. Appalled by his compatriot's frivolous treachery, and doubtless by the swagger-stick, he said enough about his activity to warrant his captivity for the duration. Another by-product of the famous diary was derived from the fact that it mentioned Brugada, the Spanish Press Attaché in London, in compromising terms. Brugada was the last person to want a scandal, and proved satisfactorily co-operative when MI5 hinted delicately that the diary might furnish the Foreign Office with a plausible pretext for declaring him *persona non grata*. He did not actually do much serious spying for MI5; but he passed on enough gossip about visiting Spaniards to earn a code-name: Peppermint.

A more spectacular success came our way soon afterwards, although I broke all the rules to achieve it and caused a ghastly mix-up which was only resolved after the war. We received an intercepted telegram showing that the Abwehr was sending two agents to South America on the Spanish SS *Cabo de Hornos*. With a carelessness which was all too frequent in Abwehr communications, their names were given in full. One was a certain Leopold Hirsch, travelling with his wife and mother-in-law, the other Gilinski. Shortly before their embarkation, a second, more mysterious message was received from the German out-station in Bilbao, confirming that Hirsch and his "ORKI companions" were ready to leave. "ORKI" was intriguing. What could it be but an organization of revolutionary international Communists—some splinter group of Trotskyists sponsored by the Germans with a view to confounding our Russian allies? We therefore passed the whole passenger list of the *Cabo de Hornos* through our records, finding at least a dozen whose careers suggested possible links with dissident Communism. Of these, perhaps half looked as if they might well be scoundrelly enough to fall in with Abwehr intrigues.

Accordingly, after consulting Cowgill, I sent a cable to the Defence Security Officer in Trinidad, where the ship was due to call, instructing him to arrest the Hirsch family, Gilinski and a string of others. I had no power whatsoever to order this, or any other arrest. The proper procedure would have been a recommendation from me to MI5; another from MI5 to the Colonial Office; an instruction "subject to local objection" from the Colonial Office to the Governor of Trinidad; and an order from the Governor of the Defence Security Officer. Fortunately, the DSO was an enthusiastic type, and acted on my orders without further question. Still more fortunately, Hirsch promptly confessed, saying, with almost certain truth, that he had nursed no intention of carrying out his German assignment but had accepted it simply to get out of Europe. In the euphoria created by this "triumph" we tended to overlook the fact that the rest of the detained men could not be induced to admit to anything remotely resembling espionage. But a search of their baggage showed that they were all smuggling in greater or lesser degree, so we had some small technical grounds for holding them, just in case.

The solution of the mystery came about a year later. My subsection officer responsible for handling all intercepted material was struck by a sudden thought. He got on the telephone to Palmer at GC & CS, and asked him to look up the relevant signal from Bilbao. Could "ORKI" possibly have been a mistake for "DREI"? Within a very short time, Palmer was back. Yes, it almost certainly was "DREI"; in fact, he could not understand how the cryptographers could have got ORKI in the first place. So, instead of Hirsch and his ORKI companions, we had Hirsch and his three companions, namely, his wife, his mother-in-law and Gilinski. By the time the British Government came to consider the claims brought by the others for wrongful arrest, I was safely out of the way, trying to penetrate the Soviet Union and the Balkan states from my comfortable base in Istanbul.

Hitherto, I have spoken only of the interception of wireless traffic. But there were several other forms of interception which, though less productive from the counter-espionage point of view, had their uses. There was the postal censorship which threw up one or two cases of interest, but less perhaps than might have been expected. There were also sophisticated techniques of opening foreign diplomatic bags. This method could not be used against the enemy directly, since German and Italian bags did not pass through British territory. But the bags of neutral states and of minor allies, such as the Poles and the Czechs, were fair game. Such operations involved several complex procedures.

First the courier had to be persuaded, by one means or another, to leave his bag in British custody. This was not so difficult as it sounds, owing to the inadequate courier systems employed by many states, and to the indiscipline of the couriers themselves. During the period that Britain was cut off from the continent, all diplomatic bags were carried by air. Delays in the departure of aircraft were an everyday occurrence, and it was always easy to engineer a delay even when flight conditions were favourable. On arrival at the airport, the courier would be confronted with an adverse weather report, or with the discovery of a technical fault in the aircraft, either of which could impose an indefinite wait. Thus he would have the choice of sitting on his bag in the airport lounge or going to the nearest town and enduring the rigours of a provincial hotel bedroom. In such circumstances, it was only courtesy on the part of the airport security officer to offer the perplexed courier the hospitality of his safe. "You can see me lock it up myself, old boy. It will be quite all right till you get back." A surprising number of couriers fell for this soft sell and went off, without encumbrance, to inspect the local talent—which, of course, the security officer was happy to provide on request.

As soon as the courier was safely out of the way, the security officer would inform the waiting experts and put the bag or bags at their disposal. Each bag and its contents were studied with minute care before they were opened. Every knot and seal was measured, copied and photographed where necessary; chemical examination was also made. Then came the task of untying the knots, breaking seals, extracting and photographing the contents. Finally, the hardest of all, was the job of replacing the contents exactly as found, with infinitesimally accurate reproduction of the original knots and seals. The Russians were exempt from this treatment, partly because their bags were invariably accompanied by two couriers, one of whom was always on duty, partly because of a belief that they contained bombs designed to obliterate the inquisitive. But the diplomatic correspondence of the South American states, of the

Spaniards and Portuguese, of the Czechs, Poles, Greeks, Yugoslavs and many others, was regularly subjected to scrutiny. Despite the extreme care used, accidents sometimes happened. On one occasion, the red seals in a Polish bag turned purple under treatment, and nothing could be done to restore them. The Poles were regretfully informed that the bag in question had been "lost." This happy ending was possible only because the Poles, following their occasional custom, had entrusted this bag to the British for onward transmission—presumably because its contents were of minor importance. It would have been much more awkward if it had been accompanied by a Polish courier.

By early 1942, the trickle of intercepted Abwehr telegrams had become a flood. This was largely the work of Dilly Knox,* who had succeeded in penetrating the secrets of the cypher machine used by the Abwehr. This comprehensive system of eavesdropping yielded fascinating glimpses of the intimate life of German intelligence officers. There was the case, for instance, of Axel, the German police dog. He had been posted from Berlin to Algeciras, presumably to guard the Abwehr out-station there from British agents sneaking across the bay from Gibraltar. On the last stage of its journey, Madrid sent a warning telegram to Albert Carbe, alias César, the head of the Abwehr post at Algeciras: "Be careful of Axel. He bites." Sure enough, a few days later, Algeciras came up with the laconic report: "César is in hospital. Axel bit him."

It was not long before we had a very full picture of the Abwehr in the Peninsula. We knew the names, pseudonyms, addresses, cover functions and real functions of most of the staff at Madrid headquarters and at the many out-stations, such as Barcelona, Bilbao, Vigo, Algeciras, etc. When our knowledge was already as comprehensive as one could reasonably expect, a maddening incident occurred which illustrates the dangers of having two separate organizations working on the same subject in the same area. I have al-

---

Alfred Dilwyn Knox, CMG, Fellow of King's College, Cambridge; d. 1943.

ready said that there were exceptions to the rule whereby service attachés in British Embassies abroad did not engage in secret intelligence work. One of the exceptions was Captain Hillgarth, RN, the Naval Attaché in Spain. There was an arrangement, prompted by Hillgarth's personal acquaintance with Churchill, by which secret funds were made available to him for undercover activity. A condition of this arrangement was that Hillgarth's only contact with SIS should be with the Chief himself. The ostensible reason for this was security; Hillgarth's sources were to be particularly sacrosanct. But the condition also helped to feed the gallant officer's illusions of grandeur. As a pseudonym for correspondence with the Chief, he chose Armada—natch!

One day, Cowgill asked me to make an appointment with the Chief to discuss an important communication from Armada. It was about the Germans in Spain. It was seldom that I saw the Chief in those days, and I was as shy in his presence as he was in mine. But I found him in a playful mood. He had been poaching on my preserves, he said; doing a spot of counter-espionage in Spain. He had given Armada authorization to buy, "for a very large sum," details of the leading Abwehr officers in Spain. Those details had been received, and he handed me a telegram—a distressingly short one, containing about a dozen names and a few particulars about each. Gustav Lenz, head of the outfit; Nans Gude, in charge of Naval Intelligence, etc., etc. I remarked, somewhat tactlessly, that the information, so far as it went, was accurate. The Chief's eyebrows rose. How did I know it was accurate? Because we knew it all already. How much more did I know? A very great deal. Why hadn't the Chief been informed? But we compiled regular monthly reports of the progress of our investigations, and a copy always went to the Chief. At this point he showed what an essentially nice man he was. "My dear Philby," he said with his characteristic quick smile, which had gone almost as soon as it came, "you don't expect me to read everything that's put on my desk!" We agreed that Armada's source should be asked for more, but of course nothing came of it. What incensed me was that I soon identified this precious source—a high official of the Dirección General de Seguridad—and knew that his price would have been very high indeed. And I had to fight to get an extra £5 a month for agents who produced regular, if less spectacular, intelligence!

One problem of intelligence is how to get it. Another, equally important and sometimes much more difficult, is how to exploit it. Picking up enemy agents as they reached British territory was all very well and good. But what about our painstaking analysis of the German establishment in the Peninsula as a whole, and the organization in Germany from which it emanated? It was borne in on me gradually that our comprehensive knowledge called for more imaginative action than had been contemplated in the past. It was not enough simply to warn MI5 of the impending arrival in Britain of Abwehr agents, or to effect the occasional capture in Trinidad. It should surely be possible to put our information to good use in disrupting, or at least seriously embarrassing, the enemy on his own chosen ground in Spain.

These thoughts were spurred by the gradual accumulation of intelligence to the effect that the Germans were contemplating an operation in Spain involving the use of advanced technical devices. The Abwehr code-name for the operation was Bodden. The Bodden is the name of the narrow strip of water separating the island of Rügen from the German mainland, not far from the wartime scientific research station at Peenemünde. Taken together with additional evidence that the Bodden experts, with their instruments, seemed to be closing in on Algeciras, this seemed a clear enough indication that something affecting the Straits of Gibraltar was brewing. We therefore consulted the formidable Dr. Jones, head of the scientific section of SIS, who studied the evidence, and pronounced fairly confidently that it indicated the installation of a device for detecting the passage of ships through the straits at night. As this would have introduced a serious new hazard into the supply position in the Western Mediterranean, I judged that the time was ripe for a new suggestion designed to scare the daylights out of the Abwehr in Spain.

I had already considered, and discarded, the possibility of put-ting SOE on to the Germans in Spain. Even if they had had the re-sources for such an operation, I doubted whether anyone on our side would really welcome a James-Bond-like free-for-all in Spain, where the authorities would have been against us. On reflection, it seemed that the diplomatic approach would be the best. We had a legitimate grievance against the Spanish Government for allowing the German intelligence a free hand on its territory, and a strong protest, based on detailed and cogent evidence, seemed quite in order. I had little hope that General Franco would take any action against his German friends; but I had no doubt at all that he would give them a friendly warning of their nakedness. My thoughts turned to General Westmacott, the Director of Extraordinary Intelligence in Compton Mackenzie's *Water on the Brain*,* and his dictum: "After all, the whole point of the Secret Service is that it should be secret." It was a good assumption that Gustav Lenz, the head of the Abwehr in Spain, would be severely shaken if his secrets could be shown to be no secrets at all.

The first step was to convince Cowgill that the operation was both worthwhile and feasible. Our indictment would have to be based largely on information derived from signals intelligence, and he was jealous of its safe-keeping, even *vis-à-vis* other British intel-ligence organizations. Yet the whole object of my proposal was that the document should be presented to an unfriendly Spanish Gov-ernment in the hope that it would be shown to the Germans. To my great relief, Cowgill reacted favourably. He took my draft, in which I had been at pains to conceal our sources, to the Chief, who also approved. Fortunately, the Foreign Office link with SIS at that time was Peter Loxley, who had as much vigour as charm, and he lent the project enthusiastic support. Within a reasonably short space, instructions were sent to Sir Samuel Hoare,† then British Ambas-

---

*Compton Mackenzie, *Water on the Brain* (London, Chatto & Windus, 1954).

†*Later Lord Templewood. British Ambassador in Madrid, and concerned with SIS work in Spain at a time when Philby was head of the Iberian section of SIS.*

sador in Madrid, to protest to General Franco in the strongest possible terms. He was to support his protest with a copy of my memorandum.

It is difficult to write nice things about Sir Samuel. But the truth compels me to admit that he rose to the occasion magnificently. He dressed the senior members of his staff in full uniform, and took them in a body to see the Head of State. What Franco then said to whom is not yet known. But the results were gratifying beyond expectation. Within two or three days, panicky telegrams were flying between Madrid and Berlin; all sorts of useless emergency measures were taken. There was even a report, not taken too seriously by us, that some of the chimneys of the German Embassy in Madrid were smoking unduly. The final triumph came in the form of a peremptory order from Berlin to Madrid: "The Bodden operation must be stopped in its entirety." We continued to get our signals intelligence without interruption. It was clear that the operation had not compromised our main source.

Encouraged by our success in Spain, we then launched a similar operation against the Germans in Portugal, but with only indifferent results. In the case of Spain our problem had been straightforward. General Franco, after all, was a self-declared co-belligerent on the side of the enemy. With very few exceptions, his senior officials sympathized warmly with the Axis. For that reason, we could be pretty sure that, wherever we hit, we would hurt our enemies. The Foreign Office had less than its usual crop of inhibitions about ruffling Franco's feathers, provided it had a good case; and, on the intelligence side, we had so few friends in Spain that we had little to fear from enemy reprisals. The position in Portugal was significantly different. Far from being straightforward, it was horribly complicated and fuzzy. Dr. Salazar, it is true, sympathized with the Axis. But he was far more cautious than his fellow-dictator in Spain, and pursued a more neutral line. For fear of disturbing Salazar's balancing act, the Foreign Office shrank from strong action calculated to force him down off his fence. He might only too

easily have come down on the wrong side. We had our own nar-
rower preoccupations on the intelligence side. Several senior Portuguese officials, whom we knew to be receiving money from the
Germans, were also receiving money from us. It was usually impossible to assess which side derived most advantage, if indeed any,
from this tangle. The last thing I wanted was to have the officials
come to us with a request to make good the extra-curricular salaries which they might lose through the expulsion of their German
paymasters.

In consequence, the contents of our protest, and the manner of
its presentation, were less spectacular than in the earlier case of
Spain. There was no full-dress approach of the Embassy to the wily
Doctor. Instead, the British Ambassador, Sir Ronald Campbell,*
took the matter up during a cosy meeting with the Portuguese Foreign Minister, Sampaio, who showed considerable diplomatic resources in his responses. It was, he said, extremely wrong of the
Germans to abuse Portuguese neutrality in the manner described
in our protest. Were we sure of our sources? He himself encoun-
tered the greatest difficulty in evaluating intelligence reports. The
whole matter was fraught with the most awkward difficulty. For instance, he had heard reports that other nations were not far behind
the Germans in illicit activity on Portuguese soil. If the Portuguese
Government took action against the Germans, the German Government might insist on similar action against those other nations.
Insistence of such a kind would put the Portuguese in a dreadful
dilemma. He, Sampaio, would certainly convey Sir Ronald's protest
to Dr. Salazar without delay. But, speaking personally, he doubted
whether the Doctor would take the action we requested without a
very careful examination of the whole many-sided problem. Having delivered this deft warning, Sampaio concluded with a gem of
diplomatic logic. Why, he sighed, must warring powers indulge in

*Friend of Maclean. He was British Minister Plenipotentiary in Washington when Maclean was
sent there in 1944. Then he became British Ambassador in Cairo—there when Maclean was posted to
Cairo in 1948.

espionage? If only they concentrated their whole intelligence resources on *counter*-espionage, there would be no objection from any
quarter!

Although the head of the British counter-espionage organization in Lisbon was an exceptionally able and sensitive man, many of
our Portuguese cases ended in the same indeterminate fashion.
There was the regrettable case of Stilwell, a British businessman
resident in Portugal for many years. His name came to our notice at
a time when our knowledge of the German services in Portugal was
still rudimentary. We were therefore inclined to regard the German intelligence operatives whom we had identified as much more
important than many of them subsequently turned out to be.
Among these was a certain Weltzien, a German merchant, who
loomed large in our preoccupations. After much endeavour, we
succeeded in purloining from Weltzien's office a card purporting to
come from his card-index.

We had apparently hit a bull's eye. The entries on the card
showed, in unmistakable terms, that Stilwell had, until quite recently, been in receipt of regular payments from Weltzien. But
our problem was by no means cut-and-dried. In itself the card
was no proof; it could have been a forgery. Some of us were
struck by the odd fact that the very first specimen from Weltzien's
card-index should have been right on the mark. A year or two
later, with more experience to hand, we might have hesitated
much longer than we did. But we had few spies actually in the
bag, and were anxious for more. In addition, we were so bemused
by the mysterious Weltzien that we were ready to take risks to
learn more about him. Stilwell was therefore invited to return to
England. He was arrested on arrival and brought to interrogation the following morning. His manner under interrogation was
dignified and resentful of his treatment. The sight of the famous
card shook him just about as much as an innocent man would
have been shaken. He was released without a stain on his character amid shamefaced apologies. We never got to the bottom of
the Stilwell card, although we staged a raid on Weltzien's office

with the object of stealing his whole card-index. Weltzien, however, was not caught off his guard, and the raid was as big a fiasco
as the arrest of the innocent Stilwell. We soon recovered our
poise when an increasing flow of serious intelligence proved that
Weltzien was not a key figure after all; on the contrary, a very minor
one.

Before leaving Portugal, I must recall a masterpiece of interrogation. A certain lady had entered Britain from Portugal, where
she had been known to consort with a number of Germans, including German intelligence officers. Search of her person and effects
yielded a small diary kept mostly in the form of cryptic abbrevia-
tions. The interrogator took her through the diary, entry by entry,
but she proved to be exceptionally quick-witted, stoutly denying
with considerable plausibility that any of the entries referred to
German acquaintances. Bloody but unbowed, her tormentor tried
one last desperate throw. "May I draw your attention, Mrs. —, to
your entry of such-and-such a date? It says: 'Spent all day sitting on
my fanny.' Now," after a pregnant pause, "*Who* was Fanny? In what
way was she yours? and *why* were you sitting on her?" Under the
impact of this dreadful inanity, the lady broke down and confessed
all.* Her story showed that her relations with Germans at Estoril
had indeed been intimate, but in no way inimical to the British war-
effort.

It was at about this time that I nearly got into serious trouble. I
have mentioned that Central Registry, housing the SIS archives,
was next door to Glenalmond. Bill Woodfield, who was in charge of
it, had become quite a friend of mine. I have been told that magenta
is the only colour that the rainbow lacks. If so, Bill's face would be
out of place in the rainbow. He had a liking for pink gins, which I
shared, and prudish appreciation of dirty stories. We used to fore-
gather often to discuss office politics, of which he had had a long
experience. This friendly connection paid off, and I was usually in

*No connection with FANY, the First Aid Nursing Yeomanry, a women's auxiliary service.

a position to get files rather more quickly and easily than many of my colleagues. Bill was seriously understaffed, and the people he had were often ill-trained.

There was a series of files in Registry known as source-books. These held the particulars and records of SIS agents operating abroad. It was natural for me to want information on the agents operating in the Iberian Peninsula, and my perusal of the source-books for Spain and Portugal whetted my appetite for more. I worked steadily through them, thus enlarging my knowledge of SIS activity as a whole. When I came to the source-book for the Soviet Union, I found that it consisted of two volumes. Having worked through them to my satisfaction, I returned them to Registry in the normal way.

About a week later, Bill telephoned to ask me for the second volume of the Russian source-book. After consulting my secretary, I called back to say that, according to our books, it had been returned to Registry on such-and-such a date. After further fruitless search in Registry, Bill contested the accuracy of my records, and urged me to make a further investigation. I turned our office upside-down, with negative results. Bill and I met once or twice in the evening to discuss the mystery over a few pink gins. He told me that the normal procedure on a loss of a source-book was for him to report immediately to the Chief. I managed to stall him for a few days, during which my alarm grew. I doubted whether the Chief would appreciate the excessive zeal which had led me to exhaustive study of source-books, especially as it had apparently resulted in the loss of one dealing with a country far outside the normal scope of my duties.

The lowering sky suddenly cleared. Bill telephoned me to offer a "full personal apology." It seemed that one of his secretaries handling the source-books, wishing to save shelf space, had amalgamated the two volumes into one. She had then come over queer, and gone home with a severe bout of flu. She had only just got back to the office and, on being tackled by Woodfield, had immediately remembered what she had done. I accepted the apology gracefully, and suggested meeting again that evening. We did so, and drowned the painful memory in another flood of pink gin. I remember thinking for a brief moment, duly regretted next morning, that magenta was my favourite colour.

IV. BRITISH AND ALLIED INTELLIGENCE COMPLEX

Owing to Cowgill's liking for a family atmosphere, an almost excessive cosiness marked the life and work of Section V. Officers and secretaries were put on Christian-name terms as soon as they arrived. It felt as if the office might at any moment burst into wholesome round games. While this was embarrassing at times, it had its professional uses. It was never difficult to find out what colleagues were doing; what was known to one would be known to all. It also gave me wide freedom of movement. Cowgill did not mind when or how the work was done, provided it was done—itself no mean requirement considering the volume of paper with which we were flooded. This meant that I could go up to London virtually at will. This was valuable for developing contacts with other SIS sections in Broadway Buildings, with MI5 and with other government departments interested in our work. I made a practice of going once a week, invariably with a bulging briefcase and a long visiting list. I also volunteered for night duty in Broadway, which came round once or twice a month. It was an instructive occupation because, in the course of a single night, telegrams would come in from all parts of the world, throwing new light on the operations of the service.*

Broadway was a dingy building, a warren of wooden partitions and frosted-glass windows. It had eight floors served by an ancient lift. On one of my early visits, I got into the lift with a colleague whom the liftman treated with obtrusive deference. The stranger gave me a swift glance and looked away. He was well-built and well-dressed, but what struck me most was his pallor: pale face, pale eyes, silvery blond hair thinning on top—the whole an impression of pepper-and-salt. When he got out at the fourth floor, I asked the liftman who he was. "Why, sir, that's the Chief," he answered in some surprise.

At that stage, I knew precious little of the Chief. His name was Stewart Menzies,† his rank Colonel. His office was on the fourth floor. His stationery was a vivid blue, his ink green. He wrote an execrable hand. Before becoming Chief, he had been head of Section IV, which dealt with Army intelligence. His official symbol was CSS, but in correspondence between Broadway and overseas stations he could be designated by any three successive letters of the alphabet, ABC, XYZ, etc. In government circles outside SIS, he was always known as "C." The initial was a hangover from the days of Captain Mansfield Cummings, RN,‡ the first head of the secret service in its modern form. That was the sum total of my knowledge of the Chief at the time of our first encounter in the lift. As will be seen, I came to know him much better, and I hasten to say that I look back on him with both affection and respect, though not necessarily with respect for those qualities on which he would have prided himself.

Apart from Fenwick, the agreeable but ineffectual oilman who vaguely administered the stations in Madrid, Lisbon, Tangier and

---

*One file available to night-duty officers in Broadway was especially valuable to me. It contained telegrams from the War Office to the British Military Mission in Moscow, sent over SIS channels.

†*Maj.-Gen. Sir Stewart Menzies. Head of SIS from 1939 to 1953.*

‡*Head of SIS when it was first created as an independent organization. Died in 1936.*

Gibraltar, my earliest contact in Broadway was with one of the Chief's closest cronies. He was in charge of the distribution of information obtained by rifling diplomatic bags, and of arrangements for its secure treatment by recipients. But he was also credited with being very close to the Chief, and thus having influence on policy. I was prepared to dislike him thoroughly, as I had heard appalling reports of him; his nickname was "Creeping Jesus." My first impressions tended to confirm the awful reports I had been given. He had most of the qualities I dislike most; it would be no justice to describe him as a selfish and conceited snob. Yet he had a capacity to ingratiate himself with senior members of the Foreign Office which, much to my surprise, I came to admire. Furthermore, I was increasingly drawn to him for his inability to assess the intelligence that passed through his hands. Although he was more than twice my age, he came to rely on my judgement. In my turn, I paid him all the outward signs of respect. Our personal association, despite its inherent absurdity, became quite a happy one. It was also of great value to me because, among the waffle and gossip that fills most diplomatic bags, there is sometimes a pearl of price. He would, of course, never have claimed the prerogative of using green ink; he used purple instead.

Through him, I met the famous Colonel Claude Dansey. Before the war, he had busied himself with building up the so-called "Z" organization, designed to penetrate Germany from bases in Switzerland. The most interesting thing about the "Z" system was that its communications were disastrously affected by the collapse of France. In Switzerland, Dansey had left behind to carry on the work a smooth operator named Van Der Heuvel (pronounced Hoyffl) who was alleged to be a Count of the Holy Roman Empire. He will forgive me if I have misspelt his name, either literally or phonetically, but I can claim to be in good company. When I went one day to dine with him at the Garrick, the porter had difficulty in understanding whom I wanted to see. "Ooooh," he said at last, "you mean Mr. Vanoovl," and gave me the appropriate direction.

I have already explained that Dansey had the lowest opinion of the value of counter-espionage, as well as a reputation for unnecessary combativeness. I was therefore surprised by the courtesy he showed me. It proved always to be so. Dansey was a man who preferred to scatter his venom at long range, by telephone or on paper. The only way to deal with him was to beard him in his office; a personal confrontation lowered the temperature, and made it possible to talk common sense. As soon as I grasped this, I had little difficulty with him, except to keep a straight face when he started to make cracks about Vivian, my boss's boss. Happily, our paths did not cross often, as he was good enough to strike me off his list of pet bugbears.

I made a point of seeing Vivian as often as possible. He was quite useless for immediate practical purposes, being mortally afraid of Dansey and even of his own subordinate, Cowgill. But he probably had a better mind than either, and was of a reflective temperament which led him to discourse long and widely on SIS history, politics and personalities, and on relations between SIS and MI5. He was a stickler for correct procedure, and his sermons on the subject told me more about the intricacies of government machinery than I could have learnt from the more slap-dash "result-getters," such as Dansey or Cowgill. I had little idea in the early months of my cultivation of Vivian how much it would assist me in attaining the one position in SIS which I wanted above anything the service could offer. Cowgill was to regret bitterly his premature dismissal of Vivian as a nonentity.

It was a short walk from Broadway Buildings across St. James's Park to the wartime headquarters of MI5 in St. James's Street. But the difference in style was considerable. Even the entrance compared favourably with the dingy hall at Broadway, and the first good impression was confirmed upstairs. The offices looked like offices; so far as I know, there were none of the makeshift rabbit hutches that disfigured so much of Broadway. The officers sat at desks uncluttered by dog-eared paper. At most, half-a-dozen neat files, each nicely indexed and cross-indexed, would be awaiting treatment. This had its drawbacks. At Section V, we used to complain of the inordinate detail which MI5 officers found time to pack into their long letters. Some of it, at least, was unwarranted by the significance of its subject-matter. Nevertheless, MI5 wore an air of professional competence which Broadway never matched. It may have been over-staffed, as Cowgill frequently complained. But the result of such over-staffing was that most of the officers knew what they had to do, and how to do it. The same could not be said of all too many in Broadway.

It had not always been so. After the fall of France, MI5 faced a situation for which it was quite unprepared. The British people fell victim to its own propaganda, particularly in regard to the German Fifth Column. For months after Dunkirk, the police and MI5 were swamped with reports of flashing lights, mysterious strangers, outlandish accents overheard in the pub and so on. The organization almost broke down. I first visited MI5 with Commander Peters in the autumn of 1940, when it was in its temporary quarters at Wormwood Scrubs. It was good to think that MI5 was housed in a prison, but the place was in a horrible mess. Stacks of unread correspondence littered the floors, and officers conceded that not more than a tenth would ever be read, let alone answered. Fortunately, it was all waste paper anyway. The German Fifth Column in Britain never existed.

The task of producing order from chaos was entrusted to a certain Horrocks who was imported (from the City, I believe) especially for that purpose. Inside a year, he could claim to have succeeded. I understand that he had authority over the administration in general, but my particular interest was in the archives. There he did a beautiful job. In a new home in part of Blenheim Palace, MI5 Registry was a place of delight after Woodfield's untidy labyrinth at St. Albans. Information was easily accessible in well-kept files and card-indices, and there were enough filing clerks to ensure that the work was done methodically and at a reasonable pace. I was surprised and envious to find that most of the girls knew the contents of the files for which they were responsible as thoroughly as the officers handling cases in St. James's Street. When I delicately raised the question with Woodfield, he replied that he was disgracefully under-staffed and that such attention to detail was unnecessary anyway.

Most of my work with MI5 concerned the so-called B Division of that organization. This was the place where intelligence was received and assessed, and where subsequent action was usually determined. By "action" in this context, I mean action to develop and exploit information received only, not such action as arrest. For, like SIS, MI5 had no executive power. It could not arrest suspects, but only recommend their arrest to the usual authorities. Although this made little difference in practice, since MI5's recommendations were almost invariably accepted, the formal distinction was firmly maintained in theory.

Here, I think, lies one of the most important reasons for the greater professionalism of MI5 compared with SIS. MI5 operates on British territory, and is therefore sensitive to the law of the land. It can, and often does, press for specific breaches of the law, but each one requires the explicit sanction of the government, usually in the form of a Home Office Warrant. Armed with such warrants, MI5 can arrange, for instance, to tap the telephones of private citizens or of institutions such as foreign embassies and the headquarters of the Communist Party. But it must watch its step. If MI5 makes a mistake, questions are asked in Parliament, the press launches campaigns, and all manner of public consequences ensue, of a kind distasteful to a shy and furtive organization. No such inhibitions hamper the operations of SIS in breach of the laws of foreign countries. The only sufferer is the Foreign Service which has to explain away mistakes to foreign governments, usually by simple denials.

The quality of MI5 in wartime owed much to its temporary recruits. There was a particularly good haul from the universities: Hart, Blunt, Rothschild, Masterman, and others, and the law also made a substantial contribution. Most of these fine brains returned to their normal occupations after the war; as this book is not a history, there is no need to enlarge on their excellences. But at the top of B Division, there were two professional intelligence officers who contrived throughout the war to retain the respect of their brilliant subordinates. As both have some part to play in my story, they call for a respectful mention.

The head of B Division was Guy Liddell.* "I was born in an Irish fog," he once told me, "and sometimes I think I have never emerged from it." No self-depreciation could have been more ludicrous. It is true that he did have a deceptively ruminative manner. He would murmur his thoughts aloud, as if groping his way towards the facts of a case, his face creased in a comfortable, innocent smile. But behind the façade of laziness, his subtle and reflective mind played over a storehouse of photographic memories. He was an ideal senior officer for a young man to learn from, always ready to put aside his work to listen and worry at a new problem.

Yet Liddell's career ended in disappointment. The head of MI5 during the war was Sir David Petrie, an Indian policeman of great authority and charm. When he retired, B Division would have voted to a man for Liddell to succeed him—and he had many supporters elsewhere. Instead, the government appointed Sir Percy Sillitoe,† another policeman, British this time, with less authority and less charm than Petrie. Liddell's personal disappointment was obvious, yet it was more than personal. He, like most of the MI5 professionals, maintained that MI5 was an intelligence organization, not a police outfit. The techniques for combating espionage were different from those adapted to crime. Since spies are backed by the great technical resources of governments, while criminals are not, there is clearly much to be said for that view. The government, however, took the view that the appointment of a senior policeman, trained in Whitehall procedures, would be safer. Liddell was awarded the doubtful dignity of Deputy Director, and he would have been inhuman if he had felt no resentment. I am sure

---

*No. 2 at MI5, then after the war became Chief Security Officer to the Atomic Energy Authority. A friend of Burgess and frequenter of his Rabelaisian parties.

†"An honest Copper," as Herbert Morrison called him. Before becoming Director-General of MI5 from 1946 to 1953, he was Chief Constable of Chesterfield, Glasgow and Sheffield.

that spies, had they but known it, would have rejoiced at Liddell's discomfiture. One did.

Liddell's chief assistant in B Division was Dick White. Originally a schoolmaster, he had joined MI5 between the wars. He was a nice and modest character, who would have been the first to admit that he lacked outstanding qualities. His most obvious fault was a tendency to agree with the last person he spoke to. With his usual good sense, he was content to delegate a lot of work to his subordinates, and to exercise his gifts for chairmanship with a view to keeping harmony in the division. He was one of the few officers in MI5 who, until the bitter end, maintained a reasonable personal relationship with Cowgill. His capacity for avoiding departmental fights paid off in the outcome. When Liddell became Deputy Director, White was promoted to the top of B Division. But there was more to come. In due course, White was wafted across the park to become Chief of SIS. Luckily, Dansey died before seeing a counter-espionage expert lording it, however courteously, over Broadway. If he hadn't, it would have killed him anyway.

I cultivated MI5 assiduously and, before the end of the war, I could claim many personal friends in St. James's Street. It was in every way necessary for someone to soften the collision between Cowgill and our opposite numbers; and as few others were willing to take the lead, I took it upon myself. Quite apart from immediate considerations, various long-term prospects were forming in my mind, for the materialization of which MI5 support would be helpful. I formed the habit of slipping my friends information off the record—that is to say, without Cowgill's knowledge. The rewards of such unorthodoxy were often generous.

A major battle developed in 1943, in which I found myself ranged discreetly on the side of MI5 against Cowgill. The issue was the location of Section V. We had been housed in St. Albans partly because of overcrowding in Broadway, partly because of the desirability of keeping the archives out of range of German bombers. When Woodfield moved his records to St. Albans, Cowgill moved too. His overt reason for doing so was that "a counter-espionage organization must be near its records." His real reason was that it enabled him to build up his little empire with a minimum of disturbance, free from the taint of "politics." The long lull in the bombing, however, had robbed these arguments of their cogency. There was plenty of office space available in London, and no obvious reason for not using it.

MI5 meanwhile had maintained their pressure for closer co-operation with ourselves. They laboured the virtues of "propinquity," a word that began to appear frequently in Petrie's correspondence on the subject with Menzies. It was indeed quite clear that, despite the telephone, co-operation would be more effective if the distance between us was less. This was precisely what Cowgill did not want, and for the same reasons that MI5 wanted it. He foresaw himself and his staff, back in London, dissipating their effort in "politics," at the mercy of the manoeuvres of Liddell and Co. Above all, he saw control slipping from his fingers. For my part, I was wholly in favour of the return to London. Closer contact with MI5, Broadway and other government departments, in my view, could only assist in promoting an overall grasp of intelligence work. That, as far as I was concerned, was all that mattered.

Characteristically, Cowgill overestimated his hold on the situation. He announced in St. Albans that he would take a free vote on the subject, giving all his staff a chance of pronouncing for or against London. He was even unwise enough to let outsiders know what he had done, so that the result of the vote could not have been suppressed. I assumed that a free vote entitled me to a little lobbying, and I got busy accordingly, not neglecting the secretarial staff, many of whom had begun to tire of the cloistered life in billets. The result of the vote dumbfounded Cowgill. More than two-thirds of our staff chose London—the vote, in itself, had no validity, but it did much to weaken Cowgill's determination. Within a few weeks, we were installed in offices in Ryder Street. We were two minutes from MI5 and fifteen from Broadway. If we came to work early, we could look down from our windows and see Quaglino's offloading its horrible garbage from the night before. We were just in time for the "little Blitz."

I must now go back a few months and write of an event that was to have a profound effect on all subsequent development of British intelligence work. I refer to the arrival of the Americans. Before the war, the United States lacked a regular foreign intelligence service. The Federal Bureau of Investigation was responsible for internal security only. Secret information from other countries was obtained to a limited extent from extra-curricular activity of service attachés and diplomats attached to United States embassies, who were less inhibited than the representatives of countries which had regular secret services to do the dirty work. It is now well known from published material how, in 1940, British Security Co-ordination, under William Stephenson,* was set up in New York. Its main ostensible function was to assist in protecting the security of American supplies destined for Britain; it was supposed that the large element of German origin in the United States would indulge in widespread sabotage. This supposition was not borne out. But Stephenson, who was a friend of Churchill's and wielded more real political power than any other British intelligence officer, soon found other outlets for his ample energies. One was interference with supplies destined for the Axis and with neutral shipping in which they were carried. It is probable that BSC committed more acts of sabotage than the whole German-born colony in the United States. But another outlet for Stephenson was the one towards which he devoted his best efforts: persuading the Americans that it was high time that they created an intelligence service of their own.

Stephenson, like many others, saw that the creation of such a service was, in the long run, inevitable. Short-term considerations suggested that it would be better for the British to get in on the ground floor and, by offering all possible help in the early stages, to earn the right to receive in return the intelligence that might

---

Canadian millionaire. Head of British Security Co-ordination in America.

be expected to flow from deployment of the greater resources of the United States. There was also the immediate chance of getting information through United States embassies in countries where Britain was no longer represented, such as Vichy France, the Balkans and even Germany. A true top-level operator, Stephenson was not used to footling around at the lower levels. His achievement was to stimulate the interest of Roosevelt himself, and to make quite sure that the President knew that Stephenson and his backers, among whom were SOE and MI5 as well as SIS, had a lot to offer. Thus when the Office of Strategic Services was born with General Donovan* at its head, the closest co-operation with the British was already assumed at the highest level. Whether the wartime exchange of British experience for American resources really paid off is a matter open to argument. What is beyond doubt is that the decision in favour of co-operation doomed the British services, in the long run, to junior status. That junior status has been sobering fact for many years. All SIS could do was sit back helplessly when the CIA committed the United States Administration to folly with Ngo Dinh Diem or to ridicule in the Bay of Pigs.

Stephenson's activity in the United States was regarded sourly enough by J. Edgar Hoover. The implication that the FBI was not capable of dealing with sabotage on American soil was wounding to a man of his raging vanity. He was incensed when Stephenson's strong boys beat up or intoxicated the crews of ships loading Axis supplies. But the real reason for his suspicious resentment, which he never lost, was that Stephenson was playing politics in his own yard, and playing them pretty well. He foresaw that the creation of OSS would involve him in endless jurisdictional disputes. The new office would compete with the FBI for Federal funds. It would destroy his monopoly of the investigative field. The creation and survival of the new organization was the only serious defeat suffered by Hoover in his political career—and his career had been all poli-

---

Maj.-Gen. "Wild Bill." Went to Moscow in December 1943 to discuss a project of co-operation between the two Intelligence services and talked with heads of GUR and GB.

tics. He never forgave Stephenson for the part he played as midwife and nurse to OSS.

These high decisions gradually seeped downwards and reached St. Albans. Our first visitor from the United States was a certain Kimball, of the FBI, who arrived shortly after Pearl Harbor. He talked with machine-gun speed, accusing the Navy, the Army, the State Department and the White House of having ignored FBI warnings of imminent Japanese attack. The real purpose of his visit, apart from the sales-cackle, was to announce that Hoover had decided to appoint a liaison officer in London, in the shape of a Legal Attaché of the United States Embassy, to co-operate with MI5 and SIS. After Kimball's departure, Cowgill spoke of him in derogatory terms, saying that "Hoover evidently intended to by-pass Stephenson." With more reason than usual, Cowgill regarded Hoover as another of the evil men who used intelligence as a step-ladder for political advancement, whose overtures should be treated with suspicion if not resisted outright. My loyalty to Cowgill was strained when the first Legal Attaché made his appearance. He was Arthur Thurston, a thoroughly competent operator with whom it was a pleasure to work. I had every reason to cultivate him, and he happily reciprocated the bootlegged intelligence I passed him. He was too perceptive to stay long with Hoover, preferring the political jungle of Indiana.

OSS were not far behind. After preliminary high-level talks with Donovan, Bruce, and others, we had assigned to us a small liaison party. Its head was Normal (Holmes) Pearson, a poet of Yale. He was hail-fellow-well-met, and have you heard the latest one about the girl in the train? He was terribly funny about his organization, Oh So Sexy. It was a notably bewildered group, and they lost no opportunity of telling us that they had come to school. I must have been slow to grasp the facts of inter-departmental life, as I was innocently surprised by the confidence bestowed on them by Cowgill. He gave them the freedom of our files, including the intercepted wireless traffic—which was still being doled out grudgingly to the FBI in heavily disguised form. It was difficult to see why a professional organization like the FBI should be denied intelligence which was given in profusion to the service once described by Pearson himself as "a bunch of amateur bums."

In due course, the answer became clear enough. It was quite true that Hoover had wanted "to bypass Stephenson." He did not like BSC and wanted to clip its wings. One way of achieving that end was to shift the weight of the liaison to London. In addition, he naturally wished to get close to MI5. Like the FBI's security division, MI5 was purely a counter-espionage organization. It had its worries about SIS, just as Hoover had his worries about OSS. Above all, in Hoover's eyes, its writ ran only in British territory, and its interests therefore could not clash with those of the FBI, whose jurisdiction was confined to the Western hemisphere. In short, Hoover's aim was two-fold: to move the centre of co-operation away from the United States to Britain, and to get as close as possible to MI5.

All this was highly distasteful to Cowgill. He would have liked to gather all exchange of counter-espionage information with the Americans into his own hands. Having failed in this, he wanted to restrict exchanges between the FBI and MI5 to a minimum. The ostensible reason for his attitude was fear that MI5 might pass to the FBI information derived from SIS without due regard for the security of SIS sources. I have never heard any evidence that such transactions occurred. But the line of argument had a certain plausibility, and in the stress of war a plausible argument is often good enough. Plausible or not, the argument was quite hollow, as Cowgill's liberality towards OSS showed clearly enough. Information too delicate for MI5 and the FBI should certainly have been withheld from Pearson's "bunch of bums." Yet it was not. The truth was that Cowgill saw in OSS a potentially pliable instrument which might be used to bolster his position against both MI5 and the FBI. His strength was that, however much Hoover might rave, no one in Britain could challenge his links with OSS on realistic grounds. Such a challenge would have meant MI5, for example, associating itself with Pearson's dictum on OSS. Inter-departmental good manners barred such crudities.

With respect to my own work in the Iberian Peninsula, the arrival of OSS was a pain in the neck. Apart from the time wasted in putting our information at the disposal of the newcomers, a host of problems arose from the appointment of their men in Lisbon. The first was a certain Ray Olivera, who soon made his dreadful mark. His opening move was to call on our own man, without warning, and ask for co-operation. Our man naturally asked for his credentials, in reply to which Olivera opened his bag to display its contents: God knows how many wads of dollar bills. Apart from this show of brashness, Olivera's arrival caused great confusion in the United States Embassy. Immediately after America's entry into the war, the Military Attaché in Lisbon, Colonel Solborg, had started sending agents through Spain into Occupied Europe. The Naval Attaché had naturally concentrated on shipping, and someone else started in on economic intelligence. By the time Olivera arrived, all these fields had been pre-empted, and no one was willing to withdraw in his favour. Prolonged muddle was eventually sorted out by George Kennan, then Counsellor of the United States Embassy in Lisbon. He decided that the best course was to keep the intelligence flowing and not to worry about jurisdictional disputes in Washington. Thus Solborg and the rest were confirmed in their undiplomatic activity, while counter-espionage, which no one had yet thought of, was thrown as a sop to Olivera.

The unfortunate Olivera, however, was given little time to settle down to his restricted field. He succeeded without delay in making himself so generally unpopular in Lisbon that he had to be replaced. The new man was a certain Di Lucia, who was soon giving us an immense amount of trouble. Within a very short time, he was claiming to have amassed a card-index of so many thousand suspects, a feat which never seemed to yield any positive benefit. More to the point was the discovery that one of his principal sources was an obscure and noxious person who went, in Portugal, under a false name. We knew, from the wireless traffic, that he was passing information to the Abwehr. We had also learnt, by opening the Czech diplomatic bag, that he was working for Colonel Pan, then Czech intelligence representative in Lisbon. We had spent many months devising means of warning Pan, without disclosing to him the guilty source of our knowledge. He resisted our sincere endeavours with remarkable density; "Ivory from the neck up," as Dick White tersely remarked after an unsuccessful meeting. It was a little too much when Di Lucia also put the Abwehr agent on his payroll. When, after endless prodding from us, OSS decided that Di Lucia must go the way of Olivera, they asked us to write to our man in Lisbon for a statement of the qualities desirable in an OSS representative in that hot spot. He cabled back at once: "For God's sake tell them to send a man called Smith." Against Cowgill's wishes, I showed the message to Pearson. He pretended amusement.

In the second half of 1942, news reached us that the invasion of North Africa had been decided in principle. The duty imposed on us in St. Albans was the timely provision of intelligence to the staffs of the invading armies. The intelligence particularly concerning us related, of course, to the activity of the Abwehr and the Italian military-intelligence service in North Africa, and that of their sympathizers among the special services of the Vichy regime. Cowgill saw in the development both a problem and an opportunity. The problem was to ensure that SIS intelligence was transmitted to army staffs in such a way as to safeguard the security of our sources, including wireless intercepts. Cowgill successfully argued the view that this could only be done by the attachment of the staffs of special units composed of Section V officers, or officers trained in Section V. Having won this point, he was well placed to show that his existing resources were adequate, and that he could fulfil his new duties only if he received substantially increased appropriations. From this battle, too, he emerged victorious, with the result that he was able to recruit additional staff as well as giving most of us, if not all, a welcome rise in pay.

In passing, I should mention that this increase in staff led to two wholly delightful associations. Graham Greene was brought back to reinforce Section V from Freetown, where he had been supposedly watching the intrigues of the Vichy French. He will forgive me for confessing that I cannot recall any startling achievements of his in West Africa; perhaps the French were not intriguing? I do remember, however, a meeting held to discuss a proposal of his to use a roving brothel to frustrate the French and two lonely Germans suspected of spying on British shipping in Portuguese Guinea. The proposal was discussed quite seriously, and was turned down only because it seemed unlikely to be productive of hard intelligence. Happily, Greene was posted, where I put him in charge of Portugal. He had a good time sniping at OSS, and his tart comments on incoming correspondence were a daily refreshment. At about the same time, Malcolm Muggeridge swam into our ken, wearing his usual air of indignant bewilderment. He was despatched to Lourenço Marques, too far away for my liking, where his principal adversary was the Italian Consul, Campini, an assiduous reporter of British shipping movements. I was glad when our interest in Campini died, and Muggeridge was brought back to deal with various aspects of French affairs. His stubborn opposition to the policy of the day (whatever it was) lent humanity to our lives.

Some weeks before the North African invasion, Cowgill asked me whether I would take over responsibility for the area. It had previously been included in the French section, but for reasons not very clear to me it had been decided that the transfer would be beneficial. I had no hesitation in accepting. We had achieved a fair stranglehold on the Abwehr in Spain and Portugal, and were regularly picking up its agents. There was no reason why I should not shoulder additional responsibilities. It was also satisfactory to me personally to get nearer to the active conduct of the war, and the enlargement of my field at that crucial stage suggested the hope of further extensions as the Allied armies progressed. That hope was fulfilled in due course.

My duties involved politics rather than intelligence work. The special units mentioned above were duly formed and attached to the army staffs under the title of Special Counter-Intelligence Units (or SCI units). The term, of course, was an Americanism—a concession to the fact of an American being in supreme command. We were also issued with new stamps marked Top Secret instead of Most Secret. It was a foretaste of things to come, but we were innocent enough then to feel enthusiastic about our precious Eisenhower. But the bulk of what I call, for want of a better term, our work, concerned relations with the French. For some time, there had been attached to Section V a Gaullist counter-espionage officer with ill-defined functions. Apart from giving him our most attractive secretary, on the grounds that she spoke French, we had kept him at arm's length. I do not know what obscure reasons promoted Cowgill's reserve towards Passy's Bureau Central de Renseignements et d'Action, the Gaullist intelligence organization. But when the political situation burst in our faces, when Darlan and Giraud became friends, not enemies, Cowgill passionately embraced a certain Commandant Paillole, a Vichy counter-espionage officer. In fact, Paillole proved to be a most attractive character, and his anti-Axis feeling was beyond reproach. Yet I could never understand what good intelligence purpose was served by the mountain of work involved in Cowgill's self-imposed commitment to defend Paillole against all comers. It was probably just that he could not adopt any attitude falling short of total involvement. What came of it all in the end, I do not know. Before the issue was resolved, if it ever was, I was immersed in the problems of the Italian campaign, and the Paillole Affair reduced itself to its proper parochial level.

The fact that in the year 1942–3 Cowgill had enlarged my field of responsibility to include first North Africa, and then Italy, suggested to me that I was beginning to make a career in the secret service. This was confirmed shortly after our move to London. Until then, Cowgill had delegated his work, during his rare absences on leave or duty, to his deputy, Ferguson. Ferguson had also come to us from the Indian police, though at one or two removes, and had impressed chiefly by his terror of taking decisions. It was time for Cowgill to pay an official visit to the United States, where he proposed to spend two or three weeks. On the eve of his departure, he circulated a minute to all officers in Section V. It informed them that during his absence, Ferguson would act as deputy in administrative matters, myself in the same capacity in all intelligence matters. This was the first formal intimation that I was on the ladder for promotion. Poor Cowgill!

V. On the Up and Up

A shrewd MI5 officer once minuted a paper: "This case is of the highest possible importance and must therefore be handled on the lowest possible level." During the two or three weeks of Cowgill's absence in the United States, when I sat in his chair, I had good cause to reflect on that dictum. It was not an auspicious introduction to the higher levels. Most of the routine work was relatively simple. The other heads of sub-sections seemed well on top of their intelligence problems, and required little guidance from me. But when I turned to Cowgill's own work, I ran straight into a horrible muddle, which proved an object lesson on the malign influence of office politics on intelligence. It was a foretaste of headaches to come, and is therefore worth notice in some detail.

Some weeks before his departure, Cowgill had summoned a special meeting of his sub-section heads. He informed us that he was working on a case in conjunction with Claude Dansey. The case was of great potential importance, with such marked political overtones that he proposed to go on handling it in person. But he thought that we should know the general outline, in case our own work threw up anything which might have a bearing on it. The outline given us by Cowgill was exceedingly blurred. He was obviously tired and rambled on without making much sense. It appeared that some hostile service was preparing, or had prepared, a gigantic plant. The nature and purpose of the plant was obscure. "My own view," Cowgill concluded with a sudden flash of life, "is that it has something to do with the Arabs. Whenever I look at this case, I see Arabs!" Richard Hannay was with us again.

In an hour or two I had forgotten all about the case, but Cowgill reminded me of it when briefing me immediately before his departure. From his private safe he produced a fat file, and handed it over. He asked me to go into it during his absence and "see what I made of it." I was told that it would be advisable to keep in touch with Dansey, as he was taking a personal interest in the matter. I thought it better not to ask why Cowgill was hand-in-glove with Dansey in relation to the case, though the connection was puzzling in view of Dansey's contempt of counter-espionage and all its works. I guessed that the battle-scarred Cowgill was beginning to feel lonely, and that even Dansey might prove an acceptable ally. Perhaps they were ganging up against Vivian and MI5, a combination that would have made sense in terms of office politics. When I opened the file, Dansey's interest immediately became clear, and I read on with increasing relish. It will be simpler for the reader if I tell the story in chronological order, not in the order which emerged from the file. Indeed, it took me a long time to unravel the essential threads.

By the end of 1943, it was clear that the Axis was headed for defeat, and many Germans began to have second thoughts about their loyalty to Hitler. As a result, a steady trickle of defectors began to appear at the gates of Allied missions with offers of assistance and requests for asylum. These offers and requests had to be treated with care for a number of good reasons. Himmler could have sent us a spy disguised as a defector. It would have been dangerous for the Russians to think that we were dickering with Germans; the air was opaque with mutual suspicions of separate peace feelers.

We could not encourage a flood of last-minute converts hoping to escape the war tribunals. There were strict standing instructions to British missions that no assurances should be given to any German without prior reference to London. One day, a German presented himself at the British Legation in Berne, Switzerland, and asked to see the British Military Attaché. He explained that he was an official of the German Foreign Ministry, and had brought with him from Berlin a suitcase full of Foreign Ministry documents. On hearing this staggering claim, the Attaché promptly threw him out. The German's subsequent attempts to see the Head of Chancery were likewise rebuffed. The attitude of the British officials cannot be condemned out of hand. It was barely credible that anyone would have the nerve to pass through the German frontier controls with a suitcase containing contraband official papers.

The German, however, was determined to get results. Having failed at the British Legation, he tried the Americans. Their regulations, it seemed, were more flexible than those of the British. A Legation Secretary, deciding that this was cloak-and-dagger stuff, told the visitor that he should address himself to Mr. Allen Dulles*—"four doors down on the left." Dulles, who was then head of the OSS office in Switzerland, heard the stranger's story, and sensibly asked to see the contents of the suitcase. Without hesitation, he decided that the goods were genuine. They shocked him into a lyrical state which was still on him when he drafted his official report to Washington. "If only," he wrote, "you can see these documents in all their pristine freshness!"

The documents were copied and sent to Washington, and OSS loyally made them available to SIS. Because of the Swiss angle, they were sent in the first place to Dansey. I have explained that Dansey had taken a personal interest in Switzerland since before the war. That interest had become a fierce proprietary obsession. He had resented the installation of OSS in Switzerland, and had lost no

---

Became deputy director of CIA in 1950, when Philby was in Washington. Responsible for tracking down Maclean as a Soviet agent.

opportunity of belittling Dulles's work. The sight of the Berlin papers must have been a severe shock to him; this was evident from his recorded comments. But Dansey seldom stayed shocked for long. It was clearly impossible that Dulles should have pulled off this spectacular scoop under his nose. The stuff was obviously a plant, and Dulles had fallen for it like a ton of bricks.

Plants involved operations by hostile intelligence services, and were a matter for the counter-espionage section. Dansey accordingly asked Cowgill to discuss the matter with him. What passed at their meeting was not recorded in detail. But it is evident that Cowgill left under the impression that it was to his interest to prove the spurious nature of Dulles's documents. It is also clear that he never studied the documents, then or thereafter. He was too busy and too tired. It was office politics that prompted him to play Dansey's game. His estrangement from Vivian was almost complete. His relations with the Chief, though still reasonably good, were not clearly so close as he would have wished. But Dansey's were very close indeed. By doing Dansey a good turn, by proving that Dulles had been sold a pup, he could also do himself a power of good.

Such was the picture that emerged from the messy Dansey-Cowgill correspondence. It made me think hard. About this time, a project was forming in my mind which needed a cautious approach. I was very anxious to get a certain job that would soon become available, and I could not afford to antagonize any of the people who might help me towards it. Cowgill, Vivian, Dansey, MI5, the Foreign Office, the Chief—they were all pieces of the jigsaw, and it was exceedingly difficult, from my comparatively lowly position, to see how they would fit together when the moment came for action on my part. I had, however, long since reached the conclusion that, although political manoeuvre can produce quick results, those results are lasting only if they are based on solid and conscientious work. I therefore decided to study the Dulles material on its merits. If it was unequivocally genuine or spurious, I would say so. If the outcome of my study was inconclusive, I would then reconsider the political aspects of the affair before deciding on which side to throw my own weight.

The great majority of the documents purported to be telegrams received by the German Foreign Office from its missions abroad. The obvious first step was to check with our cryptographic experts whether they had already received intercepted messages matching the Dulles material. There was no evidence in the file that this elementary step had been taken; Dansey and Cowgill had contented themselves with skimming the papers cursorily in the search for implausibilities and contradictions to buttress their advocacy of the plant theory. I remember Cowgill's instructions to keep in close contact with Dansey, and debated whether to consult him on the desirability of approaching the cryptographers. I was against it, as I thought that he would probably oppose the suggestion. When I found on rechecking the file that Dansey had minuted to Cowgill: "Passed to you for any action you may think necessary," I decided that I was well enough covered to go ahead on my own.

By that time, the Government Code & Cypher School, our cryptographic organization, had been virtually split into two departments. One, under Commander Travis,* dealt with all service traffic; the other, under Commander Denniston,† handled diplomatic messages. As the Dulles material was German Foreign Office correspondence, Denniston was my man. I chose for his scrutiny a striking series of telegrams from the German Military Attaché in Tokyo to the German General Staff which had been transmitted through diplomatic channels. They contained detailed statements of the Japanese Order of Battle and assessments of future Japanese intentions. There were about a dozen in all and, if genuine, they were clearly of the highest importance.

*Commander Sir Edward W. H. Travis, CMKG, CBE; Royal Navy 1906; served on Admiral Jellicoe's staff.

†Commander Alexander Guthrie Denniston, CMG, CBE. Head of Government Code & Cypher School, 1919 to 1943; d. 1961.

Two days later, Denniston telephoned me in a state of some excitement. He told me that three of my telegrams exactly matched intercepted telegrams which they had already deciphered, and that the others were proving of the utmost value to his cryptographers in their breakdown of the German diplomatic code. Could I get him some more? I could indeed, and began to feed the stuff to Denniston as fast as he could absorb it. When about a third of the material had passed through his hands with a steadily increasing tally of matches, and never a suggestion of anything phony, I felt that I had no choice but to circulate the documents as genuine. Accordingly, I passed them on to our sections dealing with the service departments and the Foreign Office, purposely playing down their significance, as I did not wish Dansey to get premature wind of anything unusual.

The reaction from the service departments was immediate. Army, Navy and Air Force—all three howled for more. The Foreign Office was more sedate, but also very polite. I asked the sections concerned to get written evaluations of the material from their departments. I also asked Denniston for a minute explaining the cryptographic reasons for supposing the documents to be genuine. I needed all the ammunition I could get for the inevitable and imminent confrontation with Dansey. Fortunately, enough accumulated for me to take action before Dansey heard of the affair from any other source. I thought of sending him the papers to prepare him for the shock, but rejected the idea on the grounds that he would not read them. So, with some trepidation, I asked when I could conveniently pay him a visit.

The visit lasted a very uncomfortable half-hour. As was to be expected, Dansey was furious. But he was sobered by the fact that I had studied the material and he had not. Denniston's minute deflated him a little. He did not understand the argument, but the conclusion was plainly stated. Anger mounted in him again as he read the eulogistic comments of the departments. He composed himself with some difficulty to read me a lecture. Even if the documents were genuine, what of it? I was encouraging OSS to run riot all over Switzerland, fouling up the whole intelligence field. Heaven knew what damage they wouldn't do. Such matters had to be handled only by officers with experience of the pitfalls that beset the unwary. For all he knew, OSS, if egged on in this way, could blow the whole of his network in a matter of days.

When Dansey had exhausted his reckless improvisation, I asked him with puzzled deference how OSS came into the business at all. I had not circulated the material as OSS material. Not even our own circulating sections, let alone the departments, knew that OSS were involved. They regarded it as *our* stuff, they were asking *us* for more. It seemed that the credit would be ours. When I faltered to an end, Dansey gave me a long, long stare. "Carry on," he said at last. "You're not such a fool as I thought." When Cowgill returned, I took him the file and explained what I had done. To his immediate anxious enquiry about Dansey's attitude, I explained that I had consulted him and that he had approved my action. With relief, Cowgill handed me back the file and asked me to handle any sequel. To my surprise, the case was by no means closed. Our German friend proved to be an intrepid operator, and paid several more visits to Berne with his useful suitcase.

Meanwhile, the work of my sub-sections dealing with German activity in the Iberian Peninsula, North Africa and Italy, was going smoothly owing to an increasingly easy familiarity with the subject. German agents were picked up with monotonous regularity and, so far as I know, nothing of any importance escaped our net. Although the German services were accorded full facilities by the Spanish Government and Dr. Salazar offered them amiable hospitality, precious few Spaniards or Portuguese showed willingness to stick out their necks for Fascism. Many of those who accepted missions did so simply to get out of Europe or into Britain, or both. Besides, we held the master key to German intentions in regular perusal of their signals.

The case of Ernesto Simoes may be taken as a representative example. We learnt from the German signals that they had recruited Simoes in Lisbon for service in England. His instructions were given to him in the form of microdots scattered about his clothing; his communications were to be by mail. After consultation with MI5, it was decided to allow him to run loose in England for a bit, in the hope that he might lead us to other German agents. He was therefore unmolested on his arrival, and was even given discreet assistance in finding employment in a Luton factory making parts for aircraft. The information he might have obtained there was just interesting enough to tempt a spy, without entailing much danger if anything had slipped back to the Germans by mistake. He was lodged with a married couple; the husband worked in the same factory. Arrangements were made for his movements to be watched and his mail checked.

Within a few days, Simoes settled down to a pattern of behaviour which he never subsequently varied. He would follow his landlord out of the factory when the whistle blew, and see him safely into the nearest pub. He would then hurry home as fast as his legs would carry him. He never emerged until the following morning when he accompanied his landlord to work. It only remained to establish the purpose of his haste to get home. On closer investigation, there emerged a wholly satisfactory explanation. Every evening, on reaching his lodging, he promptly laid his landlady under (so the clandestine watchers improbably maintained) the kitchen table. He would then eat a hearty meal and go to bed.

After a few weeks, it was decided that the comedy should be stopped. Simoes was pulled in. So as to leave nothing to chance, he was taken to the "tough" interrogation centre on Ham Common, where Tommy Harris was let loose on him. It was beyond Harris to be really tough with anyone, but he did his best. He told Simoes that he was in a British secret service prison; he was beyond the reach of the law; his Consulate knew nothing of his whereabouts and would never find out; he might stay there for life, if he was allowed to live; he could be starved, beaten, killed and no one would ever know. His only hope was a complete confession of his espionage for the Germans. And much of the same sort, with Harris's riotous imagination running the whole gamut. Indeed, Harris confessed to me later that he had painted such a blood-curdling picture that he had begun to frighten himself.

To all this, Simoes listened with mounting impatience, merely saying testily at intervals that he was hungry and wanted something to eat. After an hour or so, however, he reached a decision. Calling for paper and pen, he scratched out a two-page account of his contacts with the Germans in Lisbon, including his instructions, microdots, and all. He explained that he had not had the slightest intention of doing anything that might endanger himself; his only aim had been to earn good wages in wartime England which he could not have reached unaided. Harris saw that Simoes's account squared in every detail with our previous knowledge. Before he could say anything, Simoes flung his pen down. "And now," he asked belligerently, "can I have something to eat?"

Another case involving a Portuguese is of some interest in that it illustrates the trickiness of taking action on information derived from particularly delicate sources. Rogerio Peixoto de Menezes,* a clerk in the Portuguese Foreign Office, was posted for service in the Portuguese Embassy in London. Before he left Lisbon, we learnt, again from German signals, that the Abwehr had recruited him. He was given general intelligence assignments, and was told to communicate by secret-ink letters, sent through the Portuguese bag to cover-addresses in Lisbon. This presented little difficulty, since the Portuguese bag was regularly opened before it left England. Sure enough, within a few weeks, an envelope addressed to one of Menezes's cover-addresses was extracted from the bag and, on development, found to contain a message in simple secret ink. It commented fatuously on public morale, reported the existence of

---

*Burgess met him in a nightclub and in 1942 introduced him to Philby, who was responsible for his arrest in 1943.

anti-aircraft batteries in Hyde Park, and contained other trivia. It was felt, however, that even a poor fish like Menezes might one day stumble on something important, and that his activity should be stopped.

The difficulty was that Menezes might take refuge behind diplomatic immunity, and it was therefore necessary to induce Señor Monteiro, the Portuguese Ambassador, to waive any such claim. Yet the only evidence of Menezes's misconduct had been obtained by undiplomatic means. It was finally decided that Monteiro should be shown the letter, with the explanation that it had been passed to us by a contact in Lisbon. When confronted with the letter, Monteiro could scarcely have persisted in claiming immunity for Menezes, and the latter was duly brought to trial. It was obviously a pathetic case, and some of us had qualms before the verdict was pronounced; technically, the accused was liable to the death penalty. Happily, the judge was lenient; we had no reason to annoy the Portuguese. But the case ended with a nasty jolt. In a coded telegram commenting on the case (which we also read), Monteiro gave our explanations of the circumstances in which the letter had reached us. Having done so, he expressed the possibility that the diplomatic bag had been "indiscreet."

The existence of neutral diplomats was a lasting embarrassment to the British security authorities. The problem was brought to their attention early by the Duke of Alba, the Ambassador of Spain. We had regular access to the Spanish diplomatic bag, and from it learnt that Alba periodically sent to Madrid despatches on the British political scene of quite exceptional quality. As we had no doubt that the Spanish Foreign Ministry would make them available to their German allies, these despatches represented a really serious leakage. Yet there was nothing that could be done. There was no evidence that the Duke had obtained his information improperly. He simply moved with people in the know and reported what they said, with shrewd commentaries of his own. For some time, MI5 toyed with the idea of using him as a channel for deception. But his informants were just too high up. They included such people as

Brendan Bracken, Beaverbrook, even Churchill himself; they could scarcely stoop to trickery with a grandee of Spain. So there we had to leave it, cherishing a single hope. Alba's reports maintained a tone wholly friendly to Britain. It was possible that Hitler would dismiss him as an incurable Anglophile. After all, he was Duke of Berwick, too.

VI. THE FULFILMENT

At the end of Chapter IV, I mentioned that I seemed to be on the ladder for promotion. This brings me to an episode which will make sour reading, just as it makes sour writing. The first intimations of a successful career in SIS coincided with an opening in a specific direction which I could not possibly ignore.

Long before the end of the war with Germany, senior officers in SIS began to turn their thoughts towards the next enemy. Between the wars, the greater part of the service's resources had been devoted to the penetration of the Soviet Union and to the defence of Britain against what was known generically as "Bolshevism," i.e. the Soviet Government and the world-wide Communist movement. When the defeat of the Axis was in sight, SIS thinking reverted to its old and congenial channels; and a modest start was made by setting up a small section, known as Section IX, to study past records of Soviet and Communist activity. An officer named Currie, approaching the retiring age, was imported from MI5 to get the section going. He was hampered by deafness and by ignorance of SIS procedure; and the exceptional secrecy imposed on him hampered him in getting access to the papers relevant to his work. It was understood, however, that his appointment was a stop-gap one, and that, as soon as the reduction of work against Germany allowed, he would be replaced by a regular SIS officer.

For the next few weeks, virtually all my discussions with my Soviet contact concerned the future of Section IX. I wrote several memoranda on the subject, which we analysed in exhaustive detail. The situation, as I explained it then, held out two possible solutions: on retirement, Currie could be replaced by another officer, or his section could be merged with Section V. Cowgill had no doubt that the second solution would be adopted. He would talk airily of the days when we got rid of old Currie and really got down to the Communist job. I had little doubt that, in the ordinary course of events, he would be proved right. After the defeat of the Axis, there would be an economy drive, and SIS strength would be scaled down drastically. It seemed most unlikely that there would be room for two counter-espionage sections, one dealing with the vastly important Soviet problem, the other with more or less negligible odds and ends, neo-Fascism and all that. There would be pressure towards combining the sections, in which case Cowgill's seniority in the service would make him the obvious choice as head of the combined section.

My Soviet contact asked me if I would be offered a senior position in the section. I thought I probably would. But could I be certain? he persisted. To that question, I could not possibly give him a categorical affirmative. The corridors of Broadway were full of forecasts of post-war reorganization, more or less drastic, and it was impossible to know what peacetime staffing arrangements might be introduced. I might well be sent abroad to get field experience. We talked around the subject for several meetings before he posed what was to be a fateful question: what would happen if I was offered the post instead of Cowgill? I answered that it would mean a significant promotion and improve my chances of determining the course of events, including my own postings. He seemed satisfied, and said that he hoped to have definite instructions for me by the time of our next meeting.

He had. Headquarters had informed him that I must do every-thing, but *everything*, to ensure that I became head of Section IX, whether or not it merged with Section V. They fully realized this meant that Cowgill must go. I made an attempt to demur, pointing out that my access to many obscure places in the service had been gained through my refusal to engage in office intrigue. But the ar-gument failed to convince. The importance of the post was well worth a temporary loss of reputation. Besides, my friend pointed out quite rightly, within a few months Cowgill, and the manner of his going, would be forgotten. There was truth in this, but I faced it with qualms. I liked and respected Cowgill, and had much to thank him for. But he was a prickly obstacle in the course laid down for me, so he had to go. I could not deny that, just as he would have no serious challenger in the Section IX race if he stayed, I would have no serious challenger if he left.

Although my reluctance to engage in office intrigue had not been considered a decisive factor by my Soviet friends, headquarters had not simply brushed the point aside. I was enjoined to conduct my campaign against Cowgill with the greatest care. Although most of the detail was necessarily left to my own judgement and initiative, the following guidelines were laid down: I should take no overt measures to achieve my goal because, if things went wrong subsequently, I must be able to show that the position had been thrust on me. Every move in the campaign had to come, wherever possible, from someone else. In other words, I must find allies to fight my cause, and the best place to look for them was clearly among Cowgill's enemies. As I have suggested, these were not few, and the passage of time had done nothing to soften their acrimony. I felt that my hope was far from forlorn, especially as Cowgill was a proud man who flew high. If he fell at all, he would fall with a bump.

My first choice was Colonel Vivian, enfeebled as he was. His title was Deputy Chief of the Secret Service; he was Cowgill's direct superior in the service; he was responsible, in name, for all the counter-espionage activity of SIS. I have shown how Cowgill, contemptuous of his weakness, had brushed him aside, preferring to deal directly with the Chief. The slight rankled deeply with Vivian. On past occasions he had wept on my shoulder on account of his lost influence, embarrassing me deeply. But now I welcomed these sentimental little scenes, and it was not long before Vivian was asking me, quite improperly, "what to do about Cowgill." Clearly I could not match his impropriety by telling him in so many words. But I was able to divert his complaints to other quarters near the seat of power. It was useless to suggest that he have a showdown with the Chief. He was almost as afraid of the Chief as he was of Cowgill. But there were others who had the Chief's ear, or to whom the Chief had to listen.

The most likely of these was Christopher Arnold-Forster.[*] When I first joined SIS, he had been in the Naval Section, processing naval intelligence for the Admiralty. The Chief had then installed him in an office across the corridor from his own, with the title Principal Staff Officer. He may have regretted the appointment subsequently, but in fact it was one of the best he ever made. Arnold-Forster had a clear brain and an unusual capacity to see order in bureaucratic chaos, together with an admirable style, both on paper and in committee. He was also one of the bravest men I ever met. Much of his working day he gasped with agony at his desk behind a row of bottles containing strange stomach powders. I felt that, if his mind could be engaged on our problem, he would soon grasp the impossibility of a situation in which the head of the SIS counter-espionage section was permanently at loggerheads with MI5. It might be tolerated in the short run, under the stress of war, but to prolong it indefinitely into peacetime was a different matter. If Arnold-Forster got the point, I had little doubt that he would press it.

How to put it over? The best course was for Arnold-Forster to hear an authoritative MI5 view on Cowgill. So, with whom? I re-

---

[*]Hugh Christopher Arnold-Forster. Commander RN (rtd.), CMG. Assistant Director of Naval Intelligence, 1942–5.

jected Dick White, on the grounds that he was too much inclined to be all things to all men. He might easily have pulled his punches. Guy Liddell would be a far better bet. He was White's superior; he had been with MI5 so long that it almost seemed that he *was* MI5; he was always a plain speaker, and could be a relentless one. Accordingly, when Vivian next raised the subject, I reiterated that I had nothing to suggest, but thought that he would be well advised to consult Arnold-Forster. Perhaps it would help if a meeting could be arranged between Arnold-Forster and Guy Liddell? Vivian digested the idea slowly, but with dawning appreciation. Then with immense resolution he said: "You know, Kim, I'll do just that!"

How the meeting was arranged I do not know. Vivian's club was the East India and Sports, but they can hardly have lunched there. Its wartime curry and potatoes would have killed Arnold-Forster. But when I next saw Vivian, things seemed to be going well. He gave me a sly, winning smile. "I think," he said, "it was a real eye-opener for Chris!" More significant still was a telephoned invitation from Arnold-Forster to drop in and see him "next time I was free." He was too correct to raise what Wodehouse would call the *"res."* But we had a long discussion about SIS in general and its future, what scope there was for improvement and what modifications were necessary to meet the new conditions imposed by the coming peace. He was obviously appraising me, and I tried to be as sensible and straightforward as possible. Cowgill's name was not mentioned.

The next step was to canvass the Foreign Office, with which we had often had dealings, notably in connection with the diplomatic protests to Franco and Salazar against German intelligence activity in the Iberian Peninsula. A system was introduced in wartime whereby the Foreign Office seconded one of their officials for work in Broadway, in order, so to speak, to cross-fertilize the two services, to improve understanding of each other's aims and procedures. The first member of the Foreign Office to be so seconded was Patrick Reilly, and he was still at his post in Broadway at the time of which I write. I had dealt with him frequently in connection with German intrigue in neutral countries, and had no reason to believe that he thought ill of me. But I knew of no differences between him and Cowgill severe enough to justify me in counting Reilly among my allies. But my lucky star was shining bright. Cowgill, who sometimes seemed bent on self-destruction, chose this critical moment to try to propel the Chief into a wholly unnecessary row with Edgar Hoover. Such a row would clearly have affected Anglo-American relations in general. Reilly, therefore, entered the picture, and with sharp reservations about Cowgill's political good sense.

The first I heard of this new development was a tremulous summons from Vivian. He showed me a two-page letter which Cowgill had drafted for the Chief's signature. I cannot remember what the precise issue was. The memory was doubtless driven from my mind by the intemperance of Cowgill's language. The draft was a tirade against Hoover's regular practice of sacrificing intelligence needs for political advantage in Washington. Of course, there was much truth in what Cowgill said. But such things cannot be put on paper, not anyway in correspondence between the head of one service and another. At the bottom of the draft was a succinct minute from Reilly: "I submit that V's draft is wholly unsuitable and, if sent, would make CSS look ridiculous." Reilly had asked Vivian to rewrite the letter, and Vivian in turn now wanted me to put up what I suppose must be called a draft-draft. I scribbled about half a page, making the very minor point at issue in courteous terms, and we took it along to Reilly together. He passed it, without alteration, to the Chief's secretaries and I left them. Vivian told me next day that he had had "a *very* interesting talk with Patrick."

The scene was set. Vivian, now firmly propped, was out for Cowgill's blood. Arnold-Forster had been impressed by MI5's hostility to Cowgill, and had made sure that the Chief did not underrate it. MI5 itself was solid. Apart from Dick White, who was still personally affable, the rest of the personnel of MI5 knew Cowgill only as an antagonist in inter-office strife. Even White described him, kindly, as "an awkward bugger." There were also clouds lowering for Cowgill on the Bletchley horizon. He had always thought that officials of the Government Code & Cypher School were ready to dispute his control of German wireless intelligence traffic. Shortly after our return to London from St. Albans, he had clashed with two senior GC & CS officers, Jones and Hastings. On a deeply embarrassing occasion, flanked by his sub-section heads, he was badly worsted, not to say mauled, by Jones. Both took uncompromising and opposite stands. But Jones knew his brief backwards, Cowgill did not. I do not suggest that GC & CS took an active part in the drive to oust Cowgill. They were too remote. But through the operation of the old-boy network, the Chief knew well that the cryptographers would take a philosophical attitude towards Cowgill's departure.

The ordeal virtually ended one day when Vivian summoned me, and asked me to read a minute he had written to the Chief. It was of inordinate length and laced with quotations from *Hamlet*. It traced the sorry story of Cowgill's quarrels, and argued that a radical change must be made before the transition to peacetime conditions. My name was put forward as a successor to Currie. Cowgill's candidature for the appointment was specifically excluded. My own suitability for the post was explained in flattering detail. Strangely enough, the recital of my virtues omitted my most serious qualification for the job—the fact that I knew something about Communism.

For me, that was the end of the struggle. Vivian would not have dared to put such a far-reaching proposal to the Chief without Arnold-Forster's blessing; and Arnold-Forster would not have given it if he had not first prepared the ground for a favourable reception. The fact that the minute was typed and ready to go told me that the Chief was prepared to risk a major show-down with Cowgill, even to the point of accepting his resignation. I had little doubt that the next few days would bring a summons from the Chief. But I had one last move to make, if the summons came. I spent some time thinking exactly how I should make it.

My problem was that a career in clandestine service is unpredictable, if not downright hazardous. It is always possible that something will go wrong. Minor mishaps I could probably take in my stride. But if disaster struck, I did not want to be dependent solely on the loyalty of my colleagues in SIS. The particular danger facing secret service servants is the charge of insecurity, or of related offences, which are the province of MI5. In case anything should happen to me in my new job, it would be well, I reflected, if MI5 could be officially embroiled in my appointment. What I wanted was a statement from MI5, on paper, to the effect that they approved my appointment. Yet I could scarcely say all that to the Chief in so many words. In short, I was in search of a formula. After anxious reflection, I thought that I had better call to my aid the Chief's obsessive delight in inter-departmental manoeuvre.

The summons came. It was by no means the first time I had visited the *arcana*. But on this occasion, Miss Pettigrew and Miss Jones, the Chief's secretaries, seemed especially affable as I waited in their room for the green light to go on. The green light flashed, and I went in. For the first time, the Chief addressed me as "Kim," so I knew that no last-minute hitch had occurred. He showed me Vivian's minute, and out of politeness I pretended to read it. He told me that he had decided to act on Vivian's proposal and offer me the immediate succession to Currie. Had I anything to say? I had. Using the sort of I-hope-I-am-not-speaking-out-of-turn-Sir approach, I said that the appointment had been offered to me presumably because of the well-known incompatibility between Cowgill and his opposite numbers in MI5. I hoped that I would be able to avoid such quarrels in future. But who could make predictions? I would be much happier in the job if I knew for certain that MI5, the people with whom I would be dealing daily, had no objection to my appointment. It would make me just that much more confident. Besides, MI5 approval, officially given, would effectively protect the service against future criticism from that quarter.

Before I had finished my brief exposition, the Chief had got the point, with evident appreciation. He was extraordinarily quick to spot cover in the bureaucratic jungle. His critics used to say that only his grasp of tactics ensured his survival in the much-coveted control of secret funds. Before long, he was throwing my own arguments back at me with force and conviction. He dismissed me with great warmth, saying that he would write to Sir David Petrie* (then head of MI5) without delay. I left him in the hope that he would claim, and perhaps more than half believe, that the whole credit for the idea was his own. In due course, Petrie returned a very friendly reply. The Chief was delighted with it. So was I.

In launching this intrigue I hoped that Cowgill would end by getting himself out. He did. As soon as my appointment became known, he demanded an interview with the Chief. I know nothing of the details of the meeting, but I never saw Cowgill again. He had submitted his resignation once too often. It was a pointless and fatal mistake. Within little more than a year, Sections V and IX were united, under my direction. There was no Cowgill to dispute my path. If he had contented himself with a short period of eclipse, he would certainly have found another rewarding job in the service. But he had become used to riding high. As I hope I have shown, he was proud and impulsive, a man too big for his talents.

Within a few days, I was taking over from Currie, rather impatiently, I am afraid. I suggested to the Chief that, to regularize the position of the new Section IX, I should draft myself a charter for his signature. I cannot remember its exact wording. But it gave me responsibility, under the Chief, for the collection and interpretation of information concerning Soviet and Communist espionage and subversion in all parts of the world outside British territory. It also enjoined me to maintain the closest liaison for the reciprocal exchange of intelligence on these subjects with MI5. The Chief added a final clause. I was on no account to have any dealings

*Head of MI5 until the end of the war. Under his rules talented amateurs and intellectuals, such as Herbert Hart, Hugh Trevor-Roper and Stuart Hampshire, were introduced into the Secret Service.

with any of the United States services. The war was not yet over, and the Soviet Union was our ally. There was no question of risking leakage. The leakage which the Chief had in mind was a leakage from the United States services to the Russians. It was a piquant situation.

VII. FROM WAR TO PEACE

Taking charge of Section IX meant moving from Ryder Street to Broadway. The change was welcome for several reasons. Since the previous summer of 1943, when we moved up from St. Albans to London, I had enjoyed easy access to the heart of SIS. Now I was sitting right in the middle of it, in the best position to sniff the breezes of office politics and well placed to discover the personalities behind the faces that passed me in the corridors. I was also removed, by the width of St. James's Park, from the OSS counter-espionage people. When Section V moved into its Ryder Street premises, Pearson and his colleagues had taken office-space, with Cowgill's backing, in the same building. They had wearied us with their politicking, even if they sometimes amused us. Graham Greene has recalled, in a newspaper article, the OSS filing cabinet that just wouldn't stay shut. For the benefit of conscientious duty officers doing their rounds in the evening, Pearson, again with Cowgill's approval, adorned it with a discerning label: "This filing cabinet is to be considered secure." As I have already explained, my first orders were to have nothing to do with the Americans. Pearson knew it perfectly well. But that did not prevent him from extending to me persistent and embarrassing offers of hospitality. It was best for me to be well out of his way, high up on the seventh floor of Broadway Buildings.

At the beginning, I was absorbed by bread-and-butter problems: staff, office-space, equipment, etc. The reader may think that this meant starting the wrong way round; that I should have considered the size of my problem first, and then looked for the staff to handle it. But that line of thought disregards Parkinson's Law. I had no doubt that, however big the staff I engaged, I could always stretch the problem wide enough to engulf it. The important thing was to get hold of the good people while they were still available. With peacetime economies already in sight, it would be much easier to discard surplus staff than to find people later to fill in any gaps that might appear.

Currie's Section IX had consisted of four officers: himself, two girls and a near-mental case (male). One of the girls was a very nice Wren whom I retained. The other was an oddity who had come to us from Censorship. I was relieved when, shortly after my arrival, she toasted an eyeball watching an eclipse of the sun and had to leave. The near-mental case was Steptoe of Shanghai, who had covered the whole Far East for SIS between the wars. How it happened is still a mystery to me: I found it difficult to believe that he could hold any job for a week. Steptoe had been foisted on Currie by Vivian, presumably for old times' sake. But I had few qualms about standing up to Vivian on the issue; Vivian, after all, had served his purpose. Happily, Steptoe had already cooked his own goose. At Vivian's suggestion, he had been sent on a round tour of our stations in the Mediterranean to spread the gospel of Section IX. The journey had been an unqualified disaster, since Steptoe, the old hand, had behaved with such ostentatious secretiveness that some of our field representatives had great difficulty in believing that he really was a secret service officer. A number of odd telegrams and letters reached Broadway, questioning the validity of his credentials. With this ammunition to support my own representations, I had little difficulty in convincing the Chief that his service would lose little if he pensioned Steptoe off. The latter departed with a consolation prize in the shape of one of Vivian's stately letters, lauding his past services and lamenting the untoward manner of his dismissal.

I felt no apprehension in losing two members of Currie's exiguous team. The staff position was becoming easier with every Allied advance in Europe. Officers working in the offensive intelligence sections saw the objects of their offensiveness shrinking rapidly. Counter-espionage specialists working against the Axis secret services realized that they would soon have little to counter. I found myself in an unfamiliar and enviable position. Instead of having to fight for staff, I was being courted by would-be recruits to my section, sometimes by people I had no intention of employing. In short, as far as labour was concerned, it was a buyer's market.

The field for recruitment was divided into four categories. There were the duds, on whom I wasted no time. There were many, among them some of the ablest, who wanted nothing better than to get back to their peacetime jobs, and the sooner the better. I tried to talk a few of them into changing their minds and staying on, but, to the best of my recollection, with only one success. Then there was a number of experienced older officers who were anxious to stay at their desks drawing a salary for a few more years pending retirement. Finally, there was a score or so of younger men about my own age, give or take five years, who had acquired a taste for intelligence work during the war and were keen to make it a career for life.

It was the fourth category which attracted me most, and to which I gave the greatest attention. When the section finally took shape, most of the officers were well under forty. But it was clearly bad practice to staff an entire section from the same age-group in view of the problems of promotion and seniority to which such a course would give rise. So I took also a sprinkling of older men who would pass into retirement within a few years and leave gaps to be filled from the next generation. The best known of the older men in the first Section IX was Bob Carew-Hunt, to whom I entrusted the composition of background papers on the subject of Communism. He had the great advantage of being literate, if not articulate. In due course, Bob became an acknowledged authority on the subject, and was much in demand as an adviser and lecturer, both in England and the United States. At a later date, he told me that he had intended dedicating to me his first book on the subject, *The Theory and Practice of Communism*, but that he had decided that such a tribute might embarrass me. Indeed, it would have given me grave embarrassment for a number of good reasons.

I was in the middle of my recruiting campaign when Vivian told me that Jane Archer had become available, suggesting that she would make an excellent addition to Section IX. The suggestion gave me a nasty shock, especially as I could think of no plausible reason for resisting it. After Guy Liddell, Jane was perhaps the ablest professional intelligence officer ever employed by MI5. She had spent a big chunk of a shrewd lifetime studying Communist activity in all its aspects. It was she who had interrogated General Krivitsky,* the Red Army intelligence officer who defected to the West in 1937, only to kill himself a few years later in the United States—a disillusioned man. From him, she had elicited a tantalizing scrap of information about a young English journalist whom the Soviet intelligence had sent to Spain during the Civil War. And here she was, plunked down in my midst! Fortunately, Jane was a woman after my own heart, tough-minded and rough-tongued. She had been sacked from MI5 for taking the opportunity at a top-level meeting of grievously insulting Brigadier Harker, who for several years had filled the Deputy Directorship of MI5 with handsome grace and very little else. Within a short time of her joining us, a crisis in Greece called for action on the part of General Plastiras. Jane delighted me with a little jingle in which Master-Ass was pronounced to rhyme with Plaster-arse. It made me feel that we had come together in a big way. Jane would have made a very bad enemy.

He said that there was a Soviet agent in the Foreign Office—probably Maclean. He also gave information about Philby: see pp. 169–70.

To keep Jane busy, I put her in charge of the most solid body of intelligence on Communist activity available to the section at the time. It consisted of a considerable volume of wireless traffic concerning the National Liberation movements in Eastern Europe. It yielded a comprehensive and absorbing picture of the painstaking efficiency and devotion of the Communists and their allies in the struggle against the Axis. The systematic and massive support given them by the Soviet Union gave one much food for thought. Despite the efforts of OSS and SOE to buy political support in the Balkans by the delivery of arms, money, and material, the National Liberation movements refused to compromise. They would doubtless have accepted help from the Devil himself—but without going into league with him.

Apart from Bob Carew-Hunt and Jane Archer with their specialized duties, the section was split into the conventional regional sub-sections. But in those early days, there was very little secret intelligence to work on. The dearth of current material was not wholly disadvantageous. Very few officers in the service at that time knew anything about Communism, and our first task was to go back to school to learn the elements of the subject, while keeping abreast with current events through the study of overt material such as the Communist press and monitored broadcasts from Communist countries.

What little secret intelligence we got was mostly fake. There was a voluminous series of reports from France, which reached us through a lady named Poz who had behaved with prodigious valour during the German occupation. I had the honour of meeting her once, and she turned out to be quite a dish with eyes that dilated miraculously when she made a point. She claimed to have an agent on the Central Committee of the French Communist Party, from whom her reports emanated. They purported to show that the French Communists never took a step without direct instructions from the Soviet Embassy in Paris. Such a view was doubtless acceptable to a chic reactionary like Poz; but the language of the reports was that of Action Française, not Humanité—or anything like it. It took an awfully long time for the obvious fact of forgery to sink in, and meanwhile SIS went on paying. The chief beneficiaries of the operation were the SIS officers who, for political reasons, wanted the reports circulated and believed, fake or not.

I have already described how far the unsatisfactory relations between SIS and MI5 contributed towards my appointment to Section IX. It was now necessary for me to continue the good work, and place our relations on a new and friendly basis. My opposite number in MI5 was Roger Hollis, the head of its section investigating Soviet and Communist affairs. He was a likeable person, of cautious bent, who had joined MI5 from the improbable quarter of the British-American Tobacco Company, which he had represented in China. Although he lacked the strain of irresponsibility which I think essential (in moderation) to the rounded human being, we got on well together, and were soon exchanging information without reserve on either side. We both served on the Joint Intelligence Sub-Committee which dealt with Communist affairs, and never failed to work out an agreed approach to present to the less well-informed representatives of the service departments, and the Foreign Office.

Although Hollis had achieved little in respect to Soviet activity, he had been successful in obtaining an intimate picture of the British Communist Party by the simple expedient of having microphones installed in its King Street headquarters. The result was a delicious paradox. The evidence of the microphones showed consistently that the Party was throwing its full weight behind the war effort, so that even Herbert Morrison, who was thirsting for Communist blood, could find no legal means of suppressing it.

At the beginning of 1945, when the section was adequately staffed and housed, the time came for me to visit some of our field stations. My object was partly to repair the damage done by Steptoe, partly to discuss with our station commanders ways and means of getting the information required by Section IX. The first part of my mission was easily achieved, simply by telling all concerned that my first action in taking over the section had been to get Steptoe sacked—a news item that won universal approval. But the second part was much more difficult. Our real target was invisible and inaudible; as far as we were concerned, the Soviet intelligence services might never have existed. The upshot of our discussions could be little more than a general resolution to keep casting flies over Soviet and East European diplomatic personnel and over members of the local Communist parties. During my period of service, there was no single case of consciously conceived operations against Soviet intelligence bearing fruit. We progressed only by means of windfalls that literally threw the stuff into our laps. With one or two exceptions, to be noted later, these windfalls took the form of defectors from the Soviet service. They were the ones who "chose freedom," like Kravchenko who, following Krivitsky's example, ended up a disillusioned suicide. But was it freedom they sought, or the flesh-pots? It is remarkable that not one of them volunteered to stay in position, and risk his neck for "freedom." One and all, they cut and ran for safety.

These trips, which covered France, Germany, Italy, and Greece, were to some extent educative, since they gave me insight into various types of SIS organizations in the field. But after each journey, I concluded, without emotion, that it would take years to lay an effective basis for work against the Soviet Union. As a result, it is the trivial incident, rather than any real achievement, that remains brightest in my memories of that summer. There was the wineglass of chilled Flit which I drained in Berlin; my host had proffered it in the belief that it was Niersteiner. My visit to Rome was marred by an interminable office wrangle over the Passport Control Officer's transport. Was he entitled to an official car or was he not? In Bari, I was instrumental in getting a pet bugbear chosen for air-drop into Yugoslavia; but instead of breaking his neck, he covered himself with glory. In Larissa, I watched one of the atmospheric marvels with which Greece is so generous: two separate and distinct thunderstorms, one over Ossa, the other over Olympus, while around us the plain of Thessaly rippled quietly under the clearest of blue skies. Meanwhile, back in grimy Broadway, events were in train that were to claim a great deal of my attention.

The accumulating shocks of war had swept away the amateurish service of previous years, although some of its survivals were a long time dying. With victory in Europe, the large wartime service contracted rapidly, and what was left of it had to be reshaped. As the head of a section, I was now regarded as an officer of some seniority—especially as my section was clearly going to be larger, by a long chalk, than any other. The penalty was that I was drawn increasingly into administration and policy-making. Doubtless there are expeditious means of administering organizations and framing policies; but we had not yet found them. I spent a frightening number of mornings and afternoons busily doodling in committee, with only one ear on the proceedings.

As this book is primarily a record of my own experiences, I have so far mentioned the higher levels of the service only occasionally, when their sometimes unaccountable interventions affected my work. Before going on to describe the reorganization of SIS which took place after the war, it is necessary to take a closer look at my elders and betters, beginning with the Chief, now Major-General Sir Stewart Menzies.

I think that I have already made it clear that I look back on the Chief with enduring affection. He was not, in any sense of the words, a great intelligence officer. His intellectual equipment was unimpressive, and his knowledge of the world, and views about it, were just what one would expect from a fairly cloistered son of the upper levels of the British Establishment. In my own field, counter-espionage, his attitudes were schoolboyish—bars, beards and blondes. But it was this persistent boyish streak shining through the horrible responsibilities that world war placed on his shoulders, and through the ever-present threat of a summons from Churchill in one of his whimsical midnight moods, that was his charm. His real strength lay in a sensitive perception of the currents of White-hall politics, in an ability to feel his way through the mazy corridors of power. Capable officers who knew him much better than myself spoke of his almost feminine intuition—by which I do not mean that he was anything but a whole man.

The Chief's skill in this respect first became common knowledge in SIS when he repelled a determined assault launched by the three service Directors of Intelligence, his colleagues on the Joint Intelligence Committee. The burden of their complaint was that secret intelligence obtained from SIS was inadequate and something would have to be done about it. There was surely some substance in their allegations; there never was an intelligence service that could not have done with improvement. But the Chief knew that it would be useless to contest the accusations against him point by point. His basic weakness was that he had to look over his shoulder so often. Not a few senior officers were after his job; one of these was said to be Admiral Godfrey,* sometime Director of Naval Intelligence.

The Chief had no intention whatever of turning his office upside down to please the services. But he was astute enough to know that real danger lurked somewhere along the corridors. Characteristically, rather than meet it head on, he resorted to suppleness and manoeuvre. Conceding much of his colleagues' criticisms, he invited each of the service Intelligence Directors to send to his staff a senior officer. These officers would be given the rank of Deputy Directors. They would be given full access to all aspects of work of SIS bearing on their particular provinces. They would be free to make any sort of recommendations they liked, and their recommendations would be given the most sympathetic consideration. The Chief, or so he said, had no doubt that, with specialist senior officers of the Military, Naval and Air Intelligence Directorates at his elbow, the requirements of the services would soon be fully covered.

It was a handsome offer, which the services could hardly have refused. It was also a shrewd one. The Chief knew well that no service Intelligence Director in his right mind would part with a se-

---

Director of Naval Intelligence 1939–42, then became Flag Officer Commanding Royal Indian Navy.

nior officer of value to himself—certainly not in conditions of total war. It could be expected with the utmost confidence that the officers seconded to SIS would be expendables, if not outright duds. Once they were bedded down in Broadway Buildings, they could be shunted out of harm's way. I do not suppose that the Chief for a moment doubted that he could achieve a happy ending; and the event proved him wholly right.

So we got our three service commissars, as they were promptly dubbed. Deputy Director/Army was a certain Brigadier Beddington. Within a few weeks, he was engrossed in the problem of checking the ranks of Army officers on the strength of SIS. As a civilian, I had no official contact with him, so I cannot say what lay behind his fleshy face. But I had one small brush with him that suggested that I was lucky to be out of his reach. In those days of clothes rationing, I tried to save the elbows of my two or three civilian suits by wearing in the office the tunic of my war correspondent's uniform. Thus attired, I once entered the office lift with Beddington. We were not on speaking terms—he was that kind of a man—but I noticed a pair of widening eyes wander up my tunic and come to rest on my virgin shoulder-straps. Within half an hour, I received a visit from one of Beddington's underlings, who asked me for details of my military service. I explained how I had come by my tunic and why I was quite entitled to wear it without badges of rank.

The representative of the Air Ministry, Air Commodore Payne,* was more difficult. Payne went to the United States, where his assignment, satisfactorily prolonged, took him as far west as California—Hollywood, according to some.

Deputy Director/Navy, Colonel Cordeaux, was a Marine officer, and the best of the three commissars. He was a footballer of parts, having played in goal for Grimsby Town. With the Chief's encouragement, he soon settled down to conscientious, if somewhat stodgy, direction of SIS operations in and around Scandinavia. It was nice to see at least one of the commissars taking an

Later Air correspondent to the Telegraph.

interest in the work of our service to the extent of actually doing a little himself. From the Chief's point of view, it was satisfactory that Cordeaux, confined to his tight little corner of Northern Europe, was ill-placed to promote revolutions within SIS.

Not long after the Deputy Directors had settled down in their respective spheres of harmless obscurity, there were further changes at the top. I have already shown that Vivian's star was waning rapidly. It became absurd that he should continue under the style of Deputy Chief. He was therefore kicked downwards and sideways into a sinecure created for him, as Adviser on Security Policy. He clung on for years regardless of pride, writing long minutes which nobody read, hoping against vain hope to retire with a K. His place was taken by Dansey. But, to assuage Vivian's feelings, which were very easily hurt, Dansey became, not Deputy Chief, but Vice-Chief. Dansey's former position, that of Assistant-Chief, was now filled by a new and unaccountable intrusion from outside the service in the diminutive shape of General Marshal-Cornwall. At the time of his induction into the service, he was the senior General in the British Army. If he does not figure more prominently in this narrative, it is because his influence was ineffectual where it was not unfortunate. It was he who, through some inexplicable quirk, sustained the long and vicious vendetta against the Passport Control Officer in Rome on account of his wretched car.

Peace soon brought new faces. Marshal-Cornwall left unregretted, almost unremarked. Dansey retired with a knighthood, to experience in quick succession the states of marriage and death. It came to me, when I heard that he was dead, that I had really rather liked him. Nefarious as his influence on the service was, it gave me a pang to think that that crusty old spirit was still for ever. Dansey's place as Vice-Chief was filled from outside by the appointment of General Sinclair,* formerly Director of Military Intelligence. The

---

*John "Sinbad" Sinclair, head of SIS after the Churchill reshuffle in 1953. Forced to resign after the frogman incident of 19 April 1956 in Portsmouth harbour when Commander Crabbe disappeared while investigating the hull of the Soviet cruiser Ordzhonikidze.

Chief, on hearing criticism of the appointment, characteristically remarked: "Why, I have stifled War Office criticism for five years." The vacancy caused by Marshal-Cornwall's departure was filled by another outsider, Air Commodore Easton.

For both these newcomers I soon felt a respect which I had been unable to extend to their predecessors. Sinclair, though not over-loaded with mental gifts (he never claimed them) was humane, energetic and so obviously upright that it was impossible to withhold admiration. Easton was a very different proposition. On first acquaintance, he gave the impression of burbling and bumbling, but it was dangerously deceptive. His strength was a brain of conspicuous clarity, yet capable of deeply subtle twists. Regarding them from time to time in the light of antagonists, I could not help applying to Sinclair and Easton the obvious metaphor of bludgeon and rapier. I was not afraid of the bludgeon; it could be dodged with ease. But the occasional glimpse of Easton's rapier made my stomach flop over. I was fated to have a great deal to do with him.

Before these last appointments were made, a serious attempt had been launched to put the whole organization on a sound footing. I have indicated that the pre-war service had been a haphazard and dangerously amateur affair. There was no regular system of recruitment, of training, of promotion or of security at the end of a career. The Chief took whom he could when and where he could, and all contracts of service were subject to termination at any time. In such conditions, it was impossible to attract a regular flow of recruits of the requisite standard. No wonder that the personnel of the service was of uneven quality, ranging from good through indifferent to downright bad. The war had been a rude awakening. The service had to be vastly increased in numbers, and many able people passed through its ranks, dropping ideas as they went. But the strength of the service had been achieved by a succession of improvisations under the day-to-day stress of war. Almost everything that was done could have been done better if there had been time for reflection. Now the time was ripe. The end of the war in Europe had relieved the pressure for immediate results, yet the government was still alive to the value of intelligence. It was essential to use the remaining months of 1945 to hammer out a new structure for the service before the government sank back into post-war lethargy. The Chief himself had doubtless been thinking along these lines. When it was presented to him that there was considerable support for the idea in the service, he appointed a committee to advise him on the subject. The so-called Committee of SIS Reorganization began its meetings in September 1945.

The ringleaders of the movement had been Arnold-Forster and Captain Hastings, RN, a senior and influential officer of the Government Code & Cypher School. Although not a member of SIS, Hastings had a legitimate interest in its activity, in view of wartime lessons on the need for close liaison between the cryptographers and SIS. His appointment also had the advantage of bringing a fresh mind to the debates in committee. David Footman* was brought in to look after the political needs of the service, while Colonel Cordeaux represented the "G" sections. I was also invited to serve, not because of any aptitude for committee work (which I detested), but because, Vivian excepted, I was the senior counter-espionage officer in the service. Our secretary was Alurid Denne, a careful, not to say punctilious, officer who could be relied on for complete impartiality because he had a comfortable niche awaiting him in the Shell Oil Company.

Most of us wanted Arnold-Forster to occupy the chair. Apart from his willpower, his enthusiasm and his clear mind, he had acquired, as Principal Staff Officer to the Chief, a better knowledge than any of us of the organization as a whole. But the Chief, leery of Arnold-Forster's brains and wishing to keep any proposals for reform within bounds, had kept a bombshell in reserve for us. To our utter astonishment, he announced that our Chairman would be Maurice Jeffes, the Director of Passport Control. As the official responsible for the issue of visas, Jeffes was in frequent contact with

---

*No. 2 in Section 1 of SIS, later became head of Section 1. Burgess introduced him to Philby just after Philby had returned from Spain in 1939. Afterward Emeritus Fellow of St. Antony's College, Oxford.

our counter-espionage people; but his general knowledge of the service, of its possibilities and limitations, was nothing to write home about. As for his abilities, I do not suppose that he himself would have claimed to be more than a capable if colourless administrator. But there we were. The Chief had spoken.

In saying that Jeffes was colourless, I must explain that I use the term in a purely metaphorical sense. Some years before the formation of our committee, he had been the victim of a singular accident. A doctor, inoculating him against some disease, had used the wrong serum, with the result that Jeffes's face had turned a strange purplish blue. The process was apparently irreversible, and Jeffes was stuck with his gun-metal face. During a visit to Washington, the honest fellow had been much incensed when the management of a hotel tried to cancel his booking on the ground that he was coloured. To be quite fair, Jeffes did little to interfere in the course of our debates, and never obtruded his authority as Chairman. It was impossible not to like him, and we soon got used to his spectacular presence at the head of the table.

Much of my time during the following months was taken up by the committee. Our deliberations had now become hopelessly academic, and do not call for detailed notice. But a few comments may perhaps throw light on some of the general problems confronting the organization of intelligence. Our first task was to clear up untidy survivals from the bad old days. During the war, finance and administration had gone separate ways with inadequate coordination. The "G" sections were generally messy, those concerned with Western Europe working for Dansey, the rest directly with the Chief. Looking at it from the other direction, Dansey was nominally Vice-Chief of the service as a whole; but in fact he was interested only in the production of intelligence in Western Europe. It was clear that the structure of the service as a whole stood in need of drastic streamlining.

But before we could deal with this first problem, a matter of fundamental principle had to be decided. Should the primary division of the service be along vertical lines, with regional organizations

responsible for the production, processing, assessment and circulation of information relating to their respective regions? Or should
it be along horizontal lines, between the production of information
on the one hand, and its processing, assessment and circulation on
the other? I confess that I still do not know the right answer to this
question. But at that time my own interest was heavily engaged. If
the vertical solution were adopted, work against the Soviet Union
and Communism generally would be divided regionally. No single
person could cover the whole field. I therefore threw my weight
behind the horizontal solution, in the hope of keeping, for the
time being at any rate, the whole field of anti-Soviet and anti-
Communist work under my own direct supervision.

In favour of the case for a horizontal solution, I had a strong ally
in David Footman. In fact, it was he, in his dry and incisive way, who
made most of the running, with myself in support where necessary.
My argument was, briefly, that counter-espionage was one and indivisible. A case in Canada might throw light on another one in
Switzerland—as indeed one did shortly thereafter; an agent working in China one year might turn up in Peru the next. It was essential, therefore, to study the subject on a world-wide basis. I also
made use of the less valid, though not wholly baseless, point that
the production of intelligence should be kept separate from its assessment, on the grounds that production officers naturally tended
to regard their geese as swans. There was, of course, much to be
said on both sides of the question; but the body of service opinion
in favour of the vertical division was weakly represented in committee, and the horizontal solution was finally adopted. I knew at
least one colleague who might have turned the tide against us, and
I had been at some pains to have him excluded from the committee
membership.

Once that question of principle was decided, the rest was fairly
simple, if arduous, donkeywork. We recommended the creation of
five Directorates of equal status: (1) Finance and Administration;
(2) Production; (3) Requirements, so-called because in addition to
assessing information and circulating it to government departments,

it passed back to the Directorate of Production the "requirements" of those departments; (4) Training and Development, the latter concerned with the development of technical devices in support of espionage; (5) War Planning. We drew up a system of ranks within the service, with fixed pay-scales and pensions on retirement. We threw on the Directorate of Finance and Administration the responsibility for systematic recruiting in competition with the regular civil service and industry, with particular attention to graduates from the universities. By the time our final bulky report was ready for presentation to the Chief, we felt that we had produced the design of something like a service, with enough serious inducements to tempt able young men to regard it as a career for life.

The Chief did not accept all our recommendations. There was still a certain amount of dead wood which found no place in our plan but which he could not bring himself to cut out. But, by and large, the pattern sketched above was adopted as the basic pattern of the service. For all its faults, it was a formidable improvement on anything that had gone before. As for myself, I had no cause for dissatisfaction. One of the minor decisions of the committee was the abolition of Section V.

VIII. THE VOLKOV CASE

I now come to the Volkov case, which I propose to describe in some detail, both because of its intrinsic interest and because it nearly put an end to a promising career. The case began in August and ended in September of 1945. It was a memorable summer for me because it yielded me my first sights of Rome, Athens and Istanbul. But my delighted impressions of Istanbul were affected by the frequent reflection that this might be the last memorable summer I was destined to enjoy. For the Volkov business, which was what took me to the Bosphorus, proved to be a very narrow squeak indeed.

I had scarcely settled down to my desk one August morning when I received a summons from the Chief. He pushed across at me a sheaf of papers and asked me to look them through. The top paper was a brief letter to the Foreign Office from Knox Helm, then Minister at the British Embassy in Turkey. It drew attention to the attachments and asked for instructions. The attachments were a number of minutes that had passed between and within the British Embassy and Consulate-General, from which the following story emerged.

A certain Konstantin Volkov, a Vice-Consul attached to the Soviet Consulate-General in Istanbul, had approached a Mr. Page, his opposite number in the British Consulate-General, and asked for asylum in Britain for himself and his wife. He claimed that, although nominally a Vice-Consul, he was in fact an officer of the NKVD. He said that his wife was in a deplorably nervous state, and Page remarked that Volkov himself was less than rock-steady. In support of his request for asylum, Volkov promised to reveal details of the headquarters of the NKVD, in which apparently he had worked for many years. He also offered details of Soviet networks and agents operating abroad. *Inter alia,* he claimed to know the real names of three Soviet agents working in Britain. Two of them were in the Foreign Office; one was head of a counter-espionage organization in London. Having delivered himself of his shopping list, he stipulated with the greatest vehemence that no mention of his approach should be relayed to London by telegram, on the grounds that the Russians had broken a variety of British cyphers. The rest of the papers were of little interest, representing only off-the-cuff comments by various members of the Embassy, some of them quite flippant in tone. What proved to be of some importance later was that the Embassy had respected Volkov's stipulation about communications, and had sent the papers home, securely but slowly, by bag. Thus it was over a week after Volkov's approach to Page that the material was examined by anyone competent to assess its importance.

That "anyone" was myself; and the reader will not reproach me with boasting when I claim that I was indeed competent to assess the importance of the material. Two Soviet agents in the Foreign Office, one head of a counter-espionage organization in London! I stared at the papers rather longer than necessary to compose my thoughts. I rejected the idea of suggesting caution in case Volkov's approach should prove to be a provocation. It would be useless in the short run, and might possibly compromise me at a later date. The only course was to put a bold face on it. I told the Chief that I thought we were on to something of the greatest importance. I would like a little time to dig into the background and, in the light of any further information on the subject, to make appropriate recommendations for action. The Chief acquiesced, instructing me to report first thing next morning and, in the meanwhile, to keep the papers strictly to myself.

I took the papers back to my office, telling my secretary that I was not to be disturbed, unless the Chief himself called. I very much wanted to be alone. My request for a little time "to dig into the background" had been eyewash. I was pretty certain that we had never heard of Volkov; and he, presumably to enhance his value to us, had framed his shopping list in such vague terms that it offered no leads for immediate investigation. Still, I had much food for thought. From the first, it seemed to me that the time factor was vital. Owing to Volkov's veto on telegraphic communications, the case had taken ten days to reach me. Personally, I thought that his fears were exaggerated. Our cyphers were based on the one-time pad system, which is supposed to be foolproof, if properly used; and our cypher discipline was strict. Yet, if Volkov so wished, I had no objection to ruling out swift communication.

Another train of thought soon claimed my attention. The case was of such delicacy that the Chief had insisted on my handling it myself. But, once the decisions had been taken in London, all action would devolve on our people in Istanbul. It would be impossible for me, with slow-bag communications, to direct their day-to-day, hour-to-hour actions. The case would escape my control, with unpredictable results. The more I thought, the more convinced I became that I should go to Istanbul myself, to implement the course of action that I was to recommend to the Chief. The action itself required little thought. It involved meeting Volkov, bedding him down with his wife in one of our safe houses in Istanbul, and spiriting him away, with or without the connivance of the Turks, to British-occupied territory in Egypt. By the time I put the papers in my personal safe and left Broadway, I had decided that my main recommendation to the Chief would be that he should instruct me to go to Istanbul to continue handling the case on the spot. That evening, I worked late. The situation seemed to call for urgent action of an extra-curricular nature.

Next morning, I reported to the Chief that, although we had several Volkovs on file, none of them matched our man in Istanbul. I repeated my view that the case was of great potential importance. Dwelling on the delays involved in communication by bag, I recommended, rather diffidently, that someone fully briefed should be sent out from London to take charge of the case on the spot. "Just what I was thinking myself," replied the Chief. But having raised my hopes, he promptly dashed them. The previous evening, he said, he had met Brigadier Douglas Roberts in clubland. Roberts was then head of Security Intelligence (Middle East), MI5's regional organization based in Cairo. He was enjoying the fag-end of a spell of home leave. The Chief had been well impressed by him, and his intention, so he told me, was to ask Sir David Petrie, the head of MI5, to send Roberts straight out to Istanbul to take charge of the Volkov case.

I could find nothing to say against the proposal. Although I had formed no very high opinion of Roberts's ability, he had all the paper qualifications for the task on hand. He was a senior officer; his Brigadier's uniform would doubtless impress Volkov. He knew the area and had worked with the Turkish secret services, whose co-operation might prove to be necessary. Above all, he spoke fluent Russian—an unassailably strong point in his favour. In despondent mood, I went through other aspects of the case with the Chief, notably the need for getting Foreign Office approval for our plan of action. As I left, the Chief asked me to be available in the afternoon, since he hoped to see both Petrie and Roberts in the course of the morning.

During the lunch interval, I railed against the wretched luck that had brought the Chief and Roberts together the previous evening. There seemed nothing that I could do. Suspenseful as it would be,

I just had to sit back and let events take their course, hoping that my work the night before would bear fruit before Roberts got his teeth into the case. But I was in for yet another lesson in everyday philosophy. On return to Broadway, I found a summons from the Chief awaiting me. He looked thoroughly disconcerted and plunged immediately into his story; from his first words, I realized that luck, against which I had railed so bitterly, had veered sharply in my favour. Roberts, it appeared, though doubtless as lion-hearted as the next man, had an unconquerable distaste for flying. He had made his arrangements to return by boat from Liverpool early the following week. Nothing that the Chief or Petrie could say would induce him to change his plans. So we were back where we started from that morning.

I had originally hoped that I could so manoeuvre the discussion with the Chief that he himself would suggest my flying to Istanbul. But the Roberts interlude spurred me to direct action. So I said that, in view of the Brigadier's defection, I could only suggest that I should go out in his place. It would not take me long to brief my deputy on any outstanding business. I could leave as soon as all the necessary clearances had been obtained. With obvious relief, the Chief agreed. Together we went to the Foreign Office, where I was given a letter to present to Knox Helm, asking him to give me all reasonable facilities for the fulfilment of my mission. My only other call was on General Hill, the head of our Coding Section. He supplied me with my own personal one-time cypher pads, and lent me one of his girls to refresh me in their use. This caused a little extra delay—not altogether unwelcome, since it gave me more time to adjust my thoughts to action in Istanbul. Three full days elapsed between the arrival of the Istanbul papers in Broadway and the take-off of my aeroplane bound for Cairo en route for Istanbul.

My neighbour on the aeroplane was taciturn. Few aircraft companions bother me long, however talkative they may be by nature. For me, flying is conducive to reflection, and I had plenty to occupy my mind. For some time, I tossed around in my mind a problem which baffled me then and baffles me to this day: namely, the oddness of the reaction, shared by the Embassy in Turkey, the Foreign Office, the Chief and Sir David Petrie, to Volkov's terror of communication by telegraph. The oddness of their reaction consisted in the fact that they eschewed telegrams mentioning Volkov, and *only* telegrams mentioning Volkov. Telegraphic correspondence on every other subject under the sun, including many that must have been Top Secret, went on gaily as before. If we believed Volkov's warning, we should have concluded that all telegraphy was dangerous. If we disbelieved it, we should have instructed our station in Istanbul to take the necessary action without delay. As it was, the only result of Volkov's tip was to delay, by two or three weeks, action on his own behalf. The answer obviously lay deep in the psychology of wishful thinking. Not being an expert on codes and cyphers, I concluded that it was no business of mine to draw attention to the gross inconsistency of our conduct. Anyway, there were more immediate problems to be considered.

It had been agreed at the Foreign Office that I should use Page for the purpose of re-establishing contact with Volkov and arranging a rendezvous. To the latter, I would be accompanied by John Reed, a First Secretary of the Embassy, who had earlier served in Moscow and passed one of the Foreign Office exams in Russian. These arrangements were made subject to the approval of the Ambassador, Sir Maurice Peterson, whom I knew from Spanish days; but the Foreign Office warned me in pressing terms to approach Helm, the Minister, first. Helm, it appeared, had begun life in the Consular Service, and was still touchy about matters of status and protocol. I did not anticipate much difficulty from Helm, in which I was not altogether right. The crux of my problem, it seemed to me, was the interview between Volkov and myself, with Reed in attendance. If it ever took place, Reed would get the shock of his life if Volkov started reeling off names of Soviet agents in British Government service. It would be charitable, I thought, to spare him such surprises. How to make sure?

There was obviously no means of making sure. But I thought that I had a slender chance if I played it right. I decided that my first objective was to get hold of Reed and convince him that my mission was of a severely restricted scope. I was not authorized to discuss with Volkov the details of his information. It would be positively dangerous if he made disclosures prematurely, that is, before he was safe on British soil. My instructions were to prevent at all costs any deviation of the interview into such channels. I was in Istanbul solely to get Volkov away to safety, where he could be interrogated by those qualified for the job. I thought that I could string Reed along further by hinting that we were by no means satisfied that Volkov was not a provocateur. It would be most unfortunate, therefore, if his information was given currency before we could assess its authenticity. I felt that I could do no better. An expert, of course, could have driven a coach-and-four through my fabrications. But Reed was not an expert, and he might prove pliable. Towards evening, my rising spirits were given another boost. The pilot announced on the intercom, that, owing to electrical storms over Malta, we were being diverted to Tunis. Subject to improved weather conditions, we would fly on to Cairo via Malta next day. Another twenty-four hours! My luck was holding.

On the afternoon of the following day, we arrived at last in Cairo, too late to catch the onward plane for Istanbul. So it was not until the day after that, a Friday, that I reached my destination. I was met at the airport by Cyril Machray, the head of our Istanbul station, whom I had to brief on the nature of my mission. Such were the relations between the Foreign Service and SIS in those days that nobody in the Embassy or the Consulate-General had thought of consulting him about Volkov—and, of course, we had not dared to telegraph him from London. We called together that afternoon on Knox Helm, to whom I presented the letter from the

Foreign Office. But if I expected enthusiastic support for our plans, I was soon disabused. Some years later, after Helm had got his Embassy, in Budapest, a colleague told me that he was the most helpful and understanding of Ambassadors. But when I saw him, he was still only a Minister, and as prickly as a thorn-bush. He demurred stubbornly. Our suggestions might well cause embarrassment to the Embassy; he would surely have to consult the Ambassador before I went any further. He asked me to call on him next morning (another day wasted), then hospitably took me home for drinks. Also of the party was the Military Attaché, who suggested that I should dine with him at the Park Hotel; he also evidently had his troubles with Helm.

When I called on Helm next morning, he looked at me accusingly. "You never told me that you knew the Ambassador!" After that, our conversation scarcely got off the ground, but I gathered from Helm's manner that there were also reservations in Peterson's mind. Rather grudgingly, he told me that the Ambassador wanted me to spend the following day, Sunday, with him on the yacht *Makouk*. It would put off from the Kabatash landing-stage at 11 A.M. Meanwhile, I was to do nothing. So the whole weekend was shot.

Most visitors to Istanbul know the *Makouk,* the Ambassadorial yacht, originally built for Abbas Hilmi of Egypt. It was a large, flat-bottomed vessel, well suited to the smooth waters of the Nile, but it rolled somewhat in the swell of Marmara. There were several other guests on board, and it was not until after lunch, when we were anchored off Trotsky's Prinkipo, that I could talk to Peterson in conditions of reasonable privacy while the other guests gambolled with the porpoises. As he did not break the ice, I did so myself, remarking that I had heard that he had some objections to the plans I had brought with me from London. What plans? he asked—a question that gave me another sidelight on Helm. He listened attentively to my exposition, and then asked one question: had we consulted the Foreign Office? But yes, I answered. The Foreign Office had approved everything, and I had brought Helm a letter asking him to offer all reasonable facilities. "Then there's no more to be said," he replied. "Go ahead." The last excuse for the delay had gone.

That evening, Machray and I discussed the plan of campaign in detail. We exchanged several ideas for spiriting Volkov away, some involving Turkish co-operation, some not. It seemed clear that we could not decide definitely which was the best plan until we had spoken to Volkov himself. Much might depend on his own position and his particular circumstances—his hours of work, the degree of freedom of movement he enjoyed, etc. The first step was to establish contact with him, and clearly our best instrument was Page, of the Consulate-General, whom Volkov had approached in the first place. Next morning, accordingly, Machray invited Page to come over to his office, and I explained to him as much as he needed to know, namely, that I would like him to make an appointment for me to see Volkov some time that afternoon in conditions of greatest secrecy. (I did not want a morning appointment, because I needed time to brief John Reed on the lines already described.) We discussed several possible places for the meeting, but opted finally for the simplest. Page said that he frequently had routine consular business with Volkov. It would be perfectly normal practice for him to invite Volkov over to his office for a talk. At last, as Page reached for the receiver, zero hour had arrived.

Page got on to the Soviet Consulate-General, and asked for Volkov. A man's voice came faintly on the line, but Page's half of the conversation meant nothing to me. But Page's face was a study in puzzlement, telling me that a hitch had developed. When he put the receiver down, he shook his head at me. "He can't come?" I asked. "That's funny." "It's a great deal funnier than you think," Page answered. "I asked for Volkov and a man came on, saying he was Volkov. But it wasn't Volkov. I know Volkov's voice perfectly well, I've spoken to him dozens of times." Page tried again, but this time got no farther than the telephone operator. "She said he was out," said Page indignantly. "A minute ago, she put me on to him!"

We looked at each other, but none of us could find a constructive idea. I finally suggested that there might be some flap on at the Soviet Consulate-General, and that we had better try again the following day in hopes of better luck. I began to feel strongly that, somewhere along the line, something decisive had happened. I whiled away the afternoon by personally encyphering a brief report to the Chief.

Next morning, we met again, Machray, Page and myself, and Page telephoned the Soviet Consulate-General. I heard the faint echo of a woman's voice, then a sharp click. Page looked foolishly at the silent receiver in his hand. "What do you make of that? I asked for Volkov, and the girl said 'Volkov's in Moscow.' Then there was a sort of scuffle and slam, the line went dead." On hearing this, I was pretty certain that I knew what had happened. The case was dead. But I was anxious to clinch the matter, even if only to make my report to the Chief look better. I therefore asked Page to make one final, desperate effort. Would he mind calling at the Consulate-General and asking for Volkov in person? Page by now was determined to get to the bottom of the matter, and readily agreed to call on the Russians. Within an hour, he was back, still puzzled and angry. "It's no bloody good," he reported. "I can't get any sense out of that madhouse. Nobody's ever heard of Volkov!" We broke up, and I sat down to encypher another telegram for the Chief. After confessing defeat, I asked his permission to wind up the case and return to London.

During the homeward journey, I roughed out a report which I would present to the Chief, describing in detail the failure of my mission. Necessarily, it contained my theory of Volkov's disappearance. The essence of the theory was that Volkov's own insistence on bag communications had brought about his downfall. Nearly three weeks had elapsed between his first approach to Page and our first attempt to contact him. During that time, the Russians had ample chances of getting on to him. Doubtless both his office and his living quarters were bugged. Both he and his wife were reported to be nervous. Perhaps his manner had given him away; perhaps he had got drunk and talked too much; perhaps, even, he had changed his mind and confessed to his colleagues. Of course, I admitted, this was all speculation; the truth might never be known. Another theory—that the Russians had been tipped off about Volkov's approach to the British—had no solid evidence to support it. It was not worth including in my report.

IX. THE TERRIBLE TURK

My strategic position at the head of R5 could not last for ever. In making its recommendations on future staff policy, the Committee on SIS Reorganization had decided in favour of versatility rather than specialization. It laid down that, so far as possible, all officers should feel equally at home in offensive and defensive work, both at headquarters and in the field. Such a system might result in some loss of expertise as officers were periodically switched from pillar to post. But that loss, it was thought, would be outweighed by the greater flexibility offered by a staff made up of all-rounders. It is perhaps needless to remark that, when this staff policy was adopted, the three senior officers of the service, the Chief, Vice-Chief and Assistant-Chief, had no experience of counter-espionage and no practical knowledge of work in the field. But I was not senior enough to benefit from any such dispensation. As all my work for SIS had been concerned with counter-espionage at headquarters, I was obviously due for an early change of scene.

It was therefore no surprise when General Sinclair summoned me towards the end of 1946, and told me that my turn had come for a tour of duty overseas. I had already decided that I could not reasonably resist a foreign posting without serious loss of standing in the service, and such loss of standing might well have prejudiced my access in the long run to the sort of intelligence I needed. When I heard from Sinclair that I had been chosen to take charge of the SIS station in Turkey, with headquarters in Istanbul, I felt that things might have been very much worse. Istanbul was then the main southern base for intelligence work directed against the Soviet Union and the Socialist countries of the Balkans and Central Europe. Although I would no longer be right in the middle of my main field of interest, I would not be so far off-centre.

Sinclair told me that my successor at R5 would be the same Brigadier Roberts who had crossed my path briefly during the Volkov affair. He had relinquished his post as head of Security Intelligence Middle East (SIME), and was available for service at home. He took over from me in leisurely fashion, and questioned me more closely on the clubs of London than on the work of the section. His firmest claim to fame, as head of R5, was his success in persuading Maurice Oldfield,* an officer of high quality from SIME, also to join SIS. Within a few weeks of his installation as Roberts's deputy, Oldfield had earned the nickname "Brig's Brains."

In preparation for my overseas tour of duty, I was attached to the training section of one of the officers' courses. It was only the second or third course to be arranged under the aegis of the new Director of Training and Development, our old friend John Munn, and the syllabus has been drastically modified since. The training staff consisted in the main of officers drawn from SOE, and their tuition was conditioned by their experience of SOE in wartime. The course was of considerable interest, although I derived little immediate benefit from it. The conditions of peacetime espionage in Istanbul were far removed from the hazards of wartime work for SOE in Occupied Europe. I had personally drafted most of the lectures on the Soviet intelligence services, and was sometimes in the

---

* *Lt. Col. Intelligence Corps, Middle East, 1941–6, then worked for the Foreign Office in the Far East (Singapore). Counsellor, Foreign Office, after 1965.*

embarrassing position of having to prompt the instructor from the floor of the lecture hall. It was frustrating to have to eliminate from my drafts all knowledge based on personal experience. As I had to spend half my time keeping an eye on R5, I missed the various tests and examinations to which the other students were subjected. That was perhaps fortunate. It would have been awkward if an officer of my seniority had regularly come bottom of the class.

The training course and the hand-over to Roberts were completed in January 1947, and at the end of the month I found myself at the Airways Terminal drinking what passed for coffee at a savage hour of the morning. There I stuck, off and on, for ten days. Snow and bitter cold gripped the country; the weather and mechanical trouble caused delay after delay. But I could call myself lucky. It was the period of the famous Dakota crashes, when every paper, it seemed, brought news of a fresh disaster. For several mornings, I shared the vigil with a group of nuns bound for Bulawayo. Their departure was finally announced one perishing morning—and perish they did, every one of them. I was a happy man when I felt the warm breath of the desert and Cairo airport under my feet.

Since joining the service over six years earlier, I had taken perhaps ten days' leave. With the pressure of work momentarily lessened, I decided to fly down, en route for Istanbul, to visit my father in Saudi Arabia. He met me in Jidda and took me briefly to Riyadh and Al Kharj. It was my first acquaintance with the country to which he had devoted the greater part of his life. Neither then nor thereafter did I feel the slightest temptation to follow his example. The limitless space, the clear night skies and the rest of the gobbledygook are all right in small doses. But I would find a lifetime in a landscape with majesty but no charm, among a people with neither majesty nor charm, quite unacceptable. Ignorance and arrogance make a bad combination, and the Saudi Arabians have both in generous measure. When an outward show of austerity is thrown in as well, the mixture is intolerable.

I have indulged in this digression to answer certain writers who have attributed the unusual course of my life to the influence of my father. It is possible that his eccentricities enabled me, in early youth, to resist some of the more outrageous prejudices of the English public-school system of forty years ago. But very little research would show that, at all the decisive turning-points in my life, he was thousands of miles out of reach. If he had lived a little longer to learn the truth, he would have been thunderstruck, but by no means disapproving. I was perhaps the only member of his wide acquaintance to whom he was never rude, and to whose opinions he invariably listened with respect—even on his own precious Arab world. I never took this uncritically as a compliment. I have heard it said, possibly wrongly, that Winston Churchill gave weight to the opinions of his own son, Randolph.

It was with no pain at all that I left the useless desert for the riotous wonder of Istanbul. My colleagues were scattered around the dreary apartment blocks of Pera, but I had no intention of following their lead. Within a few days I had found a delightful villa in Beylerbey, on the Asiatic shore of the Bosphorus, a place of such loveliness that I agreed without demur to pay an exorbitant rent. It was next door to the landing-stage, and for three years I was to commute daily between Asia and Europe by ferryboat, through the everchanging pattern of gulls and shearwaters, mists, currents and eddies. The old Turkey hands, of course, were aghast. But it is a good working rule, wherever you are, to ignore the old hands; their mentalities grow inward like toenails. I had no cause to regret the choice of my remote Asian hide-out. Indeed, my example was soon followed by some of the more imaginative spirits.

I was disguised as a First Secretary of the Embassy, and here I should indulge in a short digression. I have already mentioned that the cover of Passport Control Officer for SIS officers had become widely known before and during the war, and one of the recommendations of the Committee on SIS Reorganization had been that we should move away from it. Since that time the great majority of SIS officers abroad have been posted as First, Second or Third Secretaries, according to seniority. (Since my time, one or two of the more important posts, such as Paris and Washington, have been dignified with Counsellor rank.) A few have been stashed away as simple attachés or as junior Information Officers. Meanwhile, most of the tainted Passport Control Officers working in the legitimate line of visa duty have been re-christened visa officers. Most of them are now formally free of intelligence duties, though in fact working links between the visa officers and SIS personnel are still maintained.

The change of disguise was accompanied by a change in the system of symbols designating overseas personnel. Until the reorganization, all countries had borne a two-digit number: for example, Germany was 12-land, Spain 23-land. The representatives in those countries bore the corresponding five-digit symbol: the head representative in Germany was 12,000, in Spain 23,000, while their subordinate officers and agents would have other five-digit symbols in the 12,000 and 23,000 brackets. This system, it was believed, had become as compromised as the Passport Control cover. There is the well-known legend that Abwehr officers in Istanbul had been heard singing: "Zwölfland, Zwölfland uber alles."

Be that as it may, the system was completely overhauled. Each country was now given a symbol consisting of three letters of the alphabet, the first of which (for reasons unknown to me) was invariably B. Thus the United States was BEE-land, Turkey, BFX-land. The head representative in each country was distinguished by the addition of the figures 51, and his subordinates by other two-digit symbols, e.g., 01, 07, etc. Thus, as head of the SIS station in Turkey, I found myself wearing, with an odd sense of discomfort, the designation BFX/51. Whichever way you looked at it, in longhand or typescript, it seemed horribly ungainly.

So I was First Secretary of the Embassy, with no known Embassy duties, alias BFX/51. In all, we were five officers, with the appropriate secretarial staff. In addition to a capable and companionable deputy and a sturdily enthusiastic junior (Second and Third Secretaries respectively), there was an ebullient White Russian of boundless charm and appalling energy (Attaché). Finally, there was the Passport Control Officer, who was responsible directly to Maurice Jeffes in London for visa affairs, but to me for his intelligence duties. So far as I was concerned, he acted as liaison officer with the Turkish services. He was an old Turkey hand, bearing the honoured name of Whittall; he spoke fluent Turkish; but he was far too nice to liaise with the Turks. Short mention should also be made of Whittall's secretary, who had a passion for cats and a highly personal filing system. When I asked her for a paper, she would say mildly: "I *think* it is under the white cat," and by God, it would be.

The Turkish services were known as the Security Inspectorate, and our relations with them conditioned almost all our intelligence activity in Turkey. They knew of us, and tolerated our activity, on the understanding that it was directed solely against the Soviet Union and the Balkans, not against Turkey. As will be seen, this undertaking was often honoured in the breach. In order to ensure the benevolence of the Inspectorate, we paid its Istanbul office a monthly subsidy, camouflaged as payment for the enquiries carried out by the Inspectorate on our behalf. Since we got precious little return for it in terms of intelligence, it is fairly obvious that our subvention merely inflated the salaries of the senior Inspectors in Istanbul. It was worth it, if only as hush-money.

The headquarters of the Inspectorate were at Ankara, presided over at that time by a bulging, toad-like bureaucrat whom we referred to as Uncle Ned. It was my misfortune to visit him on duty about once a month. Our meetings soon took on a regular pattern of mutual frustration. I would start by requesting facilities for this or that operation, for passing an agent, for example, from Eastern Turkey into Soviet Armenia. He would clear his throat, whisper to his interpreter, shift his buttocks and call for coffee. He would then propose that I should give him the agent and the money. He would carry out the operation and give us the results. As simple as that. When I came to know enough Turkish to realize what was going on, these interviews usually ended in my having a row with my interpreter, whom nothing would induce to be sufficiently rude. He had some excuse. He was not on the diplomatic list, and had reason to fear Uncle Ned's ill-will.

The head of the Istanbul office of the Security Inspectorate was known to us as Aunt Jane. He was a person of considerable interest to me, as it was in his area that most of my clandestine activity would have to take place. But he never succeeded in filling me with excessive alarm. He was an easy-going, rather shop-soiled *roué*, interested above all in his gallbladder and, of course, money. After a few weeks, I was content to leave the routine contact with Aunt Jane to Whittall, intervening myself only on special occasions. About twice a year, I arranged a party for him, and he proved to be the ideal guest. He would arrive in a police launch half an hour before the appointed time, down two or three quick whiskies and vanish on a plea of urgent work while the other guests were arriving.

My contacts with Uncle Ned, Aunt Jane, and their colleagues confirmed a suspicion I had already formed, namely, that the security services of the minor powers lack the resources and experience for effective action. Even Tefik Bey of Erzurum, probably the best of the Security Inspectorate officers, made a sorry mess of the only operation I ever entrusted to him. Yet the Turks were supposed to have one of the better services. I have even read recently, in John Bulloch's *Akin to Treason*,* that Lebanese security is "very efficient"— a misuse of language by any standard. If they were really efficient, they would start by stamping out the trade in forged documents that flourishes under their noses in Beirut.

Aunt Jane's office had certain supervisory functions over the Inspectorate office in Adrianople, which produced a trickle of low-grade information from Bulgaria, largely the product of tolerated smugglers and the odd refugee. But its importance was due principally to the fact that Istanbul was an active transit area. A large proportion of the refugees from the revolutions in the Balkans and Central Europe found their way eventually to Istanbul, where it was the responsibility of Aunt Jane and his officers to screen them and pump them for any information they might possess. Some of the reports derived from these sources were passed on to us by the Turks, but their quality was uniformly disappointing. This was

---

*John Bulloch, *Akin to Treason* (London, Arthur Barker Ltd.), 1966.

partly due to the ignorance of the refugees themselves, partly to the inexperience of the interrogators who failed to ask the significant questions. Repeated efforts to get official access to these refugees ourselves, before they dispersed to their various destinations, were frustrated by Turkish lethargy. We were driven to hunt them down on our own—a process which, quite unnecessarily, wasted an immense amount of time.

For much of our intelligence on the Balkan states, we had to rely on nationals of those states resident in Istanbul. A surprising number of Bulgarians, Yugoslavs and Rumanians claimed to have established espionage organizations in their own countries before passing into exile themselves. They were more than willing to put such networks at our disposal, provided we put up the necessary funds for activating them. The war, of course, had shown all Europe that there was money in espionage, and during the forties an unwary purchaser could have spent millions in Istanbul on intelligence fabricated within the city limits. The Americans had been largely responsible for pushing up the price of forgery, but by 1947 SIS's appetite for faked intelligence had become jaded. Much of our time was spent in devising means of smoking such operations into the open, so that we could judge what sort of price to put on their work. We rarely succeeded, and I am pretty sure that, in spite of the care we took, several of the exiles made regular monkeys of us.

I had been told in London not to concentrate too much attention on the Balkans. My first priority was the Soviet Union. I played with several ideas of getting tip-and-run agents into the Russian Black Sea ports by means of merchantmen calling at Odessa, Nikolaev, Novorossisk and elsewhere. But the main assault, I decided, would have to be on the Eastern frontier, which offered the possibility of infiltrating agents into the Soviet Union along a wide front. Most of the summer of 1947, therefore, was devoted to a personal reconnaissance of the frontier regions, with a view to discovering what sort of help the Turks could offer us and what sort of obstacles we would have to meet. Such a reconnaissance also served a secondary purpose: a topographical survey of the frontier marches of Turkey for which the armed services were clamouring. This was before the Americans took over Turkey and, among other things, carried out an aerial survey of the whole country. We were still pretty ignorant of the state of communications in the extensive region east of the Euphrates.

The topographical survey was of interest to SIS for different reasons. Our War Planning Directorate, thinking in terms of global war against the Soviet Union, was busy with projects for setting up centres of resistance in regions which the Red Army was expected by them to overrun and occupy in the early stages of war. Turkey was one of the first countries to be considered in this respect. The mountains of Anatolia are broken up by a series of level plains, lozenge-shaped and generally running along an east-west axis, ideal stepping-stones for a Soviet invader's airborne troops. The prospects of successful resistance anywhere east of Ankara were rated very low. The best we could hope for in Turkey, therefore, was the establishment of guerilla bases from which Soviet communications, running through the plains, could be harried. Our planners needed far more detailed information than was available on the nature of the terrain in Eastern Turkey: how broken was it? How much forest cover? What water and food resources?

An enquiry of this nature raised delicate problems. It implied an Anglo-American intention to abandon Turkey to its fate as soon as war broke out. However relentless the logic of such military thinking, it would hardly have appealed to the Turks. Indeed, it was believed that, if they had got any inkling that such plans were in existence, the resulting storm would blow away their illusions about the West and force them to come to terms with the Soviet Union. This part of the survey, therefore, had to be carried out with almost crippling discretion. Fortunately, the Turks remained unaware of my activity in this respect. If they had shown interest, it seems doubtful whether they would have believed my only possible line of defence, namely, that I was interested solely in the communications of an Allied army advancing into Georgia.

In any case, I decided that my beginnings should be modest.

After the first summer of reconnaissance, I would be better equipped for a more ambitious programme in 1948. The first hurdle was jumped when Uncle Ned, after a characteristic show of reluctance, gave me permission to visit Erzurum, from which Tefik Bey directed operations of the Security Inspectorate throughout the eastern region. The requirements of the topographical survey dictated travel by road; fortunately, my transport park in Istanbul included a heavy Dodge truck which looked as if it could withstand the shocks of a primitive road-and-track system which was all that existed east of Ankara in those days. After a courtesy farewell call on Uncle Ned in the capital, I struck out due east instead of taking the main road which runs through Kayseri to Sivas. My road took me through Boghaz Köy, thus lending the trip a little cultural uplift. It also enabled me to take a look at the unfrequented country between Yozgat and Sivas.

The notebooks which I filled during those journeys would have made nice material for one of Rose Macaulay's "Turkey books." Turkey east of the Euphrates had scarcely moved out of the nineteenth century. The Armenians, it is true, had been obliterated, and many of the Kurds as well. But you could still stand on the foothills of Palandöken and look across Erzurum towards the Camel's Neck and the Georgian Throat, and almost hear the thunder of Paskevich's guns forcing the eastern defiles. All that was about to be swept away. The Americans, with their missile-launching pads and U2s, were poised to move in.

My first call in Erzurum was at Tefik Bey's office. He was a pleasant enough colleague with a more lively interest in his work than either Uncle Ned or Aunt Jane. But our discussions gave me little ground for hope about our prospects of infiltrating agents over the Soviet border into Georgia or Armenia. Like his opposite number in Adrianople, Tefik relied on the occasional tip-and-run agent, the occasional refugee, and professional smugglers. He spoke gloomily of the thoroughness with which the Russians had protected their frontier, of the numerous watch-towers and of the continuous ploughed strip on which illicit frontier-crossers must leave tracks.

His own intelligence maps showed the poverty of his resources. A few Soviet units in the immediate vicinity of the frontier had been identified, most of them tentatively. Penetration in depth had not even been attempted, let alone achieved. The *tabula* was depressingly *rasa*.

The talks with Tefik yielded one strong negative conclusion. To achieve penetration in depth, by which I meant the establishment of resident agents in Erivan, Tiflis,* and the eastern ports of the Black Sea, it was useless to look for agent-material locally. The population on the Turkish side of the border was just too backward to serve our purposes. Besides, Tefik had combed the area for years, and it was silly to think that I could find material of promise where he had failed. We would clearly have to concentrate on, say, Georgian and Armenian emigré communities to find agents of sufficient ability to be trained in our requirements. My first recommendation to headquarters was that our stations in Paris, Beirut, Washington, and other centres where refugees tended to congregate be instructed to institute a search.

Another hint of Tefik's gave me an idea in a different direction. He spoke of the magnificent views of Erivan to be obtained from the Turkish frontier. It occurred to me that if the armed services in London were so interested in a topographical survey of Turkey, they might also take kindly to a long-range photographic reconnaissance of the Soviet frontier area. Before I left Erzurum, I had begun to rough out a memorandum outlining the general idea of an operation on such lines. I called it Operation Spyglass. There was little doubt in my mind that it would be approved, if only because it would give our technical people a chance of trying out some of their latest equipment in the camera line.

I returned to Istanbul reasonably well content with the results of my trip. Very little had been achieved towards penetrating the Soviet Union, but at least I had some ideas on the subject to keep headquarters quiet for a time. The real gain was Spyglass. I strongly

*Erivan, now called Yerevan, the capital of Armenia; Tiflis, now called Tbilisi, the capital of Georgia.

doubted whether it would contribute much to the benefit of the armed service. But it would give me a cast-iron pretext for a long, hard look at the Turkish frontier region.

The reception of my proposals at headquarters was wholly favourable. I had learnt long before, while working for *The Times,* some of the tricks of dressing implausible thoughts in language that appealed to the more sober elements in the Athenaeum. An emissary was sent from London to Paris to discuss the problem with Jordania, sometime head of the independent Republic of Georgia that came into fleeting existence in the confusion following the great October Revolution. Jordania was the most widely acknowledged leader of the Georgian emigration, and it would have been very difficult for us to recruit Georgian volunteers without his blessing. Our request, of course, put him in a very awkward position. He had claimed so often that his people, with a few minor exceptions like Stalin and Ordzhonikidze, were wholeheartedly anti-Soviet that he could scarcely express doubts on the nature of the welcome they would receive in their native country. It was no business of ours to discourage him, and we gratefully accepted his promise to furnish suitable men. But our emissary obviously had his misgivings. In a telegram which he sent me describing the results of his mission, he dismissed the Elder Statesman succinctly as a "silly old goat."

We were indeed to have our troubles with Jordania. By now, I had a reasonably clear vision of our future proceedings. We would start with a few tip-and-run raids, lasting a few days or perhaps weeks. Their object would be to explore the possibilities of conspiratorial existence in Georgia. Could safe houses be found? Was it possible to obtain a legal identity by purchase or otherwise? Could reliable courier lines be established? If these preliminary sallies went well, a start could be made with setting up, by gradual stages, a resident network, its shape and style to be dictated by the results of the early reconnaissances. What Jordania had in mind it was not easy to discover. We suspected that he wanted to burden his men from the beginning with bundles of stirring leaflets at which the Foreign Office might have looked very askance indeed. So it became a sort of Chinese tea party. We had to be polite to Jordania because he was in a position to deny us recruits. On the other hand, without our help he would not get any of his people into Georgia at all. Our emissary soon came to know the London-Paris air schedules by heart, and to confess to a dawning dislike of the very sight of Paris. Thus, with deep mutual suspicion, the venture was launched.

My Spyglass proposals were described as "extraordinarily interesting." This was very gratifying. It meant that I should spend most of the following summer, when the diplomatic corps came down to Istanbul from Ankara, at the opposite end of Turkey. Sir David Kelly, the Ambassador, now deceased, was a shy man with an acute and sensitive mind.

It also meant that I could ask for almost any amount of equipment with a reasonable assurance of getting it. The main item was, of course, the camera. Having no technical knowledge of photography, I could not specify the make; I simply described what I wanted it to do and left the rest to headquarters. In addition, I put in for two jeeps, lightweight tents, miscellaneous camping equipment, compasses and whatnot. Our technical people, always inclined to think that their ingenuity was insufficiently exploited, went to work with a will, and even sent a lot of stuff which I had not asked for, "to be tried out." Throughout the winter an imposing number of packing-cases were hacked apart in our store-room. The show-piece was the camera. I had imagined some small and highly sophisticated instrument which might, with luck, be invisible from the Soviet watch-towers at a distance of a hundred yards or so. When I first clapped eyes on it, it looked as big as a tram. My reaction was a quick decision that I was not personally going to hump such a monster over the blazing foothills of Ararat and Aladag. My tough young junior was clearly the very man to come with me and do the heavy work.

Meanwhile, during the winter and spring, I was cast back on the meagre resources of intelligence available in Istanbul itself. Following standard procedure, I began by sounding members of the resident British community. It was rough going. There are, of course, British residents abroad, businessmen, journalists and so on, who are prepared to stick their necks out. There was a Swinburne and a Wynne. But these are usually the lesser fry and their potentialities are limited. The big men, with their big potentialities, are usually unhelpful. They have too much to lose; they have duties to themselves, to their families; they even have duties to their damned shareholders. They would usually agree to pass on anything that "came their way"—invariably valueless gossip. But patriotism was not enough to induce them to take the risks involved in the systematic search for intelligence; and I could not offer them anything like the inducements they received from, say, the oil companies or civil-engineering firms. My patience would be tried by requests from headquarters for information about Turkish harbours which had actually been built by British concerns.

Our lack of success in Istanbul threw into higher relief the importance of our plans for Georgia. Here at least there was some progress to record. Jordania, rather to my surprise, made good his promise of furnishing men, and I was informed in due course that two recruits were undergoing training in London. My task was to clear matters with the Turks and, after several discussions with Uncle Ned, arrangements were made for the reception of the agents in Istanbul and their onward journey to Erzurum. But on one crucial point Uncle Ned proved immoveable. Tefik Bey would take control of the operation in Erzurum and himself make all arrangements for infiltrating them over the frontier. Uncle Ned insisted that I should not accompany them on the grounds that my own safety might be endangered. As he had given me permission to travel the whole frontier area in connection with Spyglass, the pretext was absurd. His obvious purpose was to get the agents to himself for the last forty-eight hours in pursuance of some scheme of his own. Thus, the luckless Georgians would cross the frontier with one assignment from Jordania, another from ourselves and yet another from the Turks. Everyone was conspiring to weight the scales heavily against them. I gave way with very bad grace just as I thought that Uncle Ned was getting ready to threaten cancellation of the whole business.

In due course, we foregathered in Erzurum: Tefik Bey, myself and the two Georgians. The latter were alert and intelligent enough, but their backgrounds inspired little confidence. They were both in their twenties and had been born in Paris. They knew Georgia only by hearsay, and shared the myths of other emigrés about conditions in their country. One of them was notably subdued. Tefik Bey explained with maps that he proposed to infiltrate them in the neighbourhood of Pozof, a Turkish village facing the Soviet garrison town of Akhaltsikhe. We discussed the time of crossing with reference to the moon. We examined the arms and equipment with which the Georgians had been furnished in London. I wondered who would first lay hands on the little bags of sovereigns and napoleons—the Russians or the Turks. When I got Tefik alone, I questioned the wisdom of putting them over the frontier directly opposite a garrison town, but he countered with the observation that the terrain in that sector was ideal. Just because it was ideal, I asked, would it not be more heavily patrolled? He shrugged his shoulders. I was in a very weak position to argue as I had no personal knowledge of the frontier in that sector. For all I knew, Tefik might be right. Anyway, it was essential that I should be soon doing everything possible to ensure the success of the operation.

So the two Georgians went off under the escort of a Turkish officer to Ardahan and points north. All I could do was bite my nails in Erzurum. One of Tefik's men was put to following me at a respectful distance of some fifty yards, so I amused myself by walking briskly about the countryside during the hottest part of the day, watching him take off his hat, then his tie and finally his coat. I happened to be with Tefik when the expected telegram came from Ardahan. The two agents had been put across at such-and-such a time. So many minutes later, there had been a burst of fire, and one of the men had fallen—the other was last seen striding through a sparse wood away from the Turkish frontier. He was never heard of again.

By contrast, the Spyglass venture was wholly enjoyable. Under the escort of Major Fevzi, one of Tefik's officers, we started at the extreme eastern end of the line, where the frontiers of the Soviet Union, Turkey and Iran meet, and worked our way gradually westward. Our technique was simple. We pinpointed our position on the map every few miles and swung the camera in a wide arc across Soviet territory. For the first day or two, I was expecting a burst of machine-gun fire at any moment. The Soviet frontier guards might have been excused for mistaking our instrument for a light mortar. As far as Tuzluca we followed the course of the Aras, with its teeming population of marshbirds, with Ararat on our left and Algöz on our right. Then we worked up the valley of the Arpa Cay, past the ancient Armenian capital of Ani, as far as Digor, opposite Leninakan. At this point, I decided that I had already taken too long a busman's holiday, and that the western half of the frontier should wait until the following year. We drove back to Erzurum with a night-stop at Kars, where Fevzi startled me by suggesting a visit to a brothel.

X. The Lion's Den

I never did the second half of Spyglass. In the summer of 1949, I received a telegram from headquarters which diverted my attention to quite different matters. The telegram offered me the SIS representation in the United States, where I would be working in liaison with both CIA and FBI. The intention was to upgrade the job for a significant reason. The collaboration between CIA and SIS at headquarters level (though not in the field) had become so close that any officer earmarked for high position in SIS would need intimate knowledge of the American scene. It took me all of half an hour to decide to accept the offer.

It would be a wrench to leave Istanbul, both because of its beauty and because it would mean leaving a job considerably less than half accomplished. But the lure of the American post was irresistible for two reasons. At one stroke, it would take me right back into the middle of intelligence policy-making and it would give me a close-up view of the American intelligence organizations. These, I was beginning to suspect, were already of greater importance from my point of view than their British opposite numbers. I did not even think it worth waiting for confirmation from my Soviet colleagues.

The event justified my action. No doubt was expressed anywhere of the unlimited potentialities of my new assignment. It was arranged that I should leave for London at the end of September and, after a month's briefing at headquarters, sail for America at the end of October.

In London I found that Jack Easton had the general supervision of relations between SIS and the American services, and it was from him that I received most of my instructions. I appreciated, not without misgivings, his command of the elusive patterns of Anglo-American co-operation. But the range of collaboration was so wide that there was scarcely a senior officer in the whole organization who had not got some axe to grind with me. I was lunched at many clubs on business pretexts. The discussions over the coffee and port covered many subjects, but all my hosts had one thing in common— the desire for a free trip to America. I did not discourage them. The more visitors I had in Washington, the more spies I got my finger into. That, after all, was my aim in life.

Apart from these diverting interludes, my briefing caused me serious preoccupation in more than one respect. It became clear from Easton's succinct expositions of the situation that my path in Washington was likely to be thorny. I was to take over from Peter Dwyer, who had spent several years in the United States. I knew him for a brilliant wit, and was to learn that he had a great deal more to him than just wit. During the war, he had succeeded in the prickly task of establishing close personal relations with many leading figures in the FBI. These relations, maintained after the war, had given the SIS representation in Washington a bias towards the FBI at the expense (so some thought) of CIA. As the FBI, taking its cue from the prima donna Hoover, was childishly sensitive on the subject of CIA, it was extremely difficult for Dwyer to keep a balance without exposing himself to snarling charges of double-crossing his old friends.

One of my new jobs was to tilt the balance in the opposite direction. CIA and SIS had agreed to close collaboration over a wide range of issues which inevitably meant more day-to-day contact than SIS would have with the FBI. Nothing about this change of policy could be acknowledged, of course. My assignment was therefore to tighten links with CIA and loosen those with the FBI without the FBI noticing. It did not take much reflection to convince me that such a task was impossible and absurd. The only sensible course was to get in with CIA on subjects of common interest and take on the chin the unavoidable resentment of Hoover's men. A corollary of this was that it would be dangerous to be too clever since the cards would be stacked too heavily against me. It would be better to play it silly and be ready to apologize freely for the bricks which my position would force me to drop from time to time.

My briefing on the counter-espionage side also aroused grave anxiety in my mind. This was given me by the formidable Maurice Oldfield, and included a communication of the first importance. Joint Anglo-American investigation of Soviet intelligence activity in the United States had yielded a strong suggestion that there had been a leakage from the British Embassy in Washington during the years 1944–5, and another from the atomic energy establishment in Los Alamos. I had no ideas about Los Alamos. But a swift check in the relevant Foreign Office list left me in little doubt about the identity of the source from the British Embassy. My anxiety was tempered by relief, since I had been nagged for some months by a question put to me by my Soviet contact in Istanbul. He had asked me if I had any means of discovering what the British were doing in a case under investigation by the FBI—a case involving the British Embassy in Washington. At the time of asking, there was nothing that I could have done. But it seemed, after my talk with Oldfield, that I had stumbled into the heart of the problem. Within a few days, this was confirmed by my Russian friend in London. After checking with headquarters, he was left in no doubt that information from the FBI and my own referred to one and the same case.

A careful study of the files did something to allay my immediate fears. As SIS was not supposed to operate inside the United States, investigation of the leads provided by the source was in the hands of the FBI. Characteristically, they had put in an immense amount of work resulting in an immense amount of waste paper. It had so far occurred neither to them nor to the British that a diplomat was involved, let alone a fairly senior diplomat. Instead, the investigation had concentrated on non-diplomatic employees of the Embassy, and particularly on those locally recruited, the sweepers, cleaners, bottle-washers and the rest. A charlady with a Latvian grandmother, for instance, would rate a fifteen-page report, crowded with insignificant details of herself, her family and friends, her private life, and holiday habits. It was testimony to the enormous resources of the FBI, and to the pitiful extent to which those resources were squandered. It was enough to convince me that urgent action would not be necessary, but that the case would require careful watching. Something drastic would certainly have to be done before I left Washington. Heaven knew where my next appointment would lie; I might well lose all control of the case.

My last call in London was at the Chief's office. He was in the best of form, and amused me with malicious accounts of the stickier passages in Anglo-American intelligence relations during the war. This turned out to be more than just pointless reminiscence. He told me that the news of my appointment to the United States appeared to have upset Hoover. I was then rated a fairly senior officer in the service, which Dwyer (most undeservedly) was not. Hoover suspected that my appointment might herald unwanted SIS activity in the United States. To allay his fear, the Chief had sent him a personal telegram, assuring him that there was no intention of a change of policy; my duties would be purely liaison duties. The Chief showed me the telegram, then gave me a hard stare. "That," he said, "is an official communication from myself to Hoover." There was a pause, then he continued: "Unofficially . . . let's discuss it over lunch at White's."

With my briefing as complete as could reasonably be expected, I sailed on the SS *Caronia* towards the end of September. I had a memorable send-off. The first thing I saw on the foggy platform at Waterloo was an enormous pair of moustaches and behind them the head of Osbert Lancaster, an apparition which assured me of good company on the voyage. Before we sailed, I was called to the ship's telephone. Jack Easton was on the line to tell me Dwyer had just telegraphed his resignation. It was not clear why, but I had been warned. Finally, a case of champagne was delivered to my cabin with the card of a disgustingly rich friend. I began to feel that I would enjoy my first Transatlantic crossing.

I made my first slip almost immediately after entering American territorial waters. An FBI representative had come out in the pilot's launch to greet me. I gave him a glass of Tio Pepe which he sipped unhappily while we made polite conversation. I was later to learn that the men of the FBI, with hardly an exception, were proud of their insularity, of having sprung from the grass-roots. One of the first senior G-men I met in Washington claimed to have had a grandpappy who kept a general store at Horse Creek, Missouri. They were therefore whisky-drinkers, with beer for light refreshment. By contrast, CIA men flaunted cosmopolitan postures. They would discuss absinthe and serve Burgundy above room temperature. This is not just flippancy. It points to a deep social cleavage between the two organizations, which accounts for at least some of the asperity marking their exchanges.

My FBI friends saw me through the landing formalties and bedded me down in a hotel with a view of Central Park. Next day at Pennsylvania Station, I boarded the train for Washington. The sumach was still in flower and gave me a foretaste of the famous fall, one of the few glories of America which Americans have never exaggerated because exaggeration is impossible. Peter Dwyer met me and explained, over our first bourbon, that his resignation had nothing to do with my appointment to succeed him. For personal reasons, he had long wanted to settle in Canada, where a congenial government post was awaiting him. The news of my posting to Washington had simply determined the timing of his northward move to Ottawa. So we started on a pleasant footing. Nothing could exceed the care and astuteness with which he inducted me into Washington politics.

It is not easy to make a coherent picture of my tour of duty in the United States. Indeed, such a picture would give a wrong impression of the type of work I was engaged in. It was too varied, and often too amorphous, to be reduced to simple terms. Liaison with the FBI alone, if it had been conducted thoroughly, would have been a full-time job. It was the era of McCarthy in full evil blast. It was also the era of Hiss, Coplon, Fuchs, Gold, Greenglass and the brave Rosenbergs—not to mention others who are still nameless. Liaison with CIA covered an even wider field, ranging from a serious attempt to subvert an East European regime to such questions as the proper exploitation of German documents relating to General Vlasov. In every question that arose, the first question was to please one party without offending the other. In addition, I had to work in with the Royal Canadian Mounted Police, and with individuals in the Department of External Affairs who were dickering with the idea of setting up an independent Canadian secret service.

Where to begin? As the end of my story chiefly concerns the FBI, I should perhaps concede to CIA the beginning. The head of the organization when I arrived was Admiral Hillenkoetter,* an amiable sailor who was soon to give way to General Bedell Smith,† without leaving much of a mark on American intelligence history. The two divisions with which I had most to do were the Office of Strategic Operations (OSO) and the Office of Policy Co-ordination (OPC). In plain English, OSO was the intelligence-gathering division and OPC was charged with subversion. There was also a little work with the planning division, associated with the name of Dick Helms,‡ who recently succeeded Admiral Raborn as head of the whole organization and promptly fell foul of the Senate.

The driving force of OSO at the time was Jim Angleton, who had formerly served in London and had earned my respect by

---

*CIA emerged from the disbanded OSS and Central Intelligence group in 1947. Hillenkoetter was head of CIA from 1947 to 1950 at the time when Philby was in Washington.

†Early in 1951 he presented Foreign Secretary Herbert Morrison with information about Maclean.

‡Richard Helms, director of the CIA from 1966 to 1973.

openly rejecting the Anglomania that disfigured the young face of OSO. We formed the habit of lunching once a week at Harvey's where he demonstrated regularly that overwork was not his only vice. He was one of the thinnest men I have ever met, and one of the biggest eaters. Lucky Jim! After a year of keeping up with Angleton, I took the advice of an elderly lady friend and went on a diet, dropping from thirteen stone to about eleven in three months.

Our close association was, I am sure, inspired by genuine friendliness on both sides. But we both had ulterior motives. Angleton wanted to place the burden of exchanges between CIA and SIS on the CIA office in London—which was about ten times as big as mine. By doing so, he could exert the maximum pressure on SIS's headquarters while minimizing SIS intrusions into his own. As an exercise in nationalism, that was fair enough. By cultivating me to the full, he could better keep me under wraps. For my part, I was more than content to string him along. The greater the trust between us overtly, the less he would suspect covert action. Who gained most from this complex game I cannot say. But I had one big advantage. I knew what he was doing for CIA and he knew what I was doing for SIS. But the real nature of my interest was something he did not know.

Although our discussions ranged over the whole world, they usually ended, if they did not begin, with France and Germany. The Americans had an obsessive fear of Communism in France, and I was astonished by the way in which Angleton devoured reams of French newspaper material daily. That this was not a private phobia of Angleton's became clear at a later date when a British proposal for giving Alexandre Parodi, head of the d'Orsay, limited secret information, was firmly squashed by Bedell Smith in person. He told me flatly that he was not prepared to trust a single French official with such information.

Angleton had fewer fears about Germany. That country concerned him chiefly as a base of operations against the Soviet Union and the Socialist states of Eastern Europe. CIA had lost no time in taking over the anti-Soviet section of the German Abwehr, under von Gehlen,* and many of Harvey's lobsters went to provoke Angleton into defending, with chapter and verse, the past record and current activities of the von Gehlen organization.

We also had many skirmishes over the various Russian emigré organizations, of which more later in this chapter. There was the People's Labour Alliance (NTS), which recently achieved notoriety in the case of poor Gerald Brooke.† There were the Ukrainian Fascists of Stepan Bandera, the darlings of the British. Both CIA and SIS were up to their ears in emigré politics, hoping to use the more promising groups for purposes analogous to those for which we had used Jordania. Although the British put up a stubborn rearguard action in favour of the groups with which they had been long associated, the story was one of general American encroachment in the emigré field. The dollar was just too strong. For instance, although the British had an important stake in the NTS, SIS was compelled by financial reasons to transfer responsibility for its operations to CIA. The transfer was effected by formal agreement between the two organizations, though the case of Brooke, an Englishman, suggests that SIS is not above playing around with the Alliance under the counter. Such an action would be quite in keeping with the ethics of secret service.

We had much else to discuss about Germany, since both SIS and CIA could afford to spread themselves on occupied territory. Secret activity of all kinds, including operations directed against the German authorities themselves, were financed by the Germans, as part of the payment for the expenses of occupation.

Apart from Angleton, I had one other principal contact with the counter-espionage section: he was a former FBI man whom Hoover had sacked for drunkenness on duty. The first time he dined at my

---

*Allen Dulles succeeded in acquiring ex-Nazi General Reinard Gehlen's private secret service in Germany for the purpose of infiltrating the Soviet zone.

†British lecturer imprisoned in Russia for distributing leaflets.

house, he showed that his habits had remained unchanged. He fell asleep over the coffee and sat snoring gently until midnight when his wife took him away, saying: "Come now, Daddy, it's time you were in bed." I may be accused here of introducing a cheap note. Admitted. But, as will be seen later, the same man was to play a very cheap trick on me, and I do not like letting provocation go unpunished. Having admitted the charge of strong prejudice against him, it is only fair that I should add that he co-operated well with SIS in the construction of the famous Berlin Tunnel.

As I have already said, the Office of Policy Co-ordination (OPC) was concerned with subversion on a world-wide basis. Its head was Frank Wisner, a youngish man for so responsible a job, balding and running self-importantly to fat. He favoured an orotund style of conversation which was disconcerting. I accompanied a mission which he led to London to discuss with SIS matters of common interest. When the discussions touched on issues of international concern, the Foreign Office sent representatives to watch the proceedings. At one such meeting, attended on behalf of the Foreign Office by Tony Rumbold, Wisner expatiated on one of his favourite themes: the need for camouflaging the source of secret funds supplied to apparently respectable bodies in which we were interested. "It is essential," said Wisner in his usual informal style, "to secure the overt co-operation of people with conspicuous access to wealth in their own right." Rumbold started scribbling. I looked over his shoulder and saw what he had written: "people with conspicuous access to wealth in their own right = rich people."

My relations with OPC were more active than those with OSO, which were confined mostly to finding out what they were up to. Shortly before my arrival in Washington, the American and British governments had sanctioned in principle a clandestine operation to detach an East European country from the Socialist bloc. The choice fell on Albania for several reasons. It was the smallest and weakest of the Socialist states. It was bounded on the south by Greece, with which Britain and the United States were allied and which was still technically at war with Albania. Its northern and eastern frontiers matched with Yugoslavia. Our experts considered—quite wrongly, in my opinion—that Marshal Tito, after his break with the Socialist bloc, would adopt a hands-off policy towards any changes in Tiranë. Albania, therefore, looked conveniently isolated and, moreover, it was within easy reach by sea and air from Malta. Owing to the many political implications of such a project, the State Department and Foreign Office insisted on maintaining close supervision of the operation. Subject to that supervision, the execution was the responsibility of SIS and OPC.

Both the British and the Americans were in touch with Albanian emigré groups; both sides undertook to rally their contacts in support of the counter-revolution. The British were to provide Malta as a forward base of operations, and the small boats required for the infiltration of seaborne agents. The Americans supplied most of the finance and logistical support and the use of Wheelus Field, in Libya, as a rear base and supply depot. King Idris was not let into the secret; he was then only the Amir. In the prolonged Anglo-American wrangling that followed, Malta was our trump card. "Whenever we want to subvert any place," Wisner confided in me, "we find that the British own an island within easy reach."

The wrangling concerned the political leadership of the counter-revolution. We were in the pre-Dulles era. The United States had not yet come out in open support of extreme reaction everywhere. The State Department was anxious to give the counter-revolution a democratic aspect. To this end, they stole a march on us by railroading a handful of Albanian refugees in New York into forming a National Committee and electing as its head a certain Hassan Dosti. Dosti was a young lawyer who, according to OPC, had an impeccable record as a democrat, though I failed to see what evidence there could possibly be for such an assertion. Despite repeated requests, I never came face to face with Dosti. OPC, I was told, had to handle him very carefully because he scared easily. Fine leadership material!

If the National Committee in New York filled me with misgiving, I was just as depressed by the British nominee for the leadership. He was a petty tribal chieftain named Abbas Kupi,* an old friend of Julian Amery.† From his photographs, I knew him to be whiskered and habitually armed to the teeth—made to measure for the exercise of British paternalism. I had no doubt that he could equal the feats of his ancestors in raiding unarmed caravans or sniping at heat-stricken Turkish infantrymen plodding hopelessly through the gorges. But I never shared the bemusement of the British gentleman at the sight of a tribesman. I am sure that tribal courage is legendary only in the sense that it is legend, and that the wild mountaineer is as brave as a lion only in the sense that the lion (very sensibly) avoids combat unless assured of weak opposition and a fat meal at the end of it. In short, if Dosti was a young weakling, Abbas Kupi was an old rascal. The interminable Anglo-American argument on their rival merits was intelligible only if one ignored the merits of the case and regarded it as a contest to decide whether the British or the Americans would dominate the counter-revolutionary government—if it was ever formed. When the British and Americans finally tired of the argument and looked around for a compromise, it was found that Dosti and Abbas Kupi had been so hardened in their attitudes by their respective sponsors that neither could be induced to serve under anyone else.

The day-to-day control of the operation was in the hands of a Special Policy Committee (SPC) which met in Washington. It consisted of four members, representing the State Department, the Foreign Office, OPC and SIS. The State Department appointed Bob Joyce, a convivial soul with experience of Balkan affairs; Earl Jellicoe, of the British Embassy, another convivial soul, represented the Foreign Office; Frank Lindsay, of OPC, was yet a third convivial soul; finally, there was myself. It is clear, from such a mem-

*Leader of anti-Communist legalists in Albania (supporters of King Zog). Escaped from clutches of the Communist regime. Became one of the leaders of the Albanian Freedom Movement financed by CIA and SIS—their HQ was in Greece and Italy. (While in Washington Philby made several flying visits to Greece and Italy.)

†Captain. Later Cabinet Minister. Fought alongside Albanian partisans after the German occupation of 1943.

bership, that our meetings were less than formal. Lindsay set the tone by remarking, at our first meeting, that the first Albanian he ever saw was hanging upside down from parallel bars. Even in our more serious moments, we Anglo-Saxons never forgot that our agents were just down from the trees. Although I have said that the SPC was in control of the operation, we could never act as free agents. Headquarters never allowed me to forget SIS's commitment to Abbas Kupi, and, behind headquarters, there loomed the Bevin formula for veto: "I won't 'ave it." Doubtless, Frank Lindsay was similarly inhibited.

In such circumstances, it is perhaps surprising that the operation ever got off the ground. We did finally succeed in landing a small party on the Albanian coast with instructions to work their way inland, spy out the land, and then move southwards into Greece. It was hoped that the information they gathered on the way would help us in launching more ambitious schemes at a later date. The operation, of course, was futile from the beginning. Our infiltrators could achieve something only by penetrating the towns, which were firmly under Communist control. For bare survival, they had to hide in the mountains, where their presence would have been useful only if the country was seething with revolt. That, perhaps, was the unspoken assumption behind the whole venture, just as it was assumed more recently (when people should have known better) that a landing in the Bay of Pigs would set Cuba on fire. In the end, a few members of the party did succeed in straggling through to Greece, where they were extricated, with immense difficulty, from the clutches of the Greek security authorities who would have shot them for tuppence. The information they brought was almost wholly negative. It was clear, at least, that they had nowhere found arms open to welcome them.

In due course, the operation was quietly dropped without having made any noticeable dent on the regime in Tiranë. It was just as well for the British and American governments that their squib proved so damp. In the event of success, they would have had endless trouble with their new protégé, not to mention serious difficulties with Greece and Yugoslavia and possibly Italy as well. Within a few years, Enver Hoxha* had done the job much more effectively, and the headache is felt in Peking. The moral seems to be that it is better to cut one's losses than give hostages to fortune. The same moral could be applied today to South-East Asia.

Political cross-purposes also bedevilled Anglo-American plans of greater potential importance than the Albanian venture; for instance, projects for the penetration and subversion of the Soviet Union itself. Both SIS and CIA had their Baltic puppets, whose rival ambitions were usually quite irreconcilable. It was with some relish that I watched the struggling factions repeatedly fight themselves to a standstill. On one occasion, the position got so dangerous that Harry Carr, the North European expert in Broadway, was sent to Washington in a desperate bid to stop the rot. His visit ended disastrously, with both Carr and his opposite numbers in CIA accusing each other, quite justifiably, of wholesale lying at the conference table. Disagreements over the Ukraine were even longer drawn out and just as stultifying.

From the years before the war, SIS had maintained contact with Stepan Bandera, a Ukrainian Nationalist of marked Fascist views, and the collaboration had developed since the war. The trouble was that, although Bandera was quite a noise in the emigré community, his claims to a substantial following inside the Soviet Union were never seriously tested, except in the negative sense that nothing much ever came of them. A first party, equipped by the British with W/T† and other clandestine means of communication, was sent into the Ukraine in 1949, and disappeared. Two more parties were

*Moscow-trained Albanian partisan leader. After the Second World War the Albanian partisans liberated themselves from German rule without the help of Russia. Then Hoxha seized power, using British and American arms to defeat his nationalist compatriots. On 10 November 1945 Britain and America recognized his provisional government on the understanding that he would hold free elections. Hoxha set up a People's Socialist Republic and deposed King Zog: the result was a Communist-dominated national assembly. In 1946 Hoxha accused Britain and America of imperialist aggression after British destroyers appeared off Albania. Later Philby was suspected of having passed information to Hoxha about the arrival of the invasion force, because every expedition was met and defeated without any difficulty.

†Wireless telegraph.

sent the following year, and remained equally silent. Meanwhile, the Americans were beginning to nurse serious doubts about Bandera's usefulness to the West, which the failure of the British-sponsored parties to surface did nothing to allay.

The American attack on the alliance between Bandera and SIS gathered strength in 1950, and much of my time in the United States was spent in transmitting acrimonious exchanges between Washington and London on the rival merits of obscure emigré factions. CIA proffered three serious objections to Bandera as an ally. His extreme nationalism, with its Fascist overtones, was a handicap which would prejudice Western dealings with other groups inside the Soviet Union, for example, the Great Russians. He was alleged to have his roots in the old emigration and to lack all contact with the new, "more realistic" emigration which the Americans were busy cultivating. Finally, he was accused flatly of being anti-American. The British plea that Bandera was being used solely for the purpose of gathering intelligence, and that such a use could have no political significance, was brushed aside by the Americans, who argued that, whatever the nature of the connection, its very existence must inflate Bandera's prestige in the Ukraine. They professed fears that any reinforcement of Bandera's following must risk splitting the "resistance movement" in the Ukraine, with which they were themselves working.

The weakness of the American case was that it rested on bald statement, and very little else. The results produced by the "more realistic" emigration, and by the "resistance movement" in the Ukraine, were scarcely less meagre than the results of the British-Bandera connection. It is true that CIA claimed to have received some couriers from the Ukraine in the winter of 1949–50, but the wretched quality of their information suggested rather that they were tramps who had wandered into the wrong country. In 1951, after several years of hard work, CIA were still hoping to send in a political representative, with three assistants, to establish contact with the "resistance movement." They had also scratched together a reserve team of four men, to be sent in if the first party vanished without trace.

In order to resolve Anglo-American differences on the Ukrainian issue, CIA pressed for a full-scale conference with SIS, which was duly held in London in April 1951. Rather to my surprise, the British stood firm and flatly refused to jettison Bandera. The best that could be agreed, with unconcealed ill-temper on the American side, was that the situation would be re-examined at the end of the 1951 parachute-dropping season, by which time, it was hoped, more facts would be available. Within a month, the British had dropped three six-man parties, the aircraft taking off from Cyprus. One party was dropped midway between Lwów and Tarnopol; another near the headwaters of the Prut, not far from Kolomyya; and a third just inside the borders of Poland, near the source of the San. In order to avoid the dangers of overlapping and duplication, the British and Americans exchanged precise information about the timing and geographical co-ordinates of their operations. I do not know what happened to the parties concerned. But I can make an informed guess.

Some eight years later, I read of the mysterious murder of Bandera in Munich, in the American zone of Germany. It may be that, despite the brave stand of the British in his defence, CIA had the last word.

XI. The Cloudburst

The FBI was in sorry shape when I reached Washington. It had caught a Tartar in the small person of Judith Coplon, a brilliant young woman employed in the Department of Justice, against whom they were trying to bring home espionage charges. When the evidence against her, obtained largely by illegal telephone-tapping, had hardened sufficiently to justify her arrest, Hoover sanctioned the necessary action and Coplon was pulled in. She was caught in the act of passing documents to a contact, and the case against her seemed open and shut. But in their haste the FBI had neglected to take out a warrant for her arrest, which was therefore in itself illegal. The FBI could only effect arrests without warrant if there was a reasonable presumption that the suspect was contemplating imminent flight. As Coplon was picked up in a New York street, walking away from a station from which she had just emerged, the purpose of imminent flight could not have been imputed to her by any conceivable stretch of imagination.

The illegality of the arrest was duly lambasted in court, but worse was to follow. Coplon, though caught red-handed, was resolved to fight to the end. She dismissed her first counsel on the grounds that he was too conciliatory to the prosecution; he was probably aiming, not at acquittal, which seemed a hopeless prospect, but at a mitigation of sentence. Coplon would have none of it. With a second counsel to assist her, she went over to the counterattack and began harrying the FBI witnesses. She tied them in such knots that they admitted to tapping not only her telephone, but telephones in the headquarters of the United Nations. The court proceedings began to damage the public image of the FBI so severely that Hoover incontinently dropped the charges. It was characteristic of him that he reacted to the fiasco by finding a scapegoat. Harvey Flemming, the principal FBI witness at the trial, was fired. But Coplon went free. It was the triumph of a brave woman. Whenever her name was mentioned thereafter in the Department of Justice, an abusive adjective was attached.

The failure of the FBI in the Coplon case was by no means unique, or even unusual. I cannot speak of the record of the FBI in checking crime in the United States. With that side of its activities I had nothing to do. But I had a great deal to do with its counterespionage work, and its record in the field was more conspicuous for failure than for success. Hoover did not catch Maclean or Burgess; he did not catch Fuchs, and he would not have caught the rest if the British had not caught Fuchs and worked brilliantly on his tangled emotions; he did not catch Lonsdale; he did not catch Abel for years, and then only because Hayhanen delivered him up on a platter; he did not even catch me. If ever there was a bubble reputation, it is Hoover's.

But Hoover is a great politician. His blanket methods and ruthless authoritarianism are the wrong weapons for the subtle world of intelligence. But they have other uses. They enable Hoover to collect and file away a vast amount of information about the personal lives of millions of his fellow-countrymen. This has long been common knowledge, and it has brought Hoover rich dividends from the purse of the American taxpayer. There are few people in the world without skeletons in their cupboards which they would prefer to remain decently forgotten. The covert record shows that a distressing number of American congressmen have pasts that do not bear minute scrutiny. And what about the covert record held by Hoover? The mere existence of the huge FBI filing system has deterred many from attacking Hoover's totalitarian empire.

I am speaking of the McCarthy period. It might have been thought that Hoover would have resented the infringement of his monopoly by a Senator who claimed to have effected, single-handed, deep penetration of the Communist conspiracy in the State Department and other branches of the United States Government. Not so. Hoover knew that by merely opening his mouth he could have blasted McCarthy's pretensions for ever. But why should he have done so? By raising a nationwide spy-fever, McCarthy was creating conditions in which no congressman would dare to oppose increased appropriation for the FBI. What Hoover really thought of McCarthy became evident at my first meeting with him when I put the question point-blank. "Well," said Hoover in reply, "I often meet Joe at the racetrack, but he has never given me a winner yet."

My first house in Washington was off Connecticut Avenue, almost directly opposite that of Johnny Boyd, the Assistant Director of the FBI in charge of security. It seemed a good idea to camp at the mouth of the lion's den for a short spell—but only for a short spell. The house was a small one, and I was soon arguing the need for moving to larger quarters at a safer distance, eventually settling on a place about half a mile up Nebraska Avenue. Boyd was my principal contact with the FBI, and I saw him several times a week, either in his office or at home. He was one of Hoover's original gunmen in Chicago—"the guy who always went in first" when there was shooting to be done—and he looked the part. He was short and immensely stocky, and must have been hard as nails before he developed a paunch, jowls and the complexion that suggests a stroke in the offing. He had no intellectual interests whatsoever. His favourite amusement was to play filthy records to women visiting his house for the first time. He had other childish streaks, including the tough, direct ruthlessness of a child. By any objective standard, he was a dreadful man, but I could not help growing very fond of him.

Boyd lost no time in letting me know that he disapproved of my close contact with CIA. He seemed genuinely disgusted with its cosmopolitan airs. "What do they teach them in CIA, son?" he said to me one evening. "Why, how to use knives and forks, how to marry rich wives." He also had a deep suspicion of the social graces of the United States Navy. But, as I had thought in London, I got on with him provided that I did not try to be clever and endured his heavy taunts about my CIA friends. The first time I felt the rough edge of his tongue was (very fortunately) just before Peter Dwyer left for Ottawa. It so happened that the MI5 representative in Washington, Geoffrey Paterson, and we, received parallel instructions from London to take up a certain matter with the FBI. Paterson got in first and received a brush-off; he was told it was none of London's business. When Dwyer and I arrived soon afterwards to raise the same question, Boyd gave us a wicked look. "So that's the game," he said, laying down his cigar and purpling. "Geoffrey comes in and I give him a flea in the ear. Then what happens? Then you two come along and try it on . . ." There followed a ten minutes' tongue-lashing against which all protests were useless. His fury was quite sincere, although out of all proportion to the nature of the issue which we had been told to discuss with him. What enraged him was a simple matter of office politics. It was his job to play MI5 and SIS off against one another so as to exploit any differences between us. And here we were, clearly ganging up against him. Yet that same evening he telephoned to ask me over to drink bourbon deep into the night. Not a word was said about the unpleasantness of the morning.

A sluggish trickle of information about the Embassy leakage continued to reach us. Apart from Dwyer, who was soon to leave, three members of the British Embassy staff had access to the material: Paterson, myself and Bobby Mackenzie,* the Embassy Security Officer, who was an old colleague of mine from Section V days. In the FBI, the officials concerned were Ladd, Lishman, who was

*Sir Robert Mackenzie.

then head of the anti-Communist section, and Bob Lamphere, a nice puddingy native of Ohio who was responsible for the detailed analysis of the case on the American side. We were still far from identifying the source in the British Embassy, but during the winter of 1949–50 the net began to close around the Los Alamos source. The choice seemed to lie between two scientists of great distinction: Dr. Peierls and Dr. Fuchs.* It was Dwyer's last direct service to SIS that, by a brilliant piece of analysis of the known movements of the two men, he conclusively eliminated Peierls. Thereafter, the finger pointed unwaveringly at Fuchs.

The usual trouble arose over the nature of the evidence, which was not valid in law, but Fuchs, unlike Judith Coplon, provided the evidence against himself. Shortly after Dwyer had identified him as the Los Alamos source, he set sail for England on a routine visit. He was arrested on arrival and passed to William Skardon of MI5, for interrogation. Skardon succeeded in winning his confidence to such an extent that Fuchs not only confessed his own part in the business, but also identified from photographs his contact in the United States, Harry Gold. From Gold, who was also in a talkative mood, the chain led inexorably to the Rosenbergs who were duly electrocuted. It is worth mentioning that Eisenhower explained his refusal to reprieve Ethel Rosenberg on the grounds that, if he did, the Russians in future would use only women as spies. It was an attitude worthy of the most pedestrian of United States' presidents.

There was another remarkable casualty of the Fuchs case. Hoover, who had contributed nothing to his capture, was determined to extract maximum political capital from the affair for himself. To that end, he needed to show that he had material of his own, and such material could only be obtained through the interrogation of the prisoner by one of his own men. He announced his intention of sending Lishman to London to question Fuchs in his cell. Paterson

*Rudolf Peierls (later Sir Rudolf), Berlin-born physicist who emigrated to England in the 1930s and worked on the Manhattan Project; Klaus Fuchs, atomic scientist who was instrumental, through his confession, in uncovering the espionage ring in which he was involved with Harry Gold, David Greenglass, and Julius (and allegedly Ethel) Rosenberg.

and I both received instructions to tell him that such a course was quite out of the question. Fuchs was in custody awaiting trial, and it was just impossible to arrange for his interrogation by anyone, let alone by the agent of a foreign power. I found Hoover in a state of high excitement, and in no mood to be impressed by the majesty of British law. He refused to budge. Lishman was sent to London, with peremptory instructions to see Fuchs, or else. The answer was "or else." When I heard that Lishman was back, I called at his office, a fairly grand, carpeted affair. Someone else was in his chair. Lishman himself I found a few doors farther down the corridor, writing on the corner of a desk in a small room tenanted by four junior agents. The poor devil was bloody and very bowed. He looked at me as if it had been my fault. Such was life under Hoover.

In the summer of 1950, I received a letter from Guy Burgess. "I have a shock for you," he began. "I have just been posted to Washington." He suggested that I should put him up for a few days until he had found a flat for himself. This posed a problem. In normal circumstances, it would have been quite wrong for two secret operatives to occupy the same premises. But the circumstances were not normal. From the earliest days, our careers had intertwined. He had collected money for me at Cambridge after the revolt of the Austrian Schützbund in February 1934. I had put forward his name as a possible recruit for the Soviet service, a debt which he later repaid by smoothing my entry into the British secret service. In between, he had acted as courier for me in Spain. In 1940, we had worked closely together in SIS, and he had paid me a professional visit in Turkey in 1948. Our association was therefore well-known, and it was already certain that any serious investigation of either of us would reveal these past links. It seemed that there could be no real professional objection to him staying with me.

There was another consideration which inclined me towards agreeing with Burgess's suggestion. I knew from the files that his record was quite clean, in the sense that there was nothing recorded against him politically. But he was very apt to get into personal scrapes of a spectacular nature. A colleague in the Foreign Office,

now an Ambassador, had pushed him down the steps of the Gar-
goyle Club, injuring his skull. There had been trouble in Dublin
and in Tangier. It occurred to me that he was much less likely to
make himself conspicuous in my household than in a bachelor flat
where every evening would find him footloose. I had scarcely
replied to signify agreement when Mackenzie showed me a letter
he had received from Carey-Foster, then head of the Foreign Office
security branch, warning him about Burgess's arrival. Carey-Foster
explained that his eccentricities would be more easily overlooked
in a large Embassy than in a small one. He gave a summary of his
past peccadilloes, and said that worse might be in store. "What does
he mean 'worse,'" muttered Mackenzie. "Goats?" I told him I knew
Guy well, that he would be staying with me, and that I would keep
an eye on him. He seemed happy that there was someone else who
was ready to share the responsibility.

In the light of what was to come, my decision to fall in with
Burgess's suggestion looks like a bad mistake. I have indeed given it
much thought in the past fifteen years. It will not do to plead that
the twist events were to take a few months later were utterly unforeseeable; security precautions are designed to give protection
from the unforeseeable. But, on reflection, I think that my decision
to accommodate Burgess speeded by a few weeks at most the fo-
cussing of the spotlight on me. It also lent vigour to the letter which
Bedell Smith sent to the Chief insisting on my removal from the
scene. It may even have been lucky that suspicion fell on me prematurely, in the sense that it crystallized before the evidence was
strong enough to bring me to court.

Burgess's arrival raised an issue that I could not decide by myself. Should he or should he not be let into the secret of the British
Embassy source which was still under investigation? The decision
to initiate him was taken after I had made two lone motor trips to
points outside Washington. I was told that the balance of opinion
was that Guy's special knowledge of the problem might be helpful.
I therefore took Guy fully into our confidence, briefing him in the
greatest detail, and the subject remained under constant discussion

between us. My difficulty was that I had only seen Maclean twice, and briefly, in fourteen years. I had no idea where he lived, how he lived, or indeed anything at all about his circumstances. But it is now time to turn to the case, to explain how it stood, and the problems involved.

The development of the affair was giving me deep anxiety. It was beset by imponderables, the assessment of which could be little better than guesswork. We had received some dozen reports referring to the source, who appeared in the documents under the code-name Homer, but little progress had been made towards identifying him. The FBI was still sending us reams about the Embassy charladies, and the enquiry into our menial personnel was spinning itself out endlessly. To me, this remains the most inexplicable feature of the whole affair. There was already evidence that the Foreign Office had been penetrated. Both Krivitsky and Volkov had said so. There was, of course, nothing to suggest that the three sources referred to the same man. There is still no basis for that supposition. But if the assumption had been made, if in particular the Krivitsky material had been studied in relation to the Washington leak, a search among the diplomats would have started without loss of time—perhaps even before I appeared on the scene.

But another feature of the case was even more puzzling. I must confess to having enjoyed a great advantage in that I was pretty certain from the beginning who was involved. But, even discounting that advantage, it seemed to me quite obvious from the nature of the reports that we were not dealing with the petty agent emptying waste-paper baskets and snatching the odd carbon. Some of the reports dealt with political problems of some complexity, and on more than one occasion Homer was spoken of with respect. There could be no real doubt that we were dealing with a man of stature. The reluctance to initiate enquiries along these lines can only be attributed to a genuine mental block which stubbornly resisted the belief that respected members of the Establishment could do such things. The existence of such a block was amply borne out by the commentaries that followed the disappearance of Maclean and

Burgess—and for that matter my own. Explanations of extraordinary silliness were offered in preference to the obvious truth.

Yet I knew quite well that this bizarre situation could not go on for ever. One day, any day, somebody in London or Washington would look into his shaving mirror and find inspiration there. Once investigation of the diplomats started, it would certainly yield the right answer, sooner or later. The great question was: How soon? How late?

From discussion with my friends at meetings outside Washington, two main points emerged. First, it was essential to rescue Maclean before the net closed on him. That was accepted as an axiom. No question was raised about his future potential to the Soviet Union in the event of his escape. It was quite enough that he was an old Comrade. Some readers, prisoners of prejudice, may find this hard to swallow. I do not ask them to do so. But they cannot blame me if they suffer unpleasant shocks in future cases. Second, it was desirable that Maclean should stay in his post as long as possible. After his departure, it was said blandly that he was "only" head of the American Department of the Foreign Office, and thus had little access to high-grade information. But it is nonsense to suppose that a resolute and experienced operator occupying a senior post in the Foreign Office can have access only to papers that are placed on his desk in the ordinary course of duty. I have already shown that I gained access to the files of British agents in the Soviet Union when I was supposed to be chivvying Germans in Spain. In short, our duty was to get Maclean to safety, but not before it was necessary.

But there were two further complications. I had been sent to the United States for a two-year tour of duty, and I could therefore expect to be replaced in the autumn of 1951. I had no idea what my next posting would be; it could easily have been Cairo or Singapore, far out of touch with the Maclean case. Groping in partial darkness as we were, it seemed safest to get Maclean away by the middle of 1951 at the latest. The second complication arose from Burgess's position. He was emphatically not at home in the Foreign

Office, for which he had neither the right temperament nor the right personality. He had been thinking for some time of getting out, and had one or two irons in the fire in Fleet Street. As a result, his work at the Foreign Office had suffered, so much so that it looked like a close thing between resignation and dismissal. In any case, he was anxious to get back to England.

In somebody's mind—I do not know whose—the two ideas merged: Burgess's return to London and the rescue of Maclean. If Burgess returned to London from the British Embassy in Washington, it seemed natural that he should call on the head of the American Department. He would be well placed to set the ball rolling for the rescue operation. It would have been possible for him to have resigned in Washington, and returned to London without fuss. But it might have looked a bit odd if he had gone back voluntarily shortly before the disappearance of Maclean. Matters had to be so arranged that he was sent back, willy-nilly. It was the sort of project in which Burgess delighted, and he brought it off in the simplest possible way. Three times in one day he was booked for speeding in the state of Virginia, and the Governor reacted just as we had hoped. He sent a furious protest to the State Department against this flagrant abuse of diplomatic privilege, which was then brought to the attention of the Ambassador. Within a few days, Burgess was regretfully informed that he would have to leave.

As soon as the possibility of Burgess helping in the rescue operation emerged from our discussions, great attention was paid to my own position. Despite all precautions, Burgess might be seen with Maclean and enquiry into his activity might lead to doubts about me. There seemed very little that could be done about it, but it occurred to me that I could help to divert suspicion by making a positive contribution to the solution of the British Embassy case. Hitherto, I had lain low, letting the FBI and MI5 do what they could. Now that the rescue plan was taking shape, there was no reason why I should not give the investigation a nudge in the right direction.

To that end, I wrote a memorandum to Head Office, suggesting that we might be wasting our time in exhaustive investigations of the Embassy menials. I recalled the statements of Krivitsky to the best of my ability from memory. He had said that the head of the Soviet intelligence for Western Europe had recruited in the middle thirties a young man who had gone into the Foreign Office. He was of good family, and had been educated at Eton and Oxford. He was an idealist, working without payment. I suggested that these data, such as they were, should be matched against the records of diplomats stationed in Washington between the relevant dates in 1944–5 of the known leakages. I received a reply from Vivian, assuring me that that aspect of the case had been very much "in their minds." But there was no evidence on file that anything had been done about it, and the speed, the disconcerting speed, of later developments suggested that the idea must have been relatively new.

A match of the Krivitsky material with the reports of the Embassy leakage yielded a short list of perhaps six names which was sent to us by London, with the comment that intensive enquiries were in progress. The list included the names of Roger Makins,* Paul Gore-Booth,† Michael Wright and Donald Maclean. (It may be objected that Maclean was not at either Eton or Oxford. He was not. But MI5 did not attach too much weight to that detail, on the ground that foreigners often assume that all well-born young Englishmen must go to Eton and Oxford.) The list provided Bobby Mackenzie with one of his finest hours. He offered me short odds on Gore-Booth. Why? He had been educated at Eton and Oxford; he had entered the Foreign Office in the middle thirties; he was a classical scholar of distinction to whom the code-name Homer would be appropriate; Homer, in its Russian form of Gomer, was a near-anagram of Gore; as for ideals, Gore-Booth was a Christian

---

* *Chairman of Atomic Energy Commission. Foreign Office man involved in the investigation into the flight of Burgess and Maclean.*

† *Head of British Information Services in America. Afterward Permanent Under-Secretary at the Foreign Office.*

Scientist and a teetotaller. What more could I want? It was a neat bit of work, good enough, I hoped, to give London pause for a few days.

Burgess packed up and left. We dined together on his last evening in a Chinese restaurant where each booth had "personalized music" which helped to drown our voices. We went over the plan step by step. He was to meet a Soviet contact on arrival in London, and give him a full briefing. He was then to call on Maclean at his office armed with a sheet of paper, giving the time and place of rendezvous, which he would slip across the desk. He would then meet Maclean and put him fully in the picture. From then on, the matter was out of my hands. Burgess did not look too happy, and I must have had an inkling of what was on his mind. When I drove him to the station next morning, my last words, spoken only half-jocularly, were: "Don't you go too."

MI5 were not particularly impressed by Mackenzie's brainwave about Gore-Booth. Confronted by their short list, they were looking for the odd man out, the man who conformed least to pattern. It was intelligent procedure, and it led them to put Maclean at the top of the list. He had never enjoyed the social round of the diplomatic corps. He had preferred the society of independent minds. By contrast, the others on the list were depressingly conformist. In communicating to us their conclusions, MI5 informed us that Maclean would probably be approached when the case against him was complete. Meanwhile, certain categories of Foreign Office paper would be withheld from him, and his movements would be put under surveillance. These last two decisions, taken presumably to soothe the Americans, were foolish. But I saw no reason to challenge them. I judged that they might serve me in good stead if anything went wrong. I was quite right.

I was nevertheless alarmed by the speed with which the affair was developing, and at the next meeting with my Soviet contact told him of the pressing need for haste. I was also given a pretext for writing to Burgess direct. The Embassy transport officer had twice asked me what was to be done about the Lincoln Continental which

Burgess had left in the car park. So I wrote to Burgess in pressing terms, telling him that if he did not act at once it would be too late—because I would send his car to the scrap-heap. There was nothing more I could do.

One morning, at a horribly early hour, Geoffrey Paterson called me by telephone. He explained that he had just received an enormously long Most Immediate telegram from London. It would take him all day to decipher without help, and he had just sent his secretary on a week's leave. Could he borrow mine? I made the necessary arrangements and sat back to compose myself. This was almost certainly it. Was Maclean in the bag? Had Maclean got away? I was itching to rush round to the Embassy and lend a third hand to the telegram. But it was clearly wiser to stick to my usual routine as if nothing had happened. When I reached the Embassy, I went straight to Paterson's office. He looked grey. "Kim," he said in a half-whisper, "the bird has flown." I registered dawning horror (I hope). "What bird? Not Maclean?" "Yes," he answered. "But there's worse than that . . . *Guy Burgess* has gone with him." At that, my consternation was no pretence.

XII. ORDEAL

Burgess's departure with Maclean faced me with a fateful decision. From the earliest discussions of Maclean's escape, my Soviet colleagues had been mindful that something might go wrong and put me in danger. To meet such a possibility, we had elaborated an escape plan for myself, to be put into effect at my discretion in case of extreme emergency. It was clear that the departure of Burgess gave rise to an emergency. But was it extreme emergency? I had to put aside the decision for a few hours, in order to deal with two immediate problems. One was to get rid of certain compromising equipment hidden in my house. The other was to get the feeling of the FBI, since that might affect the details of my escape. Getting rid of the equipment was perhaps the most urgent task of the two, but I decided to let it wait. It would have looked very odd if I had left the Embassy immediately after hearing the news; and Paterson's telegram gave me a good excuse for testing the FBI without delay. The telegram concluded with instructions that he should inform Ladd of its contents. Paterson, doubtless thinking that his face would be pretty red by the end of the interview, asked me if I would accompany him on the grounds that two red faces might be better than one. The fact that my face was probably more grey than red did not alter the principle of the thing.

Ladd took the news with remarkable calm. A few flashes of mischief suggested that he might almost be pleased that the bloody British had made a mess of it. But I guessed that his calm masked a personal worry. Ladd had often met Burgess at my house, and had invited him back to his own. Against all the odds, they had got on well together. Both were aggressive, provocative characters; they exchanged insults with mutual appreciation. At their first meeting, Burgess had attacked the corruption and graft which, he alleged, made nonsense of the Indianapolis motor trials, and in doing so took several hefty sideswipes at the American way of life in general. Ladd positively liked it. He had probably never heard a prissy Englishman talk that way before. In the present crisis, he would not have been Ladd if he had not wondered how much "the boss," Hoover, knew about his own acquaintance with Burgess. I concluded that Ladd's personal interest would work in my favour. From him, we went to see Lamphere, whose manner was quite normal. We discussed the escape with him, and he ventured a few theories in his solid, earnest way which suggested that he was still far from the truth. I left the building much relieved. It was possible that both Ladd and Lamphere were consummate actors who had fooled me. But it was no good jumping at shadows. I had to act as if the FBI were still in the dark.

It was possible that at any moment MI5 might ask the FBI to put me under surveillance. They could easily have done so without my knowledge by using the FBI representative in London as a direct link with Washington. But here again I felt I had a few days' grace. It was most unlikely that MI5 would put a foreign security service on to me without the agreement of MI6,* and I thought that the latter would hesitate before compounding an implied slur on one of

---

*Originally the section of British Military Intelligence concerned with positive espionage. It was later the popular name for SIS.

their senior officers. I should emphasize that this was pure guess-work on my part, and remains guesswork to this day. It is supported, however, by the fact that for several days I was left in peace.

When Paterson and I got back to the Embassy it was already past noon and I could plausibly tell him that I was going home for a stiff drink. In my garage-cum-potting-shed, I slipped a trowel into my briefcase, and then went down to the basement. I wrapped camera, tripod and accessories into waterproof containers, and bundled them in after the trowel. I had often rehearsed the necessary action in my mind's eye, and had lain the basis for it. It had become my frequent habit to drive out to Great Falls to spend a peaceful half-hour be-tween bouts of CIA-FBI liaison, and on the way I had marked down a spot suitable for the action that had now become necessary. I parked the car on a deserted stretch of road with the Potomac on the left and a wood on the right where the undergrowth was high and dense enough for concealment. I doubled back a couple of hundred yards through the bushes and got to work with the trowel. A few minutes later I re-emerged from the wood doing up my fly-buttons and drove back home, where I fiddled around in the garden with the trowel before going into lunch. As far as inanimate objects were concerned, I was clean as a whistle.

I was now in a position to give attention to the escape problem. As it had never been far from my mind in the previous weeks, I was able to make up my mind before the end of the day. My decision was to stay put. I was guided by the consideration that, unless my chances of survival were minimal, my clear duty was to fight it out. There was little doubt that I would have to lie low for a time, and that the time might be prolonged and would surely be trying. But, at the end of it, there might well be an opportunity for further ser-vice. The event was to prove me right.

The problem resolved itself into assessment of my chances of survival, and I judged them to be considerably better than before. It must be borne in mind that I enjoyed an enormous advantage over people like Fuchs who had little or no knowledge of intelligence work. For my part, I had worked for eleven years in the secret service. For seven of them I had been in a fairly senior position, and for eight I had worked in closest collaboration with MI5. For nearly two years I had been intimately linked to the American services, and had been in desultory relationship with them for another eight. I felt that I knew the enemy well enough to foresee in general terms the moves he was likely to make. I knew his files—his basic armament— and, above all, the limitations imposed on his procedures by law and convention. It was also evident that there must be many people in high positions in London who would wish very much to see my innocence established. They would be inclined to give me the benefit of any doubt, and it was my business to see that the room for doubt was spacious.

What evidence, to my knowledge, could be brought against me?

There were the early Left-wing associations in Cambridge. They were widely known, so there was no point in concealing them. But I had never joined the Communist Party in England, and it would surely be difficult to prove, eighteen years after the event, that I had worked illegally in Austria, especially in view of the sickening fact that most of my Vienna friends were undoubtedly dead. There was the nasty little sentence in Krivitsky's evidence that the Soviet secret service had sent a young English journalist to Spain during the Civil War. But there were no further identifying particulars, and many young men from Fleet Street had gone to Spain. There was the awkward fact that Burgess had got me into the secret service in the first place. I had already decided to circumvent that one by giving the name of a well-known lady who *might* have been responsible for my recruitment. If she admitted responsibility, all would be well. If she denied it, I could argue that I would scarcely have named her if I had not really believed that she was responsible.

It would have been desperately difficult, of course, if the security service had been able to check the files I had drawn during my service at headquarters, since that would have proved that my interests had roamed far and wide beyond my legitimate duties. My only possible defence, that I was passionately interested in the service for its own sake, would have carried little conviction. But I knew that the tallies were periodically destroyed, and thought it very unlikely that they would have survived the holocaust of un-wanted paper that took place after the war. There were also the number of cases which I had handled, such as the Volkov case, which had gone wrong for reasons which had never been estab-lished with certainty. But every one was susceptible to explanation without reference to myself; there were two important cases, those of May* and Fuchs, which, despite my best efforts, had gone right. The cases which went right would not clear me; but they would help me to throw an essential doubt over my responsibility for the others.

The really difficult problem was to explain away my relations with Burgess. I shared very few of his tastes, very few of his friends, and few of his intellectual interests. The essential bond between us was, of course, political, and that was a point that had to be blurred to the best of my ability. To a certain extent, geography helped. While I was in Austria, he was at Cambridge; while I was in Spain, he was in London; much of the war period, he was in London, but I was in France, Hampshire and Hertfordshire; then I went to Turkey, and he only caught up with me in Washington after a year. I could therefore show that real intimacy never had a chance to grow; he was simply a stimulating but occasional companion. Even the fact that he had stayed with me in Washington could be turned to ad-vantage. Would I be such a complete fool as to advertise my con-nection with him if we shared a deep secret?

Another difficulty was the actual course of my career. The more I considered it, the less I liked it. There were the known Left-wing associations at Cambridge, and suspected Communist activity in Vienna; then the complete break with my Communist friends in England, followed all too closely by cultivation of Nazis in London and Berlin; then the choice (of all places) of Franco Spain in which

*Allan Nunn May, atomic scientist who served six years upon conviction of espionage activities.

to carve out a journalistic career; then the entry in the secret service with Burgess's help and my emergence in the service as an expert on anti-Soviet and anti-Communist work; and finally my foreknowledge of the action to be taken against Maclean and the latter's escape. It was an ugly picture. I was faced with the inescapable conclusion that I could not hope to prove my innocence.

That conclusion did not depress me unduly. A strong presumption of my guilt might be good enough for an intelligence officer. But it was not enough for a lawyer. What he needed was evidence. The chain of circumstantial evidence that might be brought against me was uncomfortably long. But, as I examined each single link of the chain, I thought I could break it; and if every link was broken singly, what remained of the chain? Despite all appearances, I thought, my chances were good. My next task was to get out into the open and start scattering the seeds of doubt as far and wide as I possibly could.

The next few days gave me plenty of opportunity. In the office, Paterson and I talked of little else, and Mackenzie joined our deliberations from time to time. I do not think that Paterson had an inkling of the truth at the time, but I am less sure of Mackenzie. He was idle but far from stupid, and on occasion I thought I caught a shrewd glint in his eyes. My part in the discussions was to formulate a theory which covered the known facts, and hammer it home until it stuck. The opening was given me by the decision of MI5, which I have already described as foolish, to withhold certain papers from Maclean and to put his movements under surveillance. Taking that as a starting-point, I made a reconstruction of the case which was at least impossible to disprove. It ran as follows.

The evidence of Krivitsky showed that Maclean had been working for at least sixteen years. He was therefore an experienced and competent operator. Such a man, ever on guard, would be quick to notice that certain categories of paper were being withheld from him and to draw disquieting conclusions. His next step would be to check whether he was being followed. As he *was* being followed, he would not take long to discover the fact. But, while these discoveries would alert Maclean to his danger, they also put him in a quandary. The object of surveillance was to trap him in company with a Soviet contact; yet without a Soviet contact, his chances of escape would be greatly diminished. While he was still meditating this problem, the Act of God occurred. Burgess walked into his room—his old comrade. (I could produce no evidence that there had been an old association between Burgess and Maclean, but the fact that they had gone together made it a wholly reasonable assumption.) The arrival of Burgess, of course, would solve Maclean's problem, since Burgess, through *his* contact, could make all necessary arrangements. This was strongly supported by the fact that it was Burgess who looked after the details such as hiring the car. And why did Burgess go too? Well, it was clear to Paterson and Mackenzie that Burgess was washed up in the Foreign Office, and pretty near the end of his tether in general. Doubtless, his Soviet friends thought it would be best to remove him from a scene in which his presence might constitute a danger to others.

Such was my story and I stuck to it. It had the advantage of being based on known facts and almost unchallengeable assumptions. The only people who could disprove it were the two who had vanished and myself. I was also happy to see that the theory was wholly acceptable to the FBI. Ladd and Lamphere both liked it, and, in a short interview I had with Hoover at the time, he jumped at it. In his eyes, it had the superlative merit of pinning all the blame on MI5. I have no doubt that he made a great deal of political capital out of it, both on Capitol Hill and in subsequent dealings with MI5. Hoover may have got few winners on his own account; but he was not the man to look a gift-horse in the mouth.

The position with regard to CIA was more indefinite. It was an FBI case, and I could not discuss its intricacies with CIA without running the risk of irritating Hoover and Boyd, both of whom I was anxious to soothe. So I confined my talks with CIA officials to the overt details of the case which became known through the press, somewhat late and more than somewhat inaccurate. I had no fear of the bumbling Dulles; years later, I was to be puzzled by President Kennedy's mistake in taking him seriously over the Bay of Pigs. But Bedell Smith was a different matter. He had a cold, fishy eye and a precision-tool brain. At my first meeting with him, I had taken a document of twenty-odd paragraphs on Anglo-American war plans for his scrutiny and comment. He had flipped over the pages casually and tossed it aside, then engaged me in close discussion of the subjects involved, referring from memory to the numbered paragraphs. I kept pace only because I had spent a whole morning learning the document by heart. Bedell Smith, I had an uneasy feeling, would be apt to think that two and two made four rather than five.

The next few days dragged. I experienced some mild social embarrassment when the news broke with all the carefree embellishments of the popular press. One of the snootier of the Embassy wives gave me a glacial stare at one of the Ambassador's garden parties. But London remained ominously silent. One telegram arrived from London saying that "it was understood" that I knew Burgess personally; could I throw any light on his behaviour? But the one I was expecting was a most immediate, personal, decipher-yourself telegram from the Chief, summoning me home. At last the summons came, but it took a most curious, thought-provoking form. An intelligence official specializing in the fabrication of deception material flew into Washington on routine business. He paid me a courtesy call during which he handed me a letter from Jack Easton. The letter was in Easton's own handwriting, and informed me that I would shortly be receiving a telegram recalling me to London in connection with the Burgess-Maclean case. It was very important that I should obey the call promptly. While the sense of the communication was clear enough, its form baffled me. Why should Easton warn me of the impending summons and why in his own handwriting if the order was to reach me through the normal telegraphic channels anyway? There is often a good reason for eccentric behaviour in the secret service, and there may have been one in this case. My reflection at the time was that, if I had not already rejected the idea of escape, Easton's letter would have given me the signal to get moving with all deliberate speed.

After a few days the telegram came. I booked passage for the following day and prepared to say goodbye to Washington for ever. I met Angleton for a pleasant hour in a bar. He did not seem to appreciate the gravity of my personal position, and asked me to take up certain matters of mutual concern when I got to London. I did not even take the trouble to memorize them. Then I called on Dulles who bade me farewell and wished me the best of luck. Ladd was next on my list and we spent some of the evening together. He seemed to be genuinely preoccupied with my predicament and kindly offered some words of advice on how to keep out of trouble in London. Part of his concern may have been due to his sense of personal involvement in the Burgess affair; but I also detected some genuine feeling for which I was grateful. Ruthless as he was, Ladd was a human being.

I arrived in London about noon, and was immediately involved in a bizarre episode. I had boarded the airport bus and taken a seat immediately next to the door. When the bus was full, an agitated figure appeared on the running-board and frantically scrutinized the passengers. He looked over my left shoulder, over my right shoulder, tried to look over my head and then looked straight at me. Dismay settled on his face and he vanished. It was Bill Bremner, a fairly senior officer on the administrative side of SIS. I knew very well whom he was looking for. If I had been two yards away from him instead of two feet, he would have spotted me. I had never been met officially before. What with Jack Easton's letter and the designation of an officer of Bremner's seniority to act as reception committee, I could not complain that I had not been warned. As the bus drove into London, the red lights were flickering brightly.

I went to my mother's flat and, after lunch, telephoned Easton. There was a perceptible gasp at the other end of the line. After a pause, Easton asked me where I was, and I told him. Was I too tired to come over to Broadway straight away? Of course not. On my way,

I took relish in the thought of the panic that must have spread when Bremner reported my non-arrival. Easton looked a bit sheepish when I entered his office. He said that my telephone call had surprised him, because he had sent Bill Bremner to the airport, "to see if he could be of any help to me." It was pretty lame, and I felt that I had won the first trick. The trick was valueless, of course, but the mere winning of it did me good. The perhaps fanciful thought has since occurred to me that part of Bremner's mission to the airport was to see that MI5 did not pull a fast one on SIS by arresting me on arrival. In view of later developments, this seems, on the whole, unlikely, so I put forward the idea for fun only.

Easton told me that Dick White was anxious to see us both as soon as possible, so we drove across the park to Leconfield House, off Curzon Street, where MI5 had set up their headquarters. This was to be the first of many interrogations, although an attempt was made, at this early stage, to conceal that ugly fact. Easton sat in while White asked the questions; the role of the former was presumably to see fair play. It may be imagined that there was some apprehension on my side, some embarrassment on theirs. I could not claim White as a close friend; but our personal and official relations had always been excellent, and he had undoubtedly been pleased when I superseded Cowgill. He was bad at dissembling, but he did his best to put our talk on a friendly footing. He wanted my help, he said, in clearing up this appalling Burgess-Maclean affair. I gave him a lot of information about Burgess's past and impressions of his personality, taking the line that it was almost inconceivable that anyone like Burgess, who courted the limelight instead of avoiding it and was generally notorious for indiscretion, could have been a secret agent, let alone a Soviet agent from whom strictest security standards would be required. I did not expect this line to be in any way convincing as to the facts of the case; but I hoped it would give the impression that I was implicitly defending myself against the unspoken charge that I, a trained counter-espionage officer, had been completely fooled by Burgess. Of Maclean, I disclaimed all knowledge. I had heard of him, of course, and might even have met him here or there, but offhand I could not have put a face to him. As I had only met him twice, for about half an hour in all and both times on a conspiratorial basis, since 1937, I felt that I could safely indulge in this slight distortion of the truth.

I offered to put a summary of what I had said on paper. It was possible that our talk was bugged, and I wanted a written record to correct any bias that the microphone might have betrayed. When I went back for my second interrogation a few days later, White gave my note a cursory glance, then edged towards the real focus of his interest. We might clarify matters, he said, if I gave him an account of my relations with Burgess. To that end, a detailed statement of my own career would be useful. As I have explained in the previous chapter, there were some awkward zig-zags to be negotiated, but I explained them away as best I could. In doing so, I gave White a piece of gratuitous information, a slip which I regretted bitterly at the time. But it is virtually certain that they would have dug it out for themselves in time, and it is perhaps just as well that I drew attention to it myself at an early stage.

This information related to a trip which I had made to Franco Spain before *The Times* sent me as their accredited correspondent. It seemed that MI5 had no record of that trip and had assumed that *The Times* had sent me to Spain direct from a desk in Fleet Street. When I corrected White on this point, he did not take long to ask me if I had paid for the first journey out of my own resources. It was a nasty little question because the enterprise had been suggested to me and financed by the Soviet service, just as Krivitsky had said, and a glance at my bank balance for the period would have shown that I had no means for gallivanting around Spain. Embedded in this episode was also the dangerous little fact that Burgess had been used to replenish my funds. My explanation was that the Spanish journey had been an attempt to break into the world of high-grade journalism on which I had staked everything, selling all my effects (mostly books and gramophone records) to pay for the trip. It was reasonably plausible and quite impossible to disprove. Burgess's connection with my Spanish venture was never found out. I had an explanation ready, but already had quite enough to explain.

When I offered to produce a second summary of our talks, White agreed, but asked me rather impatiently to harp less on Burgess and concentrate on my own record. All but the tip of the cat's tail was now out of the bag, and I was not surprised to receive a summons from the Chief. He told me that he had received a strong letter from Bedell Smith, the terms of which precluded any possibility of my returning to Washington. I learnt later that the letter had been drafted in great part by Bill, an American official, a friend of mine, whose wife Burgess had bitterly insulted during a convivial party at my house. I had apologized handsomely for his behaviour, and the apology had apparently been accepted. It was therefore difficult to understand his retrospective exercise in spite. From him of all people! After this, it was almost a formality when the Chief called me a second time and told me, with obvious distress, that he would have to ask for my resignation. He would be generous: £4,000 in lieu of pension. My unease was increased shortly afterwards when he told me that he had decided against paying me the whole sum at once. I would get £2,000 down and the rest in half-yearly instalments of £500. The ostensible reason for the deferred payments was the fear that I might dissipate all in wild speculation, but, as I had never speculated in my life, it looked a bit thin. A more likely reason was the desire to hedge against the possibility of my being sent to gaol within three years.

So there I was with £2,000 in my hands and a great black cloud over my head. I spent the summer house-hunting and settled for a small place near Rickmansworth. It was already November when the Chief telephoned me and asked me to see him at ten o'clock on the following morning. I drove up to London on a beautiful wintry morning with the hedgerows bending low under inch-thick rime. The Chief explained that a judicial enquiry had been opened into the circumstances of the Burgess-Maclean escape. The enquiry was in the hands of H.J.P. Milmo, a King's Counsellor who had worked for MI5 during the war. I was required to give evidence, and the Chief hoped I would have no objection. The mention of Milmo indicated that a crisis was at hand. I knew him and of him. He was a skilled interrogator; he was the man whom MI5 usually brought in for the kill. As I drove with the Chief across St. James's Park to Leconfield House, I braced myself for a sticky ordeal. I was still confident that I could survive an examination, however robust, on the basis of the evidence known to me. But I could not be sure that new evidence had not come to hand for Milmo to shoot at me.

On arrival at Leconfield House, I was introduced to the head of the legal branch of MI5 and then ushered into the presence of Milmo. He was a burly fellow with a florid, round face, matching his nickname, "Buster." On his left sat Arthur Martin, a quiet young man who had been one of the principal investigators of the Maclean case. He remained silent throughout, watching my movements. When I looked out of the window, he made a note; when I twiddled my thumbs, he made another note. After sketchy greetings, Milmo adopted a formal manner, asking me to refrain from smoking as this was a "judicial enquiry."

It was all flummery, of course. It crossed my mind to ask Milmo for his credentials or to suggest that the headquarters of MI5 were an odd venue for a judicial enquiry. But that would have been out of character for the part which I had decided to play; that of a co-operative ex-member of SIS as keen as Milmo himself to establish the truth about Burgess and Maclean. So, for the best part of three hours, I answered or parried questions meekly enough, only permitting a note of anger when my character was directly attacked. It was useless, I knew, to try to convince the ex–intelligence officer in Milmo; my job was simply to deny him the confession which he required as a lawyer.

I was too closely involved in Milmo's interrogation to form an objective opinion of its merits. Much of the ground that he covered was familiar and my answers, excogitated long before, left him little to do but shout. Early in the interview, he betrayed the weakness of his position by accusing me of entrusting to Burgess "intimate personal papers." The charge was so obviously nonsensical that I did not even have to feign bewilderment. It appeared that my Cambridge degree had been found in Burgess's flat during the search which followed his departure. Years before, I had folded that useless document and put it in a book. Burgess, as anyone would have told Milmo, was an inveterate borrower of books with and without the permission of their owners. The aim of the accusation was to show that I had deliberately underplayed the degree of my intimacy with Burgess. It was flimsy stuff and went far to strengthen my confidence in the outcome.

But Milmo produced at least two rabbits out of the bag which I had not foreseen, and which showed that the chain of circumstantial evidence against me was even longer than I had feared. Two days after the Volkov information reached London, there had been a spectacular rise in the volume of NKVD wireless traffic between London and Moscow, followed by a similar rise in the traffic between Moscow and Istanbul. Furthermore, shortly after I had been officially briefed about the Embassy leakage in Washington, there had been a similar jump in NKVD traffic. Taken in conjunction with the other evidence, these two items were pretty damning. But to me, sitting in the interrogation chair, they posed no problem. When asked in Milmo's most thunderous tones to account for these occurrences, I replied quite simply that I could not.

I was beginning to tire when suddenly Milmo gave up. Martin asked me to stay put for a few minutes. When I was invited into the next room, Milmo had disappeared and the MI5 legal officer was in charge. He asked me to surrender my passport, saying that they could get it anyway but that voluntary action on my part would obviate publicity. I readily agreed as my escape plan certainly did not envisage the use of my own identity papers. My offer to send the document that night by registered post was rejected because it was "too risky." William Skardon was detailed to accompany me back to my home and receive it from me. On the way, Skardon wasted his breath sermonizing the Advisability of Co-operating with the Authorities. I was too relieved to listen, though my relief was tempered by the knowledge that I was not yet out of the wood—not by a long chalk.

Several times in the following weeks, Skardon came down to continue the interrogations. He was scrupulously courteous, his manner verging on the exquisite; nothing could have been more flattering than the cosy warmth of his interest in my views and actions. He was far more dangerous than the ineffective White or the blustering Milmo. I was helped to resist his polite advances by the knowledge that it was Skardon who had wormed his way into Fuchs's confidence with such disastrous results. During our first long conversation, I detected and evaded two little traps which he laid for me with deftness and precision. But I had scarcely begun congratulating myself when the thought struck me that he might have laid others which I had not detected.

Yet even Skardon made mistakes. He began one interview by asking me for written authority to examine my bank balance. He could have got legal authority to do so whether I approved or not; so I raised no objection—especially since he would find no trace of irregular payments because no irregular payments had ever been made. But, with the authority in his hands, he began to question me on my finances, and I took the opportunity of giving him some harmless misinformation. My object in doing so was a serious one. I had been able to invent plausible explanations for most of the oddities of my career, but not all of them. Where my invention failed, I could only plead lapses of memory. I just could not remember this person or that incident. The probing of my finances gave me a chance of confirming the erratic workings of my memory. If I could not remember my financial transactions, I could scarcely be expected to remember all the details of my social and professional life.

After several such interrogations, Skardon came no more. He did not tell me that he was satisfied or dissatisfied; he just left the matter hanging. He was doubtless convinced that I was concealing from him almost everything that mattered, and I would have given a lot to have glimpsed his summing up. There was no doubt that the evidence against me was impressive, but it was not yet conclusive. That it was not so regarded emerged from yet another summons to Broadway, this time to be interrogated by Sinclair and Easton. It was distasteful to lie in my teeth to the honest Sinclair; I hope he now realizes that in lying to him I was standing as firmly on principle as he ever did. But I enjoyed my duel with Easton. After my experiences with White, Milmo and Skardon, I was moving on very familiar ground, and did not think he could succeed where they had failed. He didn't.

XIII. THE CLOUDS PART

For more than two years I was left in peace—or perhaps armed neutrality would be a better word. I had no illusions that my file was closed; but no charges had been proffered and I remained on friendly terms with a few ex-colleagues in MI5 and SIS. It was an anxious period. I had my £2,000 and the prospect of another £2,000, and perhaps two or three thousand more in the shape of insurance policies. Lucrative employment remained a distant aspiration since when I applied for work, the first question asked was always why I had left the Foreign Service. My best chance seemed to be journalism; my thoughts turned to Spain where I had made my first breakthrough. I had no doubt that I could soon pick up the threads again, and I reflected that a Spanish destination would strengthen the hands of those who still doubted my guilt. Madrid could hardly be further from the Iron Curtain. So I wrote to Skardon asking for the return of my passport. It reached me by return of post—without comment.

My Spanish venture was of short duration. I had scarcely been in Madrid three weeks when I received a letter offering me a job in the City. The salary mentioned was modest but commensurate

with my total ignorance of business procedures. So for a year I dab-
bled in general trading, commuting daily between Rickmansworth
and Liverpool Street. I was totally unsuited to the job, and was relieved when the firm for which I worked teetered towards bank-
ruptcy owing to the rash behaviour of its shipping department with
which, fortunately, I had nothing to do. My employers were happy
enough when I took myself off, thus relieving them of the burden
of my salary. From then on, I made some sort of living from freelance journalism, a most arduous occupation calling for a depressing amount of personal salesmanship—never my strong point.

This rather dreary existence was enlivened by a curious episode
which began with a letter from a Conservative MP, who asked me
to tea at the House of Commons. He told me candidly that he was
gunning for the Foreign Office in general and Anthony Eden in
particular. His own position, he said, was impregnable; he had one
of the safest seats in the country and his local Conservative Association ate out of his hand. He had heard that I had been sacked
from the Foreign Service, and had surmised that I must suffer a
sense of grievance. If I could give him any dirt to throw at the Foreign Office, he would be most grateful. There was much to the same
effect from my host, accompanied by gusts of laughter at his own
sallies. I replied that I fully understood the reason behind the Foreign Office's request for my resignation, and left abruptly.

Several times during this period, I revived the idea of escape.
The plan, originally designed for American conditions, required
only minor modifications to adapt it to European circumstances.
Indeed, in some ways it would be easier from London than from
Washington. But each time I considered the project the emergency
appeared to be less than extreme. Finally, an event occurred which
put it right out of my head. I received, through the most ingenious
of routes, a message from my Soviet friends, conjuring me to be
of good cheer and presaging an early resumption of relations. It
changed drastically the whole complexion of the case. I was no longer
alone.

It was therefore with refreshed spirit that I watched the next storm gather. It began with the defection of Petrov* in Australia and some not very revealing remarks he made about Burgess and Maclean. Fleet Street raised the familiar hue and cry after the Third Man, but this time there was a difference. Somebody leaked my name to the newspapers. It is quite astonishing, in view of the hundreds of thousands of pounds which the popular press must have spent in ferreting out trivial misinformation about the missing diplomats, that it took them four years to get on to me—and then only because of an indiscretion. One of my SIS friends told me that the leak came from a retired senior officer of the Metropolitan Police, a gentleman we both knew for his loose tongue. This idea seemed quite plausible since the crime reporters were the first to get the story. In connection with the Third Man, the *Daily Express* mentioned a "security officer" of the British Embassy in Washington who had been asked to resign from the service. It was a characteristic inaccuracy; I was never a security officer. But it was near enough to prepare me to slap a libel suit on the first newspaper to mention my name.

I soon had my first visitor from Fleet Street. He telephoned from London, asking for an interview. I suggested that he should put his questions in writing. Two hours later, he called again from the station, and I decided to show him the form. I told him that I would say nothing whatever unless he gave me a written guarantee that not a word would be printed without my approval. I explained that most of my knowledge of the Burgess-Maclean case came from official sources, and that I would therefore lay myself open to a charge under the Official Secrets Act if I discussed it. After telephoning his editor, he went away empty-handed. But then the press closed in.

I should explain that I had moved from Hertfordshire to Sussex, and was living in Crowborough, midway between Uckfield and Peter

---

*After the mysterious death of Lavrenti Beria (Stalin's right-hand man and head of Russian Secret Services) in 1953, Petrov was suspected of having taken part in a plot which Beria was hatching—to win for himself supreme power. On being recalled to Moscow to answer charges, Petrov defected in Sydney in 1954, bringing with him valuable information about Soviet agents and code systems.

Townsend at Eridge. The reporters would cover the Princess in the morning and Townsend in the afternoon, or vice versa. Either way, they swarmed round me at lunchtime. I was lucky in two ways. First, the fact that I was being pestered in such exalted company swung local opinion in my favour. My stalwart gardener offered to put a fork through any reporter I cared to indicate. Second, the regularity of the reporters' movements enabled me to avoid them by the simple expedient of advancing my clock three hours. I got up at five, breakfasted at six, had lunch at nine-thirty, and was deep in Ashdown Forest when the press converged on my house. When I got back at three, they had vanished. The system failed only once. A lady from the *Sunday Pictorial* got into the house late one Saturday night to ask for urgent comments on a "very damaging article" written by a friend, and due to appear the following morning. I declined to read it, declined comment and bundled her out of the house, stopping short of force. Next morning I bought the *Sunday Pictorial* and found not a word about me. The friend had got cold feet.

As soon as the furore began, I got in touch with my friends in SIS. They urged me to make no statement that might prejudice the case. The Government had promised a debate on the subject, and it was imperative that no spanner should be thrown into the works. They made two requests. First, that I should submit to one final interrogation, not by MI5 this time, but by two ex-colleagues in SIS. Second, that I should again surrender my passport. I agreed to both. My passport changed hands once more, and I paid two visits to London to answer questions. The interviews followed a familiar pattern which suggested that no new evidence had been turned up. Meanwhile, the fact that I had made no attempt to escape over a long period was beginning to tell heavily in my favour. With the passage of time, the trail had become stale and muddy; there was murk enough to confuse counsel.

With the spotlight focused on me, I had cut two appointments with my Soviet friends. But when the date for the third came round, I decided that they probably needed information and that I certainly needed encouragement. It had to be an all-day job. I left Crowborough early and drove to Tonbridge where I parked the car and took a train to London. I was last to board from a deserted platform. At Waterloo I descended and after a good look round took the underground to Tottenham Court Road. There I bought a hat and coat, and wandered around for an hour or two. After a snack lunch at a bar, I did the cinema trick, taking a seat in the back row and slipping out in the middle of the performance. By then, I was virtually certain that I was clean, but still had a few hours to make sure. I wandered round districts which I had never seen before, on foot, by bus, and on foot again. It had been dark for an hour or two before I finally set course for my rendezvous. What passed there is no concern of the reader.

I was strap-hanging in the underground when I read the news. Looking over my neighbour's shoulder, I saw my name in the headlines of the *Evening Standard*.* Colonel Marcus Lipton,† MP for Brixton, had asked the Prime Minister whether he was determined to go on shielding the dubious Third Man activities of Mr. Philby. My first reaction was one of intense disappointment. Lipton's remarks were privileged and I could not get at him through the courts. Furthermore, he had shattered my dream of extracting a very large sum from a Beaverbrook newspaper. But my personal chagrin was soon swallowed up in the need for action. I had already laid plans for the dispersal of my family and had to put them into immediate effect. I then holed up with my mother in her flat in Drayton Gardens and telephoned my SIS friends to tell them that I could no longer keep silent. They agreed that I would have to say something sometime, but again urged me to postpone action until after the debate in the Commons.

There were twelve days to go. I disconnected the door bell and

*On 25 October 1955.

†*Marcus Lipton first asked the Prime Minister, Sir Anthony Eden, whether he would appoint a Select Committee to investigate the circumstances of the disappearance of Burgess and Maclean. Then he asked about the Third Man activities of Philby. Eden promised a debate which took place on 7 November 1955. In the course of this debate Harold Macmillan, the Foreign Secretary, cleared Philby.*

buried the telephone under a mountain of cushions. My mother forbade me to unscrew the knocker, on the ground that it was inaudible anyway. I need not have bothered because the press had broken it from its moorings within two days. The kitchen window had to be curtained day and night because a journalist peering through from the fire-escape had scared the cook. But she was a lady of spirit and kept us well supplied throughout the siege. Meanwhile, I spent the days in careful preparation of my inevitable statement to the press. An awful lot would depend on getting the tone just right. Unless I could force Lipton to retract, I would have no option but escape.

I fully expected a favourable outcome. I had attended many press conferences before and knew them for disorderly affairs with everyone asking questions at once. It was essential for me to keep control of the proceedings for the first half-hour or so, concentrating on the Lipton issue and hammering home the enormity of the accusation from every angle. After that, I did not care what they asked me; all my answers were ready. Simple reasoning had brought me to the conclusion that Lipton's charge had been an empty one. I did him the credit of assuming, perhaps wrongly, that he would have passed any hard evidence in his possession to the proper authorities—instead of warning me by blurting it out publicly in the House of Commons. If the authorities had received such hard evidence, from Lipton or anyone else, they would have taken action already and pulled me in. Therefore, neither Lipton nor anyone else had hard evidence.* The crucial fact of the situation was the inaction of the security authorities, since they knew ten times more about the case than the combined population of Fleet Street. It was they I had to fear, not the press.

The day of the parliamentary debate came. In his speech to the House on behalf of the Government, Harold Macmillan, the Foreign Secretary, said that I had performed my official duties consci-

*In fact Lipton got his information from the Empire News, who could not name Philby without facing libel risks.

entiously and ably (which was true) and that there was no evidence that I had betrayed the interests of the country (which was literally true). That statement gave me the green light. I removed the cushions from the telephone, and asked my mother to tell anyone who called that I would be available to visitors at 11 A.M. the following day. Within twenty minutes there were half a dozen calls. Then peace. I telephoned a contact in SIS to warn him of my impending appearance in public, then went to bed and slept for nine hours.

The door bell began ringing at ten-thirty. But with the necessity for controlling the situation still in mind, I let it ring. I had said eleven o'clock and it was going to be eleven o'clock. On the dot, I opened the door and said: "Jesus Christ!" I had expected perhaps a dozen visitors. What I saw was a spiral of humanity winding down the staircase out of sight. It seemed impossible that they would all get into the living-room, but somehow they did. For some five minutes the flash of bulbs went off continuously. Then the cameramen disappeared, giving us space to breathe. When we got settled, I asked one of the reporters lolling in an armchair to yield his seat to a lady leaning against the door. He shot up as if stung by a wasp, and the lady shyly sat down. It was a lucky break for me; it confirmed my control of the meeting at the outset.

The conference was extensively reported at the time, and there is no need to recapitulate the questions and answers in detail. I began by passing round a typewritten statement to the effect that, in certain aspects, reticence was imposed on me by the Official Secrets Act. Given that reservation I was prepared to answer questions. Of the first half dozen shot at me, one mentioned Lipton and I seized on it. "Ah, Lipton," I said. "That brings us to the heart of the matter." It was not only the press which knew Graham Greene's titles. I then invited Lipton to produce his evidence for the security authorities or repeat his charge outside the House of Commons. After some twenty minutes, four or five of the reporters excused themselves politely and hurried off. Good, I thought, that looks after the evening papers. I could now relax, so threw the meeting open to questions. What did I think of Burgess? Was I a friend of

Maclean's? How did I account for their disappearance? Where were they? What were my politics? Was I the Third Man? It was easy. After an hour or so, we adjourned to the dining-room where there was beer and sherry. (Luckily, our numbers had dwindled.) There was marked friendliness by now; only the *Daily Express* reporter showed a slight excess of zeal, so I gleefully "no-commented" most of his questions. As I have since learnt that he spent eleven years on the story, "and for five of them did very little else"—I quote from Anthony Purdy's *Burgess and Maclean**—I cannot hold his importunity against him. I can only suggest that he should take a fortnight's course in interrogation with Skardon.

It was past my normal lunchtime when the last of my visitors left. The reports of the conference carried by the evening newspapers left nothing to be desired. The challenge to Lipton was down in black and white in precisely the words I had used. The favourable impression was confirmed, by and large, in the morning papers on the following day. A friendly reporter telephoned to congratulate me on my press. The ball was now in Lipton's court. On the first evening, the BBC reported that he had attended the session of the House but had remained silent. The following evening, he gave in. His exact words were given me by a parliamentary reporter who asked me if I had any comment. I told him to call back in five minutes. In my relief, my first reaction was to congratulate Lipton on a handsome apology. But I decided that it was undeservedly fulsome and settled for a more non-committal formula: "I think that Colonel Lipton has done the right thing. So far as I am concerned, the incident is now closed." I took my mother round to the local for the first time in two weeks.

The incident was indeed closed, and remained so for more than seven years. The press dropped me like a hot brick. In the light of subsequent events, it is easy to blame Macmillan, and through him the Government, for giving me a clean bill of health. But the blame lies elsewhere. No one in the Government, and particularly no one

---

*Anthony Purdy, Burgess and Maclean *(London: Secker and Warburg, 1963).*

in the security service, wanted to make a public statement as early as 1955. The evidence was inconclusive; they could not charge me and did not want to clear me. They were forced to take action by the ill-informed hullabaloo in the popular press and by the silly blunder of Marcus Lipton.

For this monumental fiasco, the Beaverbrook press bears a particularly heavy responsibility. It started the running and kept it up, blundering but relentless, in pursuance of Beaverbrook's stupid feud with Eden and the Foreign Office. It would be interesting to compare the overseas expenditure of the Foreign Service with the money squandered by the *Daily Express* in the acquisition of irrelevant snippets of information about the Burgess-Maclean case. But "it is an ill wind turns none to good." I have Beaverbrook's quirk to thank for seven years of decent livelihood, in the nick of time, and of further service to the Soviet cause.

EPILOGUE: HOME AND DRY

My experiences in the Middle East from 1956 to 1963 do not lend themselves readily to narrative form except as part of the general history of the region during that period. That would be quite a different book. But there has been much speculation about what I was doing there in addition to my work as a newspaper correspondent, and it would be unfair to the reader to leave him guessing in total darkness. At the same time, I am inhibited by the fact that I am now speaking of very recent times. If the British Government can use the fifty-year rule to suppress the publication of official documents, I can also claim the right to veil in decent discretion events that took place as little as ten or five years ago. I will therefore content myself with a few hints at the truth, adjuring the reader only not to fall flat on his face into traps of his own making. Life can be quite simple. The compelling reason for discussion at this point is that, while the British and American special services can reconstruct pretty accurately my activities up to 1955, there is positive and negative evidence that they know nothing about my subsequent career in Soviet service.

It has been generally assumed that I was working under journalistic cover for SIS. Indeed, it would have been odd if they had made no use of me at all. They habitually use journalists, and there I was, with a sound knowledge of their requirements and more anxious than anyone to be in their good books. I would like to reassure any of my Arab friends who may read this book. I do not think I did their cause any disservice by telling the British Government what they really thought; in any case, the British paid scant notice, and look where they are now (summer, 1967)!

If it would have been odd of SIS not to take advantage of my presence in the Middle East, it would have been odder still if the Soviet intelligence service had ignored me. One British journalist, shortly after my departure from Beirut, asked in print what use I could have been to the Soviet Union, and came to the astonishing conclusion that I was probably reporting on the Middle East College of Arabic Studies located in Shemlan in the hills above Beirut. With all due respect to that institution, which has achieved more notoriety than it really deserves, the most detailed information about it would have been considered by most intelligence services a poor return for seven years' work.

The fact is that the Soviet Union is interested in a very wide range of Middle Eastern phenomena. Enjoying a wide margin of priority at the top of the list are the intentions of the United States and British governments in the area. For an assessment of such intentions, I was not too badly placed.* One writer, discussing my case, commented on the fact that I seldom asked direct questions; I was the least curious of journalists. Of course! If you put direct questions on matters of substance to any American or British official you are apt to get either an evasion or a whopping great lie. But in the course of general conversation, discussion and argument, it is not impossible to get the drift of your interlocutor's thinking or to estimate with fair accuracy his standing in respect of policy decisions.

---

* *In 1963, in the House of Commons, Mr. Heath said that "since Mr. Philby resigned from the Foreign Service in July 1951 he has not had any access to any kind of official information. For the past seven years he has been living outside British legal jurisdiction."*

It is difficult, though by no means impossible, for a journalist to obtain access to original documents. But these are often a snare and a delusion. Just because a document *is* a document, it has a glamour which tempts the reader to give it more weight than it deserves. This document from the United States Embassy in Amman, for example. Is it a first-rate draft, a second draft or the finished memorandum? Was it written by an official of standing, or by some dogsbody with a bright idea? Was it written with serious intent or just to enhance the writer's reputation? Even if it is unmistakably a direct instruction to the United States Ambassador from the Secretary of State dated last Tuesday, is it still valid today? In short, documentary intelligence, to be really valuable, must come as a steady stream, embellished with an awful lot of explanatory annotation. An hour's serious discussion with a trustworthy informant is often more valuable than any number of original documents. Of course, it is best to have both.

So, after seven years, I left Beirut and turned up in the Soviet Union. Why? Maybe I was tipped off by a Fourth Man. Maybe someone had blundered. It is even possible that I was just tired. Thirty years in the underground is a long stretch, and I cannot pretend that they left no mark. The question, as far as I am concerned, can be left to history; or rather, since history is unlikely to be interested, it can be buried right now.

But the treatment which my escape had received from various publicists calls for some comment, as an illustration of the bland invention which characterizes so much of current writing on secret service matters. The writer of an article in the *Saturday Evening Post* told a stirring story of Lebanese police surveillance of my activity, involving an American confectioner (a neat touch!), breakneck taxi rides and night photography. I do not know whether the writer had his tongue in his cheek; unless I misjudged him sadly, he is too intelligent to fall for such twaddle. A later author, John Bulloch, advanced the theory that the Lebanese deliberately let me go, in collusion with the British. His only support for the theory was the statement that the Lebanese security authorities were so "very efficient" that I could not have got away without their knowledge. I am afraid that this betrays total ignorance of local conditions. Beirut is one of the liveliest centres of contraband and espionage in the world. Dozens of people make illegal crossings of the Lebanese frontiers monthly; only a few are brought to book.

Fantasies pursued me, of course, into the Soviet Union. Reports of my whereabouts have been bewilderingly various. I am living in Prague; I am living on the Black Sea Riviera; I am in a sanatorium suffering from a nervous breakdown. I am living in a *dacha* outside Moscow; I am in a big government house outside Moscow; I am hidden away in a provincial town. I accompanied the Soviet delegation to the abortive Afro-Asian Conference in 1955; I am working in a Soviet cultural institute at Bloudane, not far from Damascus. It is obvious that none of those who published such nonsense could really have believed it. But, if they were guessing, why such stupid guesses? The overwhelming balance of probability was always that I was living in Moscow and, like all the other millions of Muscovites, in a flat. Anyone who had hazarded such a trite guess would have guessed quite right.

I will conclude by mentioning a factor which has unnecessarily puzzled some Western commentators on my case. That was the liberal smokescreen behind which I concealed my real opinions. One writer who knew me in Beirut has stated that the liberal opinions I expressed in the Middle East were "certainly" my true ones. Another comment from a personal friend was that I could not have maintained such a consistently liberal-intellectual framework unless I had really believed in it. Both remarks are very flattering. The first duty of an underground worker is to perfect not only his cover story but also his cover personality. There is, of course, some excuse for the misconception about my views which I have just mentioned. By the time I reached the Middle East, I had more than twenty years' experience behind me, including some testing years. Furthermore, I was baptized the hard way, in Nazi Germany and Fascist Spain, where a slip might have had consequences only describable as dire.

CHRONOLOGY

1912   Harold Adrian Russell "Kim" Philby born on 1 January in Amballa, India, son of Harry St. John Philby, an Indian Civil Service officer who later became a renowned Arabist and converted Muslim, and Dora Philby.

1925   Philby goes to Westminster School.

1929   Enters Trinity College, Cambridge, at the age of seventeen and joins the Cambridge University Socialist Society.

1930   Guy Burgess arrives at Trinity from Eton.

1931   Defeat of the Labour Government. Philby becomes a more ardent Socialist.

1932   Becomes Treasurer of the Cambridge University Socialist Society.

1933   Leaves Cambridge a convinced Communist with a degree in Economics, then goes to Vienna, where Chancellor Dr. Engelbert Dollfuss is preparing the first "putsch" in February 1934. Philby becomes a Soviet agent.

1934   Clash between the Government and the Socialists in Vienna. On 24 February Philby marries Alice (Litzi) Friedman; then in May, after the collapse of the Socialist movement in Vienna, he returns with his wife to England. He begins work as a sub-editor on the Liberal monthly *Review of Re-*

views, and joins the Anglo-German Fellowship of which Burgess is also a member—its pro-Hitler magazine, supported by Nazi funds, was edited by Philby. To cover up his Communist background he also makes repeated visits to Berlin for talks with the German Propaganda Ministry and with von Ribbentrop's Foreign Office.

1937   In February he arrives in Spain to report the Civil War from Franco's side. In July he becomes correspondent of *The Times* with Franco's forces.

1938   Awarded the "Red Cross of Military Merit" by Franco personally.

1939   In July leaves Spain and becomes war correspondent of *The Times* at the British headquarters in Arras.

1940   In June, after the evacuation of British forces from the Continent, he returns to England. Recruited by the British Secret Service and attached to SIS under Guy Burgess in Section D. Assigned to school for undercover work at Brickendonbury Hall, near Hertford, but on its being disbanded transferred to Special Operations in London and assigned to the teaching staff of a new school for general training in techniques of sabotage and subversion at Beaulieu, Hampshire.

1941   Transferred to SIS, Section V, under Major Cowgill. Philby was put in charge of the Iberian sub-section, responsible for British intelligence in Spain and Portugal.

1942   Marries his second wife, Aileen Furse. OSS party under Norman Pearson arrives in London for liaison with British Secret Service. Philby's area of responsibility is extended to include North Africa and Italian espionage under newly formed counter-intelligence units.

1943   Section V moves from St. Albans to London.

1944   Appointed head of a newly created section (Section IX) designed to operate against Communism and the Soviet Union.

1945   The Volkov incident. Philby's position is seriously threatened by a Russian agent who offers to "talk."

1946   Takes a "field" appointment—officially to be First Secretary with the British Embassy in Turkey, actually to be head of the Turkish SIS station.

1949 Becomes SIS representative in Washington, as top British Secret Service officer working in liaison with the CIA and FBI. He sits in on Special Policy Committee directing the ill-fated Anglo-U.S. attempt to infiltrate anti-Communist agents into Albania to topple the Enver Hoxha regime.

1950 Guy Burgess arrives in Washington on assignment as Second Secretary of the British Embassy, and Philby invites him to stay at his house on Nebraska Avenue.

1951 Philby is informed of the tightening net of suspicion surrounding Foreign Office diplomat and Soviet agent Donald Maclean, whose British Embassy position in Washington at the end of the war had placed him on the Combined Policy Committee on Atomic Energy as its British joint secretary. Burgess is removed by Ambassador Franks and returns to England; then, on 25 May, Burgess and Maclean disappear from England, having escaped, via the Baltic, to Russia. Philby is summoned to London for interrogation and asked to resign from Foreign Service.

1952 In the summer the famous "Secret Trial" takes place, when Philby is questioned by Milmo.

1955 Government White Paper on the Burgess-Maclean affair. On 25 October in the House of Commons, Marcus Lipton asks about the Third Man, Philby. Harold Macmillan states that there is no evidence of Philby having betrayed the interests of Britain. Nevertheless he is dismissed from the Foreign Service because of his association with Burgess.

1956 In September he goes to Beirut as correspondent of the *Observer* and the *Economist;* most likely he is still employed by SIS. But that year Dick White, who suspects Philby of being a Soviet agent, becomes head of SIS.

1957 Aileen, Philby's second wife, dies.

1958 He marries Eleanor Brewer.

1962 George Blake is caught. Philby is now known to be a Soviet agent.

1963 On the night of 23 January Philby disappears in Beirut. The Soviet Union announces that Philby has been granted political asylum in Moscow. On 3 March, Mrs. Philby receives a cable from Philby postmarked Cairo. On 3 June *Izvestia* reports that Philby is with the Imam of Yemen. On 1 July, the British Government discloses that Philby is now known to have been a Soviet agent before 1946 and to have been the Third Man.

1965   Awarded the Soviet Union's "Red Banner Order," one of the highest honours bestowed by the USSR.

INDEX

MODERN LIBRARY IS ONLINE AT
WWW.MODERNLIBRARY.COM

MODERN LIBRARY ONLINE IS YOUR GUIDE TO CLASSIC LITERATURE ON THE WEB

THE MODERN LIBRARY E-NEWSLETTER

Our free e-mail newsletter is sent to subscribers, and features sample chapters, interviews with and essays by our authors, upcoming books, special promotions, announcements, and news.

To subscribe to the Modern Library e-newsletter, send a blank e-mail to: **join-modernlibrary@list.randomhouse.com** or visit **www.modernlibrary.com**

THE MODERN LIBRARY WEBSITE

Check out the Modern Library website at **www.modernlibrary.com** for:

- The Modern Library e-newsletter
- A list of our current and upcoming titles and series
- Reading Group Guides and exclusive author spotlights
- Special features with information on the classics and other paperback series
- Excerpts from new releases and other titles
- A list of our e-books and information on where to buy them
- The Modern Library Editorial Board's 100 Best Novels and 100 Best Nonfiction Books of the Twentieth Century written in the English language
- News and announcements

Questions? E-mail us at **modernlibrary@randomhouse.com**
For questions about examination or desk copies, please visit the Random House Academic Resources site at **www.randomhouse.com/academic**